THE JOURNEY HOME

My journey to find peace of mind and heart while fighting a war against Bipolar Disorder

LORI-ELLEN PISANI

outskirts press

The Journey Home
My journey to find peace of mind and heart while fighting a war against Bi-Polar Disorder

v5.0

The opinions expressed in this manuscript are solely the opinions of the author and do not represent the opinions or thoughts of the publisher. The author has represented and warranted full ownership and/or legal right to publish all the materials in this book.

Outskirts Press, Inc.
http://www.outskirtspress.com

ISBN: 978-1-4787-9577-3

PRINTED IN THE UNITED STATES OF AMERICA

DEDICATION:

TO: Dr. Martin Mintz, Dr. Itamar Salamon,
and Mrs. Renee Pepper, CSW-R
My gratitude and thanks are deep and profound.
You have traveled with me on my journey home and
given me the means and the will to keep fighting
the battles along the way.

TABLE OF CONTENTS

PROLOGUE

Philippians 4:13 – ***I can do all things through Christ who strengthens me.*** I put my faith in this Bible verse when I am challenged. It gives me courage. I need courage to write my story in a way that will help those who share my struggle to fight daily battles against bipolar disorder. It is the story of a fight; more like a war, with daily battles of will against a powerful enemy that has the capacity to overtake even the strongest of soldiers. My story does not have an ending, for it continues to unfold as long as I continue to live.

I never considered myself to be strong, but over the years, I have learned how to fight. Years of therapy and an effective medication protocol have provided me with the strength I need to wage war on a daily basis. There is no permanent victory, since there is no cure. And, to this day, there are times when the enemy grows stronger than I. Although this war will never be won, I now have the necessary resources and reinforcements to fight alongside me, and I'm still standing. For that, I am blessed and grateful beyond all comparable measure.

Battling bipolar disorder is not a war that one enlists to fight voluntarily. I was conscripted by inheritance. My father and sister suffer(ed) from it, although their diagnoses would come years after mine. I suspect there are more family members who have not recognized that they too have this illness, and my attempts to help them have failed.

I was the first to recognize something was seriously wrong inside my brain and that I needed help, or I would not survive. I had no one to talk to in the family about my fears and concerns. They were not safe people I could share my fears and thoughts with, for it was they whom I believed had put me in this position of helplessness and hopelessness, fear, rage, and deep pain as a child.

Bipolar disorder is characterized by severe mood swings, from the highest of highs (mania-the feeling of euphoria to a degree, the ability to manage many tasks simultaneously, a burst of creativity, energy and/or impulsive actions such as spending money without regard for the consequences) to the lowest of lows (severe depression, with suicidal thoughts or actions).

The goal is to maintain a truce between the two extremes. It is quite the challenge. A word, action, or situation can trigger me into fits of rage (hypomania) or suicidal depression. It's a spectrum disorder in that one size does not fit all. I do not experience mania as others might. I do not spend money recklessly or paint my house wild colors on a whim. My mania is experienced by bursts of creative energy and the ability to manage many tasks simultaneously. My depression however, is suicidal depression. That is a slow walk through hell, which I would never wish on another human being. I also suffer from hypomania that brings with it incredible rage. And then there are the mixed states when I am raging and depressed simultaneously. I have successfully waged my war against this illness thus far. But make no mistake, it is a war. The enemy is bipolar disorder; the victory is living a life with meaning and purpose and finding peace of mind and heart.

The very first battle is to find competent doctors to diagnose and treat this illness as early as possible. It is a complicated diagnosis and takes time to identify through treatment with a psychiatrist and psychotherapist who work together for your benefit. One can remain in a state of depression or mania for several years at a time, which makes an accurate diagnosis that much more difficult. After almost a year of treatment for clinical depression, my doctors suspected that I was bipolar in December 1996. I wasn't formally diagnosed as bipolar until February 1997. I was thirty-four years old. It takes a thorough evaluation to accurately diagnose this disorder. My correct diagnosis was a result of therapy sessions with Dr. Martin Mintz, who realized I was suffering from more than depression and referred me to his colleague, Dr. Itamar Salamon, who further evaluated me and confirmed the diagnosis.

I knew something was wrong from an early age, but relied on my faith in God to see me through the crisis periods. My faith was shaken and abandoned over the years, leaving me alone to battle against depression, rage, and mania the best way I could. It was utter desperation that led to my entering into the therapy process and subsequently, my journey.

I count my blessings that I have found the right doctors who, to this day, help me fight to survive. It may sound overly dramatic to say that this is a fight for my life. However, bipolar disorder is a serious illness, and it can take your life or your freedom if you are not vigilant about treatment and medication protocol. I learned that the hard way.

It is a lifetime journey. The worst part of it was that for so many years, I did not know what was wrong with me until I found the professional help needed to put a name to the nightmare I was living. As a child, I attributed my feelings as the consequences of how I was treated within the family. Every action they took had a reaction from me. I didn't know enough to realize that this exchange could have lasting, cumulative effects. Growing up, I lived in the moment, taking each situation as it came, and praying to God for help. I lived life in this way for decades.

I entered formal therapy in 1994, at age thirty-one. I dabbled a bit in counseling as a senior undergraduate student when I found myself huddled in the corner of my bed, unable to move, but that experience was not formal therapy but career counseling. During that time, I used prayer as my means to fight what had yet to be identified.

As my story unfolds, there came a need to enter formal, long-term therapy. I was separated from my husband, and living on my own for the first time in my life. When I told my parents that I was going into therapy, my father was quick to tell me that therapy was only for crazy people. I explained that I disagreed and planned to seek treatment. From that point on, I was labeled as weak, unstable, and misguided. I was the last to know when issues affected family members. Information regarding their situations was withheld from me because I was too unstable to handle it. "Don't tell Lori-ellen, it will make her freak out," I heard my sister say.

This attitude did not help me much, but nonetheless I continued my journey. I knew from a very early age that education was my ticket out of the nightmare of living with the people I held responsible for my pain and misery, and so I pursued it with a vengeance. I proceeded to obtain a master's degree, sixty credits beyond my master's in education, a doctoral degree in modern psychoanalysis and psychotherapy, and certification as a school administrator and supervisor from New York State.

With each graduation, my status within the family grew. They no longer believed therapy was only for the weak, and that I was unable to cope with stress or family issues. I was the only child to graduate from higher education. My siblings left college for their own reasons. I would like to think that it was my perseverance and determination that changed their perceptions of me. What I do know is that once I completed my doctoral degree, my family's perception of my abilities and strengths changed dramatically. I was no longer weak in their eyes, but competent, and successful. They put aside their feelings about therapy and medication as they saw me thrive and succeed.

In November 1997, my parents moved to Florida. I became the matriarch of the family in New York. If there was a problem, the family said, "Call Lori-ellen for help." I think it an incredible change from the place I held in the family as a child growing up. You will witness this transformation as my journey unfolds.

The path I traveled was one filled with sinkholes and obstacles. The sinkholes represent the deepest, darkest thoughts of suicide, and the obstacles were the hills (which felt like mountains) I climbed to keep fighting this illness without succumbing to it.

Perhaps you are reading this book because you too suffer from this illness or have a loved one or friend who does. If so, I urge you or anyone around you who is suffering to seek treatment and be faithful to it. Therapy appointments and medication regimes will become a part of your life. You must come to accept these intrusions--for that is what they seem at times--as necessary for your survival. Without treatment, your chances are slim with respect to leading a successful life. I experienced this first hand.

To my family – if my descriptions of you or the accounts I have written offend or hurt you, I sincerely apologize, but that is as far as I will go. I will not placate you or revise what I have written for your comfort. I spent too many years placating and subjugating myself to you in the hope that I would be accepted, wanted, important, and loved. My memories of you are mine, and they are real. You may forcefully disagree with what I have written. I accept and respect that your memories and perceptions may be quite different from mine. We are individuals who have our own unique ways of assimilating the world and events into our consciousness. I will, however, vehemently defend what I have written. The words on these pages express how I saw you as a child, who was vulnerable and desperately wanted and needed your love and acceptance.

This book is not retribution; it is an effort to put on paper what I remember and how it affected my life. My goal is to release my brain and heart from the pain I've lived with for so many years. Therapy was and is a huge help, but for me, I needed more. It isn't enough for me to share my story with a few confidants. I have a need to share my struggles with those, like me, who struggle with this illness, or have a loved one who is battling this powerful enemy. Perhaps my story can inspire someone to keep up the fight.

I have come to a place in my life where if my family decides, upon reading this book, that they no longer want or need me in their lives, I can accept it and move forward. I pray that is not the case, but nonetheless it may be the outcome.

It is also important for me to note that I have changed many names to protect people from retribution by others in their lives. Only first names, for the most part, are used for the sake of simplicity. Recitations of conversations had between the "characters" in this book are certainly not verbatim, but my recollections of their content is to the best of my ability. Key words and phrases that came to mind when remembering the events, settings, and context were the impetus for these verbal exchanges.

My goal in writing this book is not to hurt, but to heal myself and offer hope to those suffering from the affliction of mental illness.

My actions, in some cases, did hurt both others and myself. I offer my sincere apologies to those whom I have hurt by mistakes made out of misperceptions of my needs and how to meet them. I take full responsibility for everything I have done in my life and make no excuses. There are reasons, but there is never an excuse to hurt another human being.

I cannot, in all honesty, tell you that this story has a happy ending. Happiness is a fleeting emotion for me, as is peace of mind and heart. Yet I continue to strive, or fight, for these. Peace of mind and heart is the ultimate goal – one that I have not yet achieved but have hope that it will come. I wrote ***The Journey Home*** in 2010. I was forty-seven years old, and looking forward to retirement in the year 2020. I continue to live alone in homes in New York and North Carolina, and pray that I will retire to my North Carolina home in peace. ***The Journey Home*** started as just a poem written during a dark time in my life. It now provides me with the inspiration and motivation to fight my fight on a daily basis, find the courage to keep fighting when I am in pain and deeply depressed, and win some major battles along the way.

And that is the purpose of my story--to inspire hope in all those who read it or can relate to it in any way, to urge you to declare war on mental illness, and to use every available means to win your battles.

CHAPTER 1

THE JOURNEY HOME

Hello my friend,
I can see you,
Standing alone and frightened on the path that leads to my past
The sight of you brings back many memories
You are alone and shivering, yet it is warm
Your eyes are open wide, recording all that surrounds you
Your arms are wrapped tightly around you,
protecting your fragile heart
Your lips quiver as you struggle to cry out

I have heard your silent cries and have come back for you
I knew you would be waiting for me
I had much to do before I returned to travel this path once again
You are safe within my care
I am now grown and strong. I've learned how to shield us from harm
Take my hand, little one, and we will journey home together
But first we must travel the path back in time to say goodbye
Fear not, for I am with you and will lead the way

Lori-ellen Pisani

THIS IS THE first poem I've ever written. I sat at my kitchen table in my first apartment as a newly single woman, drinking coffee, smoking cigarettes and thinking about my life. The year was 1994. I was thirty-one years old, in the midst of a nasty divorce and bankrupt as a result. I was employed as a school secretary after losing my career as an elementary school teacher, and wondering why I was put on this earth only to live a life of pain. I was in a deep depression, the suicidal kind.

It was late at night, and I couldn't sleep no matter how hard I tried. As I lay in bed, I listened to a book on tape as a means of distraction. It was what I always did to clear my mind before going to sleep. Usually I couldn't get through side A of the cassette, as the reader's voice sent me into a deep sleep. This night however, it didn't work. No matter how hard I tried to focus on the story, my mind raced back to feelings and memories of helplessness, loss, and hopelessness for a brighter future. I attributed my feelings to the events surrounding my divorce proceedings and could see no way out of the mess I was in.

I was living alone for the first time in my life. There was no one to share my feelings with, lean on in times of need, keep me company, and experience intimacy with. My marriage was not entered into as two people sharing life's experiences, but my co-dependence on another as I strived to escape my house of pain and the people who made my life miserable. Now, I was truly alone and terrified at the thought of having sole responsibility for my life. I didn't think I was capable of managing even the smallest of chores like putting gas in my car or paying the bills on time. That was my husband's job. *What would I do if my car broke down?* He took care of that, too. *What if I was fired? Who would support me? Would I be alone for the rest of my life? Was life even worth living anymore?* At that point, I wasn't so sure.

My simple life as a married woman was at an end. I was, for all intents and purposes, a child in an adult body; unable to fend for myself without the aid of another, feeling abandoned and rejected. I knew these feelings well; they were my constant companions growing up. Fear, helplessness and hopelessness were back in my life again and were very powerful emotions. I was terrified by my own thoughts. I wanted desperately not to feel anything--to escape the pain that was clutching at my heart and confusing my brain. I could think of only one way out, and it would mean the loss of my life.

The hours ticked by, and when no relief came, I got up and went to sit at my kitchen table. On the table was a yellow writing pad and pen left there from making a grocery list a few days before. I sat there for a while staring at that yellow writing pad in front of me. I was thinking of writing a suicide note, but couldn't think of what I'd say. The phrase, "I'm tired," kept running through my mind. Nothing more. I was consumed by my own misery. I wanted to end my life to release myself from this pain. So much had happened to bring me to this point in time. I was weak, afraid, and exhausted.

I knew in my heart that if I didn't take control of myself, I would succumb to the plan to end my life. I'd had this feeling before. I knew it well. It was easy enough to buy a handgun. I had no criminal record, and since my excuse was that I needed it for protection (as I was not living in the safest of neighborhoods), no one would ever question it. There was no thought of leaving loved ones behind, but there was the question of God. I was always told that suicide was an unforgivable sin. Those who committed it were damned in the eyes of the Church and God. He and I weren't on the best of terms at this time. I couldn't reconcile in my mind how a loving God could allow me to get to this point once again. *Did He hate me? Was I that horrible of a human being to deserve this pain? I knew that some sins I committed in my life were grievous, but I went to confession. Didn't that count as forgiveness? Was I still being punished for sins confessed?* In the whirlwind of thoughts, I convinced myself that if I did take my own life, I'd have the opportunity to explain why I did it to God once I got to heaven's gate. Maybe, just maybe, He would accept what I did, forgive me, and let me in.

I walked over to the refrigerator to get something to drink. My throat was parched and had what felt like a golf-ball-sized lump in it. As I reached for the door, I saw the small card I received from my insurance company that had hotline numbers for various services such as 24-hour nursing care, and prescription benefits, and numbers to call in case of an emergency. I had cause to use this card in the past for medical tests that needed pre-certification. It was much more convenient than flipping through a large plan book. I never paid much attention to the other numbers on the card, but this night, I did.

I took the card down and looked at it closely. I found the 800 number for suicide prevention. I stared at it for quite some time. Should I even bother to call? I didn't have the necessary equipment to carry out my plan that night. I knew I'd have to wake up the next day and either do something about that or suffer through another day. *Could they actually help me? Who were these people on the other end of the phone, anyway? I knew they were volunteers, but how much training did they actually have?* I started to think that calling couldn't hurt, since I was desperate and didn't have an easy way out of my situation at the time.

I was uncertain of what I would say after the person on the other end greeted the caller with, "Suicide prevention hotline, how may I help you?" "Ummm, hello, my name is Lori-ellen and I want to kill myself." That line didn't sound good. Could they trace the number and send the police or ambulance to take me away? No, I needed to reply calmly to the question, so as not to raise an alarm, but hopefully get some help.

I practiced a few opening lines to help me and scribbled some notes on my yellow writing pad. I can't think under pressure and when nervous. I sometimes stutter or mix my words together. I didn't want them to think I was on drugs. I was chain smoking, but that didn't count. I needed to calm myself a bit if I was to make it through this phone call. I wanted to make sure to say that I was unhappy and felt helpless. Maybe they'd give me a referral to a psychologist on call so I could talk to him.

I put the card on the table next to the writing pad with my notes on it and took the phone off the receiver. I listened to the dial tone until it changed to a busy signal and replaced the phone on its cradle. I paced the floor, sweating, and prayed for guidance and courage. I wondered if God was listening. About ten minutes later, I picked up the phone and tried dialing the number. My hands were shaking so violently that

I misdialed twice. I put the phone down again. I wasn't ready; I was too nervous and frightened. I shook my hands out, paced the floors a few more times, and sat down once again at the table. I looked up to God and said, "Please help me make this call, Lord. I'm in pain and need help."

With a bit more conviction and courage this time, I picked up the phone again, and as carefully as I could manage, dialed the number. I listened to it ring several times and was wondering if anyone was there when the line on the other end engaged and a male voice said, "Suicide prevention hotline, how can I help you?"

There it was, the greeting I thought they would say. What else could they say?-- "Suicide prevention, do you want to kill yourself?"

After I heard the greeting, I took a deep breath, and said my practiced opening line, "I'm very unhappy and need some help."

"Will you tell me your name?" he asked.

"Lori-ellen," I replied.

"Are you alone right now, Lori-ellen, or is there anyone with you?"

"I'm alone."

"Lori-ellen, I am here to help in the best way that I can. Do you feel as though you may take your own life tonight?"

"I'm not sure."

"Do you have a plan?"

"Yes, but I don't have the things I need."

"What would you need?"

"A gun."

"Do you have access to a gun?"

"No, I didn't get it yet."

"That's a good thing."

"I guess so."

"It is so. By making this phone call, you are telling me that deep in your heart you don't want to kill yourself; you want to get the help you need to heal instead. It took great courage for you to make this call, and I admire you for it. Now, how can I help you with the process of getting help?"

"I don't know where to start."

"How did you find our phone number?"

"It was on the card from my insurance company that had a list of phone numbers on it."

"So you have insurance?"

"Yes."

"That's a good thing. It will help you greatly in your process towards healing. You won't need to worry about the cost."

"What do I do?"

"Do you have a plan book? It's the book that comes with your insurance card that has a list of doctors in every specialty."

"Yes, I have one."

"I want you to take out your plan book and look under the Mental Health section in your area. You will find a list of psychologists who take your insurance. Choose one, and first thing tomorrow morning, make the phone call to set up an immediate, emergency appointment. Tell the receptionist that the matter is urgent. If you can't get an appointment with the first doctor, go down the list until you find one who can see you. Not getting an appointment on the first call does not mean you are being cast off or rejected. Doctors are working with their schedules and may already be booked solid tomorrow. If you don't have any luck, you need to go the emergency room of the hospital closest to you. Do you understand what I'm saying?"

"Yes."

"Do you work?"

"Yes."

"Call in sick and go to that appointment or hospital. You really should take someone with you if you go to the hospital. You may be asked to stay for a few days until things settle down."

"I don't like hospitals, and that would be a career-ending move for me if my boss found out. I'm not sure I'm willing to take that step."

"Okay, but the most important thing is that you move away from thoughts of suicide and turn your attention to seeking professional help. Is there anyone, a friend or family member you can call who will come and stay with you tonight?"

"No, I don't want anyone to know."

"Well, I can understand that, but you shouldn't be alone."

"I'm not going to do anything."

"Will you make me that promise? Will you promise me that you will not harm yourself, but instead make a plan for tomorrow that is all about getting to a doctor for help? Can you make me that promise, Lori-ellen?"

"I think I can."

"Lori-ellen, obviously there is a reason you called. There is something dear to you that stopped you from acting on your plan and urged you to pick up the phone. Think about what it is that is so dear to you that prevented you from making the ultimate mistake. Can you do that for me?"

"I can try."

"Trying is all we can all do. Is there anything else I can help you with tonight?"

"No, I think I have a better plan now. Thank you."

"Good luck Lori-ellen, and remember we are only a phone call away. Good night."

"Good night." I hung up the phone.

That conversation was all of about ten minutes. It wasn't what I expected, but it gave me pause to think about what he said. There was something that made me pick up the phone. What was it that was dear to me? It wasn't how my family would feel if I died. It was something else. Something I hadn't thought of, something I treasured but made every effort not to think about in my misery.

I asked myself, "What stopped me?" over and over. It was now 3 o'clock in the morning. I was exhausted in every way. But my mind would not rest until I had my answer. I thought about the school where I had taught kindergarten since 1987. I lost my career as a teacher, but I was still working in the same school as a secretary. I saw my former students every day. They were in most of the grades by that time. They questioned me about why I wasn't in the classroom anymore. I didn't have the courage to tell them the truth, so I said that I needed a change. They begrudgingly accepted that answer.

How could I tell these young children that I hadn't followed my own dream, when I preached to them every year not to give up on theirs? I was a hypocrite, and every day that I walked into the main office rather than my classroom, I knew it. They needed to see me back on my feet, and I needed to show them that no matter what age they are, they can persevere, even when their dreams are thought to be lost. I couldn't fail them. They meant the world to me.

What would my principal, John, say to the staff and my former students? How would he explain my death? Would he lie? And what about the newspaper? Would it be reported there for my all of my former students' parents to read? How would they process the loss of their teacher in such a horrific way? How could I break the solemn promise I made to my students on the last day of every school year since 1987? I promised them that no matter how old they were, or where they were, if they ever needed me, I would come to them.

It was this solemn promise to all the boys and girls I ever taught that stopped me in my tracks from taking away the pain I was feeling. I still felt responsible for them in more ways than by teaching them reading, writing, and math. I was not only one of their teachers, but for many of them, I remained throughout their years at our school, their mentor, their life coach, and in many ways their surrogate mother.

As I thought about my former students and the solemn promise I made, my mind went to a visual of me as a six-year-old, standing on a path. The dirt path had trees on both sides, and I was standing in the middle of it. Some distance away, there I was again, only I was an adult looking at myself as a child. The adult me started to speak, and on the same pad that I was going to write my suicide note, I wrote the poem that changed my life.

I wrote what I saw, and the words flowed. I finished the poem in ten minutes and knew that whatever I wrote in the future, this was my most important work, and it remains so to this day. It captures my life story in seventeen lines and makes me promise myself that I will survive every time I read it. I keep it in a frame in my bedroom and read it when those dark thoughts creep back into my mind.

I knew there was something desperately wrong, and if I was going to survive, I needed professional help. The next day, I was determined to make that phone call. When I told the man on the phone the previous night that I didn't have a family member to stay with me, it was not because they lived too far away. It was because they would have only made matters worse.

It was a useless exercise in frustration trying to talk to my parents or siblings. All they saw was the whiny child of my youth--the child who cried every day for what they thought was no reason. There was a reason. I was a child with three siblings who mercilessly teased me and didn't understand that I took their teasing and taunts as their rejection of me. When I cried, I was told they were going to tease me more so I'd "toughen up," and "stop being such a baby." The child who had a song "Lori-ellen, Lori-ellen stop that yellin' Lori-ellen" sung to me in a whining and mocking tone over my tears of emotional pain never did toughen up.

I knew the therapy process would prove painful. In order to get the help I needed, I had to share everything that brought me to my therapist's couch. I needed to bring forth all my deepest darkest feelings, thoughts, and experiences in words said out loud, accept them, and let them go. It meant learning my patterns of behavior and response to triggers as a child to an adult and changing them in order to heal. I could not change the past, but I could have hope for relief from its vice-like grip over me by changing how I responded to stressful situations, emotional triggers, and painful memories. My journey home was about to begin.

CHAPTER **2**

TO TRUST ANOTHER

To trust another requires that you take off the suit of armor that has served to protect your heart from emotional pain

To trust another asks that you not only give of yourself, but expect that you will receive in return

To trust another means that you are free to be vulnerable – to let another embrace the wounded child within you

To trust another enables you to accept another's point of view without devaluing your own

To trust another takes all the strength and courage you can muster

To trust another is to trust yourself

Lori-ellen Pisani

TRUST IS A huge issue for me. My trust was broken too many times in the past, and to risk trying again terrified me. My family taught me that trust was easily betrayed. In my heart however, I knew that if I was going to get through this, I needed to trust someone. I needed someone not to judge me harshly for my thoughts and feelings. I wanted desperately for someone to acknowledge that what I felt was real and valid. I never had that in any previous relationship, and especially not from family. It boiled down to trusting myself enough to find a person I could open up to and be accepted. And funnily enough, a stranger was safer for me than my own family.

I looked in the mirror in my living room as I was putting on my coat for my first therapy session. *What would be my answer to the first question: "Well, what brings you here to see me?" The answer was, "everything." My whole life was the answer to why I was sitting on his couch. Could I even express myself in a way that made sense? Where would I start? How would I explain that at the age of thirty-one, I had no life--only a past that included painful memories, regrets, and the belief that the future would not be any different?*

Where would I start my story? Could I even share that deep in my heart I didn't want to live anymore, but was too afraid to commit suicide? Would he think I was crazy? Would I be committed immediately to the nearest psych hospital? The fear of being put in the hospital was overpowering. In my mind, I would lose my job and be worse off than before. It didn't have anything to do with how it might affect my family. They didn't enter into this equation, for they were the reason I came to be sitting on this couch in the first place.

I sat in his waiting room, sweating profusely. There were many forms to fill out-- insurance and a brief family and personal history. My hand shook terribly, and I was embarrassed by my poor handwriting. After filling out the requisite forms, I tried to read magazines, but only flipped through the pages. My mouth was dry, and I needed to use the bathroom but was too afraid to get up and find it. So, I crossed my legs and tried to rehearse my answer to the question about to be imposed.

The door opened, and out stepped Dr. Martin Mintz, psychoanalytic psychotherapist. He reminded me of Freud, with his white hair and beard. His voice was gentle as he asked me to enter his inner office. His office was more of a study, with bookshelves crowded with large volumes, and charcoal drawings of boats and outdoor scenes on the walls. His desk was full of papers. I remember a fireplace on one side of the room. I love fireplaces; they are comforting in that they give heat, the fire is pretty to watch, and I feel more at ease around them.

On the other side of the room were his couch and a few chairs. He took the chair set across from me at an angle, and I took a seat on the middle cushion of the couch, not too close. He flipped through the pages of the forms and put them on his knee. I couldn't tell what he was thinking. Finally, he picked up a yellow writing pad. I took a deep breath and waited for him to speak.

"So, what brings you here to see me?"

I took another breath and started with, "I don't know where to begin, but I am in deep trouble and know that I need help." I didn't tell him about the phone call to the suicide hotline. I was too ashamed. Since I wasn't sure where to start, Dr. Mintz suggested I start with my family and the home I grew up in. With all the courage I could muster, I began my story.

I was born on March 10th, 1963 at 7:07 p.m., but I wasn't alone. Seven minutes before me, my twin brother, Louis, entered the world. We were the last children born to Dan and Dianne Pisani. My eldest sister, Debby, was born April 1st, 1958, and my middle sister, Liz (short for Elizabeth), was born July 24th, 1960. My parents only wanted three children. I was a surprise.

I was named Lori-ellen, my mother said, "Because it went with Louis." There was no question as to what his name would be. Louis was the name of my paternal grandfather, and it was expected that all male children were to be named after him. My father's Christian name was Canio Louis Daniel. Canio was a name from my grandmother's side of the family, and Louis had to fit in there somewhere. My mother wasn't taking any chances, since my uncle's wife didn't follow that rule. She was outcast for a while. So, my twin was christened Louis Pisani III, and I was Lori-ellen Pisani.

Louis and I were brought home to join Debby and Liz in an English Tudor-style house on Vaughn Avenue, just down the street from the elementary school we would all attend. The front of the house had a sloping lawn that bordered the sidewalk with a large planting of pachysandra. The stone steps and slate path led up to the heavy wooden front door. The house had three floors, nine rooms, four bedrooms, two and a half bathrooms, a large living room, formal dining room, breakfast room, kitchen, office, and finished basement. The living room had a huge fireplace. It was made of cut stone and took up an entire wall. It was my favorite place in the house. The rooms were separated by curved archways and were furnished with comfortable yet traditional furniture. The floors were covered in deep red wall-to-wall carpet. The basement was finished with an old wood bar and built-in bookshelves. The main area in the basement was a large space that had a television and more seating. The backyard was large and had four patios, each on a different landing. The fourth patio had an above-ground pool. On the outside, the house was beautiful. No one would guess that on the inside were six people who by name were a family but did not know how to be one.

I moved on to talk about my siblings, the role they played in my life, and how they shaped my life living inside that house on Vaughn Avenue. I started with Debby, the oldest. As the first born, she was my father's "No.1" child. There are many pictures of her growing up. The album is filled with her and her big stuffed toys, sitting on my father's chest, sitting atop a pony, and of course the famous one most people have – Debby in the tub as a baby. The picture-taking grew more inconsistent with each child born, and by the time Louis and I came along, we could count a scarce handful.

Louis and I were also five years younger than she, and that age gap had its downside. She entered different maturational phases in her life while we were still in the previous one. For example, when Louis and I were born, Debby was entering kindergarten. She was starting school life and making friends while Louis and I were newborns.

We had little to do with each other in a positive way as children. What I do remember, however, is that as I grew older, it was she who set me up for situations that ended in my looking foolish or stupid. She was a practical joker and enjoyed telling me often how I wasn't wanted and was found by the side of the road. Her jokes and stories made everyone laugh but me. I was frightened to be around her, for fear of what she might say or do, so I kept my distance and knew that she was not the one to trust with my feelings, as they would be the topic of her next joke.

Debby shared one thing with my father that I'm sure she wishes she hadn't. She was an overweight child who struggles with this issue to this day. Just before she entered college, she went on a liquid diet for months and lost a huge amount of weight. She was unrecognizable, but gorgeous with long blonde hair, blazing green eyes, and a Roman sculpted nose. Her facial features most resemble my father's when he was a young Marine with the same green eyes and Roman nose. Her confidence soared as her weight dropped, as did her ability to be the center of attention.

She went off to study court reporting in Connecticut, but found after only one year, that college was not for her. She returned home at age nineteen. She began eating solid foods again, and consequently gained the weight back and then some. I remember a time when, for several months, Debby sat on the couch in the living room in her bathrobe and didn't speak much, if at all. She looked catatonic. For months, there were no more jokes or funny stories. She kept to herself and didn't interact with anyone. I thought it odd that my parents didn't insist on her seeing a therapist, but then again, therapy was not accepted as a legitimate treatment in my family at the time. So, my parents and the rest of us waited it out, or I should say waited her out.

We've never spoken of that dark time in her life. I can only say, as I look back, that she suffered from severe depression, and my parents did not intervene. I was in my early teens at this time and didn't know what to do. Since she wasn't talking, I didn't either. I'd sit across from her and wonder what was happening inside her head, and I felt sorry for her. Even though our interactions were mostly hurtful when I was a child, I never wanted this for her and wished that I could help. I don't know how, but Debby did come out of her depression, and resumed life with what I thought was a renewed sense of strength, but was actually a defensive posture. Before someone could hurt her by commenting on her weight, she would throw them off guard by being a sought-after companion at gatherings with her wit and infectious laugh.

She developed a personality much like my dad's. She was and is known as the "funny one" of the family. When in a group, Debby takes command of the conversation, interweaving anecdotes and impressions into her contributions to what's being said. Even I must admit, that once, at dinner with family for some holiday or other, Debby was on a roll, and I had to excuse myself and run to the bathroom, as I was laughing so hard I wet myself. She is a truly gifted comedienne, but when her impressions and mockery turn against me, I cringe and hope I don't burst into tears.

Debby loves to tell stories about each of us. They usually entail some embarrassing moment, or in my case, an incident when I cried again for "no apparent reason." To this day, she can still bring me to tears with an anecdote about one of my follies as a child, or with her mocking tone.

In 1984, while working for the general manager at a four star hotel in Manhattan, Debby married Joe, a successful businessman with drive and ambition. His success in the computer field afforded them a very comfortable lifestyle, moving from state to state and from one large home to another with big backyards and an in-ground pool at one point. He and Debby had my two nephews, Thomas and Daniel, and Debby was afforded the luxury of being a stay-at-home mom. Joe had his own issues, however. He was highly opinionated, a know-it-all, an "I can top that story" kind of guy. He was difficult to be around.

Debby stayed in the marriage for twenty years but was desperately unhappy. Near the end of their marriage, Debby was forced to work two jobs, as Joe's employment status grew unsteady. The boys were in their late teens when they finally divorced, and Debby was forced to move from her large house up on a hill to one that could fit on the first floor of her former home. Today, she works as both a teaching assistant and as a daycare provider. Thomas finished college and works for the government, and Daniel will start his first year of college. At this time (2010) I cannot say that we are closely bonded sisters, but we do have a relationship in which I do share some of my feelings and thoughts, but always with a bit of trepidation.

Next there's Liz. She is three years older than I, so my relationship with her was closer than mine was with Debby. She is tall and skinny with dark brown hair and brown eyes. Her face has sharp, sculpted features. She looks more like my mother than the rest of us kids.

As young children, we shared a bedroom. We spent many hours rearranging the furniture and setting up stores, tents, and playing all kinds of imaginary games. She often took me for rides on her blue bike. I sat on the seat with my arms around her waist while she peddled standing up to Sacconne's for Italian ices. She also taught me how to go down the slide on the playground. I was terrified, but she stayed with me, and kept encouraging me until I was able to do it without crying. She is very pretty, highly imaginative and intelligent, but she was also the black sheep of the family.

As she grew older, she became a wild child who did what she wanted without regard for the consequences. Our close relationship ended as she began middle school and I was in third grade. She had new worlds to conquer. As a young teen, she seemed to relish breaking all the rules of the house. She broke curfew, skipped school, lied constantly to my parents as to where she was and what she was doing, and ran with a rowdy crowd. She'd hang out on the west end of town, smoking pot and being cool. She asked me many times to lie for her and tell my parents that she was with a particular girlfriend rather than hanging out on the streets. She often asked me to check the mail for referral notices sent from school to advise my parents of her excessive absences and behavior problems.

She took a great deal of pride in her appearance, and boys noticed. In high school, she had boyfriends all the time. Of course, she always chose the "bad boys." Either they had fast cars and money or shared her pot addiction. She started smoking pot at about age thirteen and continued to smoke it every day of her life until her downfall in 2006.

There are too many occasions to count when my parents were called by junior high school administrators who were exasperated by her antics. My parents couldn't take the chance of having her go to the local high school. It was a huge school with too many bad influences around, so they enrolled her in a private Catholic high school. That lasted less than a year. She was expelled for cutting classes, wild behavior, and finally for calling a nun "crazy" in front of a large group of students. That was the night my father lost total control of his temper, and instead of breaking her in half, he broke half the china in the house. With each piece he smashed, he screamed expletives and muttered words I couldn't hear. It was left to Debby, Louis, and me to clean it up. Liz was sent to our room.

My father then did something that, to this day, I can't figure out. After we cleaned up the broken mess of china, my father yelled for Debby, Louis, and me to come to my parents' bedroom. One by one, he asked each one of us in a menacing tone and with glaring eyes, "Are you afraid of me?" We stood stock-still as he waited for our answers. I honestly can't remember what the others said, but when it was my turn, he took a step toward me, and I blurted out, "Yes!" Without a word, he went over to the dresser, took the money he had in his wallet, divided it into four piles, and walked out of the house.

Through all of this, my mother didn't say a word. She stood there with the rest of us, not knowing what to do. After a few minutes, she sent us away so she could be alone. We huddled in the hallway and muttered how this wouldn't have happened if it weren't for Liz and her screwed-up behavior. We peeked inside the bedroom to find her sleeping; she never heard a thing. We knew from that moment on, she was the one to watch out for. I lost the sister who was my only friend in the house. And because of what she did, I thought I had lost my father as well. He returned a few hours later after we had all gone to bed.

Liz, as I said, is very intelligent. She managed to finish high school without attending for almost half of each year. She thought of going to college, but that would take too much of her time. Instead, she enrolled in secretarial school. When she graduated, she headed straight for New York City to make her way in the world.

She met a man, Michael, who was a performance artist with big plans. Together, they built a party-planning business that was highly successful. Their clients ranged from very wealthy families throwing six-figure extravagant parties for their children's Bar Mitzvahs to large corporations using the QE 2 as their venue. Liz's creative talents were in high gear, and she thrived in this business. She didn't know it yet, but she was experiencing mania. She was living the high life, and loving it. Her boyfriend Michael, however, had a cocaine addiction and anger management problems. He was extremely abusive toward Liz both emotionally and physically, and she fled the relationship as well as the business. As far as her relationship with the rest of the family, all I can say is that it was tense. She continued to live life on her terms, and it caused a great deal of tension amongst and between everyone.

She took a job working for a single practice attorney, Bob. Although she didn't have the necessary certification, she served as both his administrative and legal assistant. She was a quick study and learned a great deal about law in a short period of time, all the while maintaining her pot addiction. It increased in its intensity over the years. At this point, she couldn't go more than a few hours without smoking a joint. Bob knew it, but didn't say a word. She was good at her job, and that's all that mattered to him. Her behavior, however, began to change dramatically in 2001.

It was just after 9/11. Liz called me in a frantic panic over what happened. She was experiencing terrible dreams and fears that the terrorists were going to get her. This was a total break from reality. She didn't even know anyone hurt or killed in the attack, but here she was, at the center of it, and their next target. I did what I could to calm her down and encouraged her strongly to seek therapy. She was out of control, and I had no idea what was wrong with her. I feared that she was having a nervous breakdown and needed to be hospitalized. She didn't agree with me at the time and remained volatile in her temperament for three more years. Finally, in 2004, she asked me to bring her to a psychiatric hospital/rehabilitation center. She believed, as did the whole family, that her addiction to pot, and being in another abusive relationship which caused her to attempt suicide had finally gotten the best of her., and she was out of control. Her breaking point was a suicide attempt after a violent argument with her boyfriend.

She spent about a month in the hospital. I went for family therapy with her, and learned that she was diagnosed as bipolar, a diagnosis she rejected out of hand, even though by that time, both my father and I were already diagnosed with this disorder. The first thing she did upon release from the hospital was smoke a joint.

For the next two years, she waged her own war on this illness, with two more hospitalizations. She was in and out of therapy and out of compliance with her medications. Her work was suffering, and she was on a fast track to self-destruction. Her ultimate downfall would come in December of 2006. That nightmare episode took years off my life.

And finally, there is Louis, my twin. As infants, he and I were put in the same crib in one of the bedrooms. We took turns rocking each other to sleep with our silky blankets tucked under our chins. Louis sucked his thumb, and I sucked my pointer finger. We both rubbed our silky blankets, he along his chin, and me between my fingers and thumb. To this day, I continue to rock myself to sleep with a piece of silky fabric in hand. I stopped sucking my finger when my grandfather, "Poppy," threatened to cut it off if I didn't stop. Louis stopped sucking his thumb when he got braces. As the braces came off, and Louis grew older, he looked more like my father. He is approximately six feet tall, with an imposing stature, although not overweight. He is very handsome. He has dark hair, piercing gray-green eyes, and a dazzling white smile. When he walks into a room, everyone notices.

When we were very young, we loved being twins. We shared everything and did everything together. As toddlers, we spoke our own language. We translated for others when they couldn't understand what we were saying. I was fiercely protective of him. He was and remains a part of me. We completed each other, each filling in gaps of the other's core personality traits. Dr. Mintz later explained this as "twinning," and it's not healthy for a relationship. It is something I needed to work on in therapy. I couldn't separate my life from his and took his issues on as my own. It was finally resolved when he married for the second time in June 2006.

When we registered for kindergarten, we sat at two different desks to be interviewed. One teacher asked Louis what he had for breakfast and I called over from where I was sitting to respond, "He had Cap'n Crunch." The teacher sitting with me asked, "What do you think you'd like about school?" and before I could respond, Louis called out, "She'll do reading, I'll do math." My mother instantly asked for us to be placed in separate classrooms and they agreed without hesitation.

My mother recalls an account of an odd exchange while at the beach. Louis and I couldn't have been more than five years old. We were there during one of our summers spent in Belmar, New Jersey. Debby, Liz, and Louis were playing in the water, and I was standing on the sand with one hand on my hip and the other shielding my eyes so I could look out over the water. My mother walked over to me and asked, "What are you doing?"

I answered, "I'm watching out for Louis."

She replied, "It's my job to look after you kids; I'm the mother."

I instantly retorted, "He's my twin, and it's my job to look after him. You don't have to."

As we grew, our relationship oscillated from intense feelings of bonding on my part and fierce fighting. Louis had it rough as the only male in the house besides my father. He was called upon to do harder chores and ordered about like a soldier. My father's way of speaking to him was critical and harsh. Although he thought all of us to be his servants, he was particularly hard on Louis. Boys don't play; they work like men. Louis was working like a man, from a very early age.

My father was a hands-on, do-it-yourself project man. He always had something for Louis to do and left him no time to play with friends or relax. I saw the look on Louis' face, and although I was experiencing the same treatment, my heart ached for him. He ran around, being yelled at and called names, all the while trying to please a demanding father. He never could, and ended most days exhausted and feeling hurt.

Perhaps the ultimate chore for Louis as a child was painting the upper half of our house. Remember, this was an English Tudor-style home, three stories high. My mother and we girls had to paint the trim on the windows and the lower portion of the house. My father, the project manager, erected a scaffold for the upper half. It was only partially secure as the poles sank into the soil, and the scaffold rocked side to side when anyone attempted to climb it.

Louis was sent up the scaffold to the roof to paint the eaves. We were only nine at the time, and I was terrified for him. But Louis couldn't be scared. There was no time, and my father expected him to get the job done that morning. He had to bring the scaffold back to the rental place the next day or pay another day's fees, and it was the last job that had to be done to finish painting the house.

My father leaned against the legs of the scaffold to steady it and ordered Louis to climb up it to the roof. The roof was made of slate and was slippery. He made it to the top and waited for the paint and brushes to be sent up on a rope pulley system my father rigged. I couldn't stop what I was doing to watch, since that might incur my father's wrath, so I kept busy painting the lower portion of the house, but prayed for Louis's safety the entire time.

I only looked up when I heard a yell. It wasn't Louis, but my father. I ran over to see what had happened, only to find my father covered in paint. Louis had not fallen off the roof, but in his haste to finish the job quickly, he knocked over the paint can, and paint poured over my father's head. He was pissed beyond all measure. At that point, Louis didn't want to come down from the scaffold for fear of what would happen.

My mother had had enough and yelled at my father to stop screaming, a bold move on her part. Believe it or not, he actually did. He ordered Louis down from the scaffold and into the house. No more was said about it, except for my father cursing repeatedly as he went inside to clean up. The next day, my father went up the scaffold to finish the job, with all of us kids holding onto it so it wouldn't fall over. It took eight weeks to paint that house, and after that, none of us kids wanted to see another paintbrush again.

As we went through elementary school, Louis and I were never in the same class. We went our separate ways during the day but came home each day to what seemed like endless rounds of fighting. I wanted to know about his day and how he was feeling, and he wanted nothing to do with me. He kept all his feelings inside and screamed at me when I'd say that I felt badly for him especially after being either cursed at or hit by my father.

He raged against me, pushed me, punched me, told me he hated me and to get away from him. All I wanted to do was comfort him, since my mother did not, but he railed against any kind of affection from me. I loved him dearly and I wanted him to know that I felt his pain, but he rejected all my efforts, thus leaving me with a feeling of rejection and abandonment. I cried often for him and for me. As we reached high school, he had football to keep him busy, and I was in the stands every Saturday cheering him on.

Louis didn't finish college; it wasn't the place where he learned best. He learned by hands-on, real-world experiences. After completing a couple of years studying business and accounting, he quit school in 1983, and went to work at the same hotel as Debby in Manhattan. He worked his way up to the night manager's position and stayed for several years. When he left that hotel to advance to a different position in another hotel, he was required perform tasks for which he was not trained, and none was provided. He quit that position and came home to sit on a chair and stare at the television for over a year. It was reliving Debby's nightmare all over again.

He refused to talk about it and turned a deaf ear to my parents screaming at him to get up and get moving. Once again, therapy was not even a consideration. My parents thought that calling him a "lazy ass" every day would be enough to get him to move. It didn't. I was of little help, as I was away at school.

After about a year and a half of sitting in that chair, he went to work for my father. He retired from his previous union position to open his own shop and took Louis on board as his partner. It was a tense working relationship, but it got Louis out of the house, and that's what mattered.

When my parents sold their home in 1997, Louis moved into his own apartment. It was close to mine, and we often took long walks together. We passed houses that we dreamed of buying and chatted about our future plans as we walked. Our relationship returned to being close once again, and I was thrilled. In 2002, Louis and I decided to take an apartment together. Principally we moved in together to save money, but my need for "twinning" once again returned. During that time, Louis reconnected with an ex-girlfriend from high school. She had a four-year-old son from a former relationship, and Louis loved playing the role of stepdad. It was a whirlwind relationship, and they married shortly after reconnecting.

I had a hard time letting go of him. I didn't care for this woman; she was loud and bawdy. She giggled incessantly, and she wasn't right for him, but outwardly I gave my support. In my heart, I knew that the marriage wouldn't last, and once again, my heart ached for him.

During his marriage, Louis grew into a very difficult person to deal with. He was stubborn, hot-tempered, and demanding. He was provocative in conversation, instigating arguments over the smallest of things. He demanded that I agree with his argument or perception even when I didn't. He had little patience and even less tolerance for anyone's shortcomings. His words could be harsh and hurtful. I considered this to be the effects of living the life we did as children, and I wanted to help him heal. He insisted that he had no ill effects from the past, and that I needed to stop insisting that he did.

When the marriage ended a year or so later, Louis came back to live with me. I still had the two-bedroom apartment we rented before he met his first wife. I had my twin back. He was with me and I could take care of him. I assumed the role of mother and wife to a degree. I cooked for him and cared for him. I lent him money when he needed it and did whatever I could to make up for years of hurt caused by our years at 42 Vaughn Avenue. It wouldn't last long.

Louis moved out after a few months into his own place nearby. I moved to a one-bedroom apartment in the same complex. About a year later, he found love again, this time on the internet. He married again four years ago, and is now the father of Evan, his son. I let him go this time, for he had found his love and has a family of his own. My "twinning" days are over.

CHAPTER 3

BROKEN HEART

How can a mother give love
When she's never known her own?
For my mother's birth permanently blinded
The mother she had known

Grandma raged against her
And her father then took flight
My mom was left to care for her
And prayed with all her might

She met a handsome soldier
Who swept her off her feet
He promised love and happiness
Those needs she longed to meet

But soon after they married
These things did disappear
Leaving mother to care for children
Feeling abandoned and in fear

She raised us all with motherly concern
But yield her heart she couldn't

For her mother and her husband
Could give her love but wouldn't

Her heart was unavailable
Though I needed her to say
I love you child with all my heart
But her pain would not give way

Lori-ellen Pisani

HOW CAN I describe my mother? She hasn't played a significant role in my story thus far. That's because I don't have many explicit memories of her as a child, other than my very first memory and her involvement in school functions. She was pretty, standing five feet seven inches tall, with thick dark-brown hair, brown eyes, and sculpted facial features. She was always thin, with long skinny legs and a willowy body.

Her role in my life was that of a mother, not a mommy. She did everything she was supposed to do. I was fed, clothed, and cared for, but I never felt love from her. She was distant in every way. When I ran to her crying, she'd send me away with the admonishment to "knock it off." I never remember being hugged as a child. She always told me not to expect love or praise from my father, but it was she who also withheld these things from me. And just like my father, compliments were not her style. She too had the gift of hurting with words as well as hands. Although she didn't call me names, she did nothing to protect me from the ceaseless and merciless taunts from my siblings. I learned quickly that she was not one I could open my heart up to. She was emotionally unavailable.

She was active in school activities. She attended all functions, chaperoned school trips, and helped with school projects. She handmade all of our Halloween costumes, and was Liz's Girl Scout Troup leader. She was a very involved and interested parent with teachers, and she volunteered for PTA fundraisers. When we got home from school however, we were sent to our rooms to do homework by ourselves. She said she didn't understand the "new math," so we were on our own. There were times that she'd play board games with us. We helped in the kitchen and ran errands with her. But these were activities done as a group, and I remember precious little that she did with me alone.

She was busy raising four children, all within a five-year age range of each other. She punished with either a slap of her hand or by wielding a belt across our legs. She needed order in the house if she was to get her work done and have some peace and quiet. Winters were the worst, as we were cooped up all day and under her feet. I tried to stay away and give her space. She didn't read stories to me at night or spend quality time doing "mommy and me" activities. I never heard the classic fairytales until I read them to my own students.

She never expressed many feelings, only those of anger or disappointment toward us, or more so, toward my father. She met him while she was working as a dental assistant. He was a Marine Corporal who looked like a Roman god and was charming. He was in the chair and fainted during a minor procedure. She thought that was funny. He didn't, but he asked her out anyway. After a few years dating, they married on October 13th, 1956. She was twenty years old, and desperate to get out of her mother's house.

She told me once that she knew the day after she married my father that she had made a mistake. "It was as if a light switch was turned off," she described to me. Gone was the handsome soldier and charmer who swept her off her feet. In his place was a demanding, difficult man who immediately started treating her with much less respect. He yelled and screamed at her, ordered her about, called her names, and humiliated her.

The name-calling and abusive language from my father towards her was relentless. Any sign of affection between the two was almost nonexistent. I often wondered how we even made it onto the scene. But in those days, it was a woman's duty to marry and have children, so that's how it was. She had four children under the age of five by the time she was twenty-eight years old.

Over the years, my mother grew in courage and began to fight back. My childhood is riddled with memories of my parents' screaming matches and name-calling. I truly believed that was how they communicated. Rarely was there any kind of conversation that didn't turn into a fight soon after it started. As children, we learned that when they were together, the fireworks were about to begin. I tried to stay clear of the explosions, or I would be brought into the middle of it. My father demanded that I or anyone else within earshot of the argument agree with him as he called my mother "a damn fool." My mother threatened with her glaring brown eyes that I'd better not say a word. Eventually, I gathered the courage to say "I'm not getting involved in this" and ran quickly away.

What I learned about my mother was that she was miserable in her marriage and had no idea what unconditional love was. She never experienced it as a child, and definitely not in her marriage. She bore her children out of obligation and didn't know how to be affectionate with us. She was a stranger to me in this way, and although our relationship today is much more affectionate, I was, and can be still, fearful of my mother's ability to hurt me with her words. I don't share many personal feelings with her. I only share my thoughts about topics, and even that can be dangerous territory. To this day, I remain more of a friend than a child, although over the years, she has mellowed, and is more forthcoming with praise and affection.

My Father's Ways

My father's ways were quite unique
In manner, style, and tone
He had ways of showing love
Unique and all his own

I remember as a tiny child
Kissing his puffed-out cheek
And wanting to think that this was love
Though the words he dared not speak

His ways were different, we'd all agree
And misunderstood, mostly by me
Perhaps it's best to believe in my mind
That his love was truly one of a kind

Lori-ellen Pisani

You may wonder--who was this man that barked orders at his children, made his wife miserable, and had the neighbors wondering if they should call the authorities? My father was a very large man. At five feet eleven inches tall, he weighed in, at his heaviest, at 350 lbs. He had a loud voice, strong arms, a big belly, gray hair, green eyes, and was strong enough to lift a car's front end off the ground. He had a tattoo of a bulldog on his right arm with U*S*M*C forever printed over the dog's head and his ID # 1305226, tattooed below its chin. When he entered a room, people actually stopped to look. His massive size and commanding presence demanded their attention.

He was a busy man, working as a business agent for a national electrical union. As a child, I never knew how to explain what my father did. When asked, I'd always say, "My father's a contractor" because he spent a lot of time negotiating contracts between the labor force in the shops he handled and management. I didn't know the term "business agent" at the time.

He let us know that his job came first and his family second. He also made it quite clear that his children were there to serve him and work. My father did not believe in "play" as he called it. We didn't have friends over much, and we were told not to make plans for the weekends. We had too many chores to do.

"Dan the Man," "Moose," "Dan," and "Connie" were the names those who knew him called him by. We all had nicknames he called us by, when he wasn't screaming our Christian names. He called Debby "No. 1" for being first-born and Liz was "Snake," since she was tall and skinny. Louis was called "Moose Head." Mine was "Spike" due to my large nose. Even my mother had a nickname--"Chicken," for her skinny legs. His favorite nicknames however for all of us were "Damn Fool" "Bimbo," and "Shit for Brains." He used these most often when we disappointed him or made a mistake. As a former Marine, he was more of the sort who believed that a spirit needed to be broken in order for character to be built.

We spent our weekends working from dawn until dusk doing yard work, painting, building or repairing one thing or another. My father barked orders and shouted expletives and insults at us as we ran as quickly as possible to get the job done, and done right. His favorite tool to use outside was the hose. If we didn't move fast enough, he'd squirt us with it and use it to point in the direction we should be running. Every Saturday, our neighbors looked out of their windows in disbelief as four kids ran serpentine around a very large house mowing lawns, raking leaves, pulling weeds, washing windows, cleaning gutters, and clipping hedges, all while our father shouted orders and called us names.

His job took him away for most of the day, and upon his return, his primary interaction with us was to make lists of chores to do on the weekends, yell, and hit us with newspapers, his belt, or any other handy object for bad behavior reported by my mother. One time, he threw me from one end of the living room to the other when he was at a loss for words. He had odd ways of punishing besides these. I remember standing with my nose to the telephone pole because I complained that one of the chores he gave me was too hard. When Liz was suspended from school, he made us all scrub the kitchen floor with our toothbrushes. If he wasn't grabbing, throwing, yelling, or hitting, he was ordering us to clean something or other with our toothbrushes.

On the flip side, he was also a master storyteller. He weaved tales that enraptured his listeners into thinking these fantastical fictions were true. Other stories had us rolling off the couch with laughter. He enjoyed scaring the hell out of us kids with his séances. We gathered around the dining room table with the lights dimmed low, while he conjured up all kinds of spirits. Somehow, he had rigged a chair or object in the room to move when he commanded it to, and we'd run screaming from the table.

There were times when he took the family on mini adventures, all in the name of food. We'd be sitting in the living room, watching TV, and he'd say, "I'm in the mood for a New York City hot dog from a guy I know on 47th Street." And as soon as he said it, we were all piling in the car ready for the adventure into the city. He did this once or twice a month with different foods – wedges at the Wedge Inn in the Bronx, ice cream from Carvelle, and pies from the Red Door Bakery. We loved his food cravings. He was in a good mood and playful on these outings. On these occasions he was more like a daddy than the father I feared.

In addition, he enjoyed playing practical jokes, almost sending one of his friends to the hospital by planting a plastic snake under the driver's side seat of his car. When Charlie got into the car, he reached down to adjust his seat, felt the snake, and nearly had a heart attack as he scrambled screaming from the car. My father played his practical jokes on family and friends alike. You never knew what was going to happen when he disappeared for a few minutes while company was in the house. My nephews still remember the jokes he played on them as children.

When my sister Debby had her two boys and the rest of us were grown, my father's demeanor changed. He visited his grandchildren often, holding them, feeding them and telling them funny stories. He was called "Poppy King," and the boys loved being around him. It was a complete 180-degree turn from how he interacted with his own kids.

And then there was the time he played Santa Claus. My nephew, Thomas, was about two years old, and my father decided to dress up as Santa Claus. But he was no ordinary Santa. As Joe kept the camera rolling, my father played the role of Santa in such a way that would make Eddie Murphy blush. He played a drunk, coked-up Santa who had lost his way. He sat on the steps slugging his whiskey, snorting cocaine, and smoking a "joint" while looking at an upside-down map of Africa to try and find his way. We could have made big money with that video, but it wasn't suited for *America's Funniest Home Videos*. It was however, funny as hell.

My father was also a dreamer. As an adult, I described him as a cross between Ralph Cramden from the TV show *The Honeymooners* and Archie Bunker from *All in the Family*. His size, temper, loud mouth, and scheming to make his fortune were combinations of these two characters. I once counted nineteen times that he used the "f" bomb in a five-minute conversation (if you could call it that) on the phone. He was never content to be a business agent for the union. He had big dreams and was determined to see all of them come true.

Strangely enough, I loved this man dearly and feared him at the same time. It was a complicated relationship that I would come to understand years later and only with the help of my therapist. Although he was mainly responsible for the beatings and many other painful/repulsive memories in my life, I craved his attention and any words of love or praise. My main mission in life was to please him. I was determined to make him happy and proud of me.

This relationship doesn't appear to make sense. Why would I love a man so dearly who had hurt and humiliated me? Why was he more important to please than my mother, who didn't taunt me? Perhaps because when he wasn't hitting, screaming, or being abusive, he was charismatic, generous, charming, and funny. It was as if he had two completely separate people living in one body. I loved one, and feared and was repulsed by the other, but I could not separate the two.

CHAPTER **4**

ESCAPE

As I fall asleep each night
I think of things to dream
I try to keep out conscious thoughts
Of anger, fear and pain

I do not want to stay awake
Reliving in my mind
Memories that will disturb my rest
Preventing sleep I need to find

Before I close my eyes to rest
I press the tape to start
I listen to the stories read
Hands clasped across my heart

I've learned this attempt is futile
This farce to escape my pain
The unconscious is awake while sleeping
Replaying memories that remain

Lori-ellen Pisani

YOU MUST UNDERSTAND that it was not possible to communicate all this information about my family in a few sessions. For almost a year of weekly sessions, I spent fifty- minutes talking about everyone in my family and my relationships with each. By 1995, Dr. Mintz knew that I was suffering from severe depression and broached the subject of referring me to Dr. Itamar Salamon, a colleague and psychiatrist, for confirmation and to begin a medication protocol. I was afraid to go, and wondered if I could stay on the meds for only a short period of time. I didn't want to be thought of as the crazy one in the family who had to be on medication because I couldn't handle life. I thought that by talking it all out, I'd feel better and could go on with my journey. I could put the past behind me and not let it affect me anymore. *Was medication the answer to why I was feeling so miserable? Could a little pill "cure" me?* I was hopeful, but a short-term solution was not what it ended up being. For the foreseeable future, I would see both Dr. Mintz for therapy and Dr. Salamon every month for a medication evaluation and follow-up. They would have need in the future for further consultation, as more of my story unfolded and my journey continued.

I trusted Dr. Mintz implicitly regarding my need to meet with him, but I feared what I would be told by Dr. Salamon and had no clue as to where to start. *How much does he know about me? Do I have to start from the beginning and go through my whole life's story again? What kind of medication would I be on? Would I need to be on it the rest of my life? Am I brain damaged? Is my whole life some kind of weird movie that I've lived and not reality? Am I insane?* These are the questions that went through my mind as I waited in his waiting room. His office was in a small cottage located on the grounds of an Episcopal church. I arrived twenty minutes early and had a cigarette before I got out of the car.

I gathered up my courage and walked into the cottage. It reminded me of the old English cottages I've seen in paintings. The ceilings were low, the rooms were small, and the doors and windows looked original to this very old building. It even smelled like an old cottage. I took a seat and attempted to look through a magazine, but only flipped the pages. *How do I start? Where do I start?* I felt like I was having déjà vu. I remembered my first meeting in 1994, with Dr. Mintz. *Would I, could I connect with this new doctor who literally had my brain in his hands?* I didn't have much time to ponder that question before the door opened and Dr. Itamar Salamon popped his head out into the waiting room and asked, "Lori-ellen?"

"Yes," I responded.

"Come on in," he said as he opened the door wider and I walked through another little waiting area that separated his office from another doctor's, and through the double doors to his office. It was cozy, with a couch, a large leather chair for me to sit in, and another smaller chair just across from mine. His desk was toward the rear of the room. There was a side door that led outside to the parking lot, and small windows with curtains behind his desk. On the end table next to my chair were a clock and a box of tissues. Dr. Salamon had on a sports jacket, dress shirt, and a bow tie. He was clearly in the same age range as Dr. Mintz, and the diplomas on the wall next to his desk assured me he knew his stuff. He pointed to the leather chair. I sat down and folded my hands in my lap. I had no idea if I should start talking or if he would put an end to my immense anxiety.

Dr. Salamon began, "I've spoken with Dr. Mintz, who asked me to speak with you about anti-depressant medications."

"Yes, it appears as though my depression is more than the average person's, and I need help to manage it," I replied.

"You're right. When a person's depressive mood has not lifted in several weeks, it is deemed clinical depression. The medication will help lift your mood so that you can deal more effectively with your depression."

"Will I have to be on it long?" I asked.

"Let's take things one step at a time. You need to know that it takes a few weeks to get into the bloodstream before you feel the effects."

"What am I going to feel?"

"Well, you won't be doing cartwheels, but you should feel a lift from the deep sadness you feel to a more even keel. It's very important that you follow the directions carefully, and that you remain in therapy with Dr. Mintz. You can call me at any time if you need to. I will be checking in with Dr. Mintz to see how the medication is working. You and I will meet once a month or so to evaluate the meds and determine if changes need to be made."

"Okay, I guess we should get started." We walked over to his desk where he wrote out a prescription for an anti-depressant. He reminded me that I should call if I felt the need or experienced any unusual side effects, and that he was going to be in contact with Dr. Mintz as well.

"Thank you, Dr. Salamon. I will be sure to follow the directions carefully, and I will call if I need to." We made an appointment for the next month. This gave the drug time to get into my system, and I should know if I was feeling better. I took the prescription and left his office through the side door.

I went directly to the pharmacy to fill the script, and then went home. I read about the side effects, and decided they were worth it if I was going to feel better. I took the pills and followed up with my therapy appointments and meetings with Dr. Salamon. As it happened, I needed to try a few different anti-depressants over the next year due to side effects. I kept at it, fighting my way through, and praying the whole time that something would work for me.

Dr. Mintz's chief objective at this point was to have me begin the regime of anti-depressant medications to lighten my burden and allow me to continue therapy with perhaps a better perspective and a lighter mood. I started the medication and continued to chatter away about my family during my sessions. I was feeling better, getting all my "stuff" out of my head and into the open. I thought I was on my way to completing my work and moving on with my life. How naïve....

Surprisingly, during one of my sessions, Dr. Mintz wanted to know my very first memories as a child. He needed to understand my reasoning behind the feelings I had as it related to the descriptions I provided of each family member. There was much more behind these accounts that led me toward such a profound depressive state. It would serve to open up Pandora's Box, as you will read later. At the time, however, all I could remember was the teasing, taunting, hitting, yelling, feeling unloved and unwanted.

Children are teased all the time, and most may cry but are easily soothed. They are able to reconnect with friends and family once an apology is offered. I'd seen it first hand in my own classroom. It was a firm and strict rule that my students were not to be teased by any other classmate. My explanation to them was that it was mean and hurtful and therefore unacceptable. If one of my students was teased or bullied, I immediately went into "mommy mode." I comforted the crying child and made it quite clear to the offender that he/she had made a mistake and needed to correct it immediately. My tone was firm, and my facial expressions serious and stern.

All my students were encouraged on a daily basis to come to me with any issue that hurt their feelings and I would be sure to address it. It was not unusual for them, when frustrated or angry, to call out "Mom!" to get my attention. I'd smile, and say, "Yes, sweetheart, what's the matter?" Once they realized what they said, they'd giggle, but press forward with what they needed from me. No one else laughed when one of my students called me "Mom." I never made that a rule; it's just the way it was.

Dr. Mintz needed to know why my reactions to what seemed like incidental matters were so extreme. there was something more--something I had not revealed. It didn't make sense. I was blocked, stopped dead in my tracks. It was easy to tell my tale through my family's lives. But that wouldn't reveal the "why" answer. *Why was I so invested in their lives and not my own? Why did it matter so much what they thought about me when others could easily dismiss them as being mean?*

I took some time between sessions to think about those things that remained vivid in my memory. Since I was so descriptive in my relationships with family members, what happened to me that I couldn't remember, but had such a profound effect on me?

I was having trouble remembering who I was as a child and the events that affected me directly. I drew a blank and it was frustrating. Tears rolled down my cheeks as I struggled to remember. Weeks passed, and I was still stumped. Although Dr. Mintz didn't want to put thoughts in my head, he knew that he needed to say something to jar my memory. In desperation for something to say, I said, "Please help me. I can't remember."

He responded, "I'm wondering if you are having such a hard time because there might be something sexual in your early life experiences that you have blocked from your mind."

I sat bolt upright upon hearing these words. I picked up my jaw, which had dropped to my chest and shouted, "What are you saying? Are you saying that I was sexually abused and can't remember? That's disgusting! Surely I would remember something like that!" Suddenly I found it hard to breathe. I started to hyperventilate and was enraged. How could he suggest such a thing! I was repulsed and horrified, embarrassed, and frightened. All these feelings came upon me at once. I wanted to bolt out the door and never return, but I was afraid to get in my car for fear that I'd ram it straight into a tree.

I wanted to scream and call Dr. Mintz a bloody quack, but the words wouldn't come out. This man that I had spent two years with was now someone to be feared. Instead of feeling comforted by telling my story as I knew it, I was thrown into a whirlwind of emotions and didn't know what to do with them. Needless to say, it was well over my allotted session time before I was calm enough to leave with the promise that I would not harm myself and would return the next day. I didn't want to make any promises. I wanted to run as far away as I could--escape to an island, never to be seen again. Reluctantly, I made the promise.

On the way home, my mind raced, searching for an answer to the sexual question. Surely Dr. Mintz had it all wrong. This couldn't be a part of my life. I didn't have sex before I was seventeen. *But why did my feelings change from the rage I experienced in his office to feelings of humiliation? Was I embarrassed by what he said? Or, did the word "sexual" trigger something more in the recesses of my mind?* After all, Dr. Mintz did explain that sexual abuse has many forms. It doesn't have to mean intercourse. It has more to do with the feelings you have after being coerced, threatened or forced into doing something that was a violation of your most personal space. That got me thinking....

CHAPTER **5**

LITTLE GIRL LOST

This little girl is lost
I have no mommy to comfort me
I have no daddy to protect me
I have no siblings who accept me
And my home is not a safe place for me

This little girl is lost
I lay in bed at night afraid to sleep
I pray each night for God's help

I pray that he will change my family's ways
And I will feel wanted and safe in my home

This little girl is lost
Gone are the carefree days of childhood

They've been replaced with tears and fear
And nightly prayers to grow up fast
I made promises to God that I will never allow
another child to feel the way I felt

This little girl is lost...
Who will find me?

Lori-ellen Pisani

MY FIRST REAL memory as a child is the day my mother told me I had to go to the hospital for an operation. The year was 1967, and I was four years old. We were sitting in the living room. She was sitting on the couch and I was sitting in front of her on an ottoman. None of the other kids was around. I never remembered my mother asking to speak to me alone. Usually, she told me what to do or sent me to my room.

She said, "Lori-ellen, come and sit with me for a minute. I need to tell you something." She took a deep breath and continued, "Lori-ellen, you have to go the hospital for an operation."

I didn't know why and asked, "What do you mean, operation? What's wrong with me?"

"Remember you have been going to see Dr. Williams for your terrible earaches? Well, you need to have that fixed, and an operation is how doctors fix things that are wrong," she answered.

The problem was that I had mass on the mastoid bone in my inner ear that did not dissolve with medication. In fact, it continued to grow in size, causing frequent and very painful ear infections. Because the mass was growing, the ear, nose, and throat doctor, Dr. Williams, determined that it needed to be removed, along with the mastoid bone.

What my mother did not tell me was that her brother, Leonard, had the same issue and as a result of his surgery, was deaf in that ear. His surgery also involved a major incision down the side of his head behind the ear. I, however, was spared this, as my doctor was pioneering a new surgery that would remove the mass and the mastoid by going through my ear canal rather than around it. This was groundbreaking surgery in 1967, and my case was included in one of the medical journals. Not only did Dr. Williams remove the mass and the bone, but he managed to preserve my hearing as well. Today, this surgery is no longer performed. I must, however, continue to be careful. I have ruptured the eardrum in that ear several times in the past, and with each rupture the risk of hearing loss is greater. I was told never to jump in pools, dive, or swim underwater, as the pressure might be too much for the eardrum. Flying also causes problems, but I use special earplugs and nasal spray to deal with the changes in cabin pressure.

"Will it hurt?" I asked.

"I don't think it will hurt any more than your earaches have hurt you."

"When do I have to go?

"We'll pack a few things in a suitcase for you, and we'll go later this morning. The hospital is not far away from the house. I'll show you as we're driving there. It's right next to the building where we go when you see Dr. Williams."

"Will I be home later?"

"No, you will have to stay in the hospital for seven days so that the doctors can make sure they fixed the problem."

"Is Louis coming too?"

"No, he doesn't have a problem with his ear, so he'll stay home and wait for you."

"Will you stay with me?"

"No, I have your sisters and brother to take care of, but I will come and see you, and I'll bring you a present when I come."

"Can I have paper dolls?" These were my favorite toys to play with.

"Yes."

"Who will stay with me?"

"Well, you like Dr. Williams, and he'll be there, and there are lots of nurses who will look after you when I'm not there. I'm sure they're very nice. There will also be other children who need to have something fixed, and they will keep you company."

"What children?"

"We don't know their names yet, because we haven't met them, but I'm sure they'll be there, and they can play with you."

"Who will make my food?"

"They have a kitchen at the hospital, and people will be there to cook your breakfast, lunch, and dinner. And you'll get to have dessert with lunch and dinner every day."

"Can I take my silky blanket?"

"Yes, and we'll take a few other things to keep you company."

Later that morning, my mother and I packed my little round black plastic suitcase with my silky blanket, pajamas, slippers, toothbrush, hairbrush, stuffed animal, and my favorite paper dolls, and headed off for the hospital. It wasn't far from the house, as my mother told me, only a few blocks away. I remember riding up in the elevator, clutching my plastic suitcase in one hand, and my mother's hand in the other.

As we exited the elevator, my mother went to a big desk and gave them my name. I couldn't see over the desk to see who she was talking to. After talking to my mother for a while, the nurse on the other side of the desk stood up and reached for my hand. My mother took me by the wrist and held my arm out to her. The nurse put a plastic bracelet on my wrist that had purple writing. There were lots of numbers and words. My mother pointed out that my name was on it and said, "Look, you have a bracelet. You can keep that." We walked down the hall to a large room with seven beds in it. Each bed was in a cubicle and each cubicle had a curtain except for one. It was next to the big window that divided the hall from the room. There was no curtain for privacy around this bed, and my mother headed straight for it.

I looked around to see that all the other beds were full of boys and girls. They didn't pay any attention to my mother or me. The television perched high on the wall so that everyone could see it was on. Cartoons were playing, and the other children were much more interested in watching TV than looking at the new girl on the ward.

My mother helped me into my pajamas and tucked me in my bed (more like a crib, but with metal railings) She stayed with me for a little while, making sure I had my silky blanket and stuffed animal, and encouraged me to watch TV. She said she would be back but didn't tell me when. She was gone.

I was frightened and felt abandoned in a place that was scary. I was trapped in a bed that had railings on the side, so I couldn't get out easily. I called for her, but the nurse came in and told me to be quiet.

Strange women in white uniforms with hats on their heads were doing things to me that I didn't like. I didn't have the word for it, but I felt violated every time a nurse took my temperature or exposed my naked body in front of the other children to bathe me. My bed was right next to the big window and anyone could see in. My private parts were exposed for all to see. I was humiliated and struggled every time she came near me. That didn't make the experience any better. I couldn't get away, and sometimes she had another nurse hold me down while she turned me over to take my temperature and held me there exposed for all to see until it was time to remove the thermometer, or finished with a sponge bath that never made me feel clean.

I cried every night. I was thankful for my silky blanket. I put my finger in my mouth, rubbed my silky blanket, and rocked myself into a fitful sleep. One morning, I remember being held down on the operating table looking up at big people with white masks on their faces and wearing blue clothes. There was a big light shining in my eyes. I screamed, and struggled against arms that were holding me down while they put the mask over my face to put me to sleep. When I woke again, I was back in my hospital bed, crying for my mother. I was to stay in the hospital for a week, but I didn't know how long a week was. Was it forever? My mother visited every day for a bit and spent time with the other children whose parents weren't there. I remember feeling jealous as she spent her time with them rather than with me. I do not have any memory of my father ever coming to see me.

By day four or so, I wanted out. I planned my escape. I thought that if I could make my way to the elevator, and out the front door when everyone was sleeping, I was on my way home. Once outside, I knew how to make my way up the hill to the corner, but I couldn't remember which way to go after that. It didn't matter to me. I was going to get out of there. When it was dark outside, I peeked out from under my covers to see that my roommates were asleep. I climbed, with some difficulty, over the rails of my bed, and packed my silky blanket in my suitcase. That was all I needed. I didn't even bother to get dressed. I didn't care. The only thing I made sure I had on were my slippers.

I knew my house wasn't far from the hospital, and I wanted to get there quickly. With my suitcase in hand, I crept out of the room. I tried to be very quiet. I thought it best to look behind me as I walked to make sure no one was following me. I didn't think there was anyone behind the desk, since I couldn't see over it.

What I didn't think to do was look ahead of me, for as I was making my way down the hall, I walked straight into a nurse on night duty. I was thigh-high to her. I looked up and saw a woman in a white nurse's uniform with bright red curly hair sticking out from under her nurse's cap, and lots of freckles on her face, arms, and hands. She looked like a scary Bozo the Clown.

She asked, "Where do you think you are going?"

I replied, "I'm going home." She immediately turned me around and marched me back to the room. The next thing I knew, my mother was standing over me telling me how disappointed she was that I would do such a thing. She made it very clear that I was to do what I was told and never ever try such a stupid thing as run away again. She then tucked me tightly back into my bed and left the room without a kiss or hug.

My stay at the hospital was traumatic, to say the least. It is responsible for the major change that took place in my psyche. I left for the hospital a four-year-old child and came back home a changed person. It was the first time being away from my family. I entered a world that was foreign to me. Strangers surrounded me; doctors and nurses prodded, poked, and hurt me. I slept in a bed that constrained me; my cries for help went unanswered by my mother or father, and my twin brother and my sisters were nowhere to be seen.

It is my very first memory, and for me it was traumatic. I didn't immediately remember it when Dr. Mintz asked me. The word "sexual" jogged it out of the recesses of my mind as I remembered how violated I felt whenever the nurses touched me.

My hospital experience left me with the first evidence of trauma – feelings of abandonment and loss of protection as my mother left me in the hospital at the very beginning of my stay and again after my attempted escape rather than taking me home. I became hypersensitive to harsh words. I felt violated due to the loss of personal privacy over my body with the demand that I comply when strangers, nurses and doctors, touched me, prodded me, and hurt me in my private places and in public view. I did not have the words to express myself then, but I had the feelings, and they weren't happy ones. It changed my world as I knew it, and it changed me forever. Even in a family of six, I was alone with my feelings and fears and had no way to express them but through my tears.

CHAPTER **6**

NOW I LAY ME DOWN TO SLEEP

Now I lay me down to sleep
I pray the Lord my soul to keep
If I should die before I wake
I pray the Lord my soul to take

Eighteenth-Century English Prayer
Author Unknown

THIS WAS MY nightly prayer. Liz taught me the words. After my hospital experience, I grew up as a child who was fearful of everything and cried whenever my siblings or parents yelled at me, teased me about my looks (buck teeth and a huge nose), my fears, or my clumsy actions. They relished this practice and made it a daily routine to see who could make me cry.

There was no sympathy the following year, when I was back in the hospital to have my tonsils and adenoids removed. This time, however, my mother stayed overnight with me. I don't think she wanted a repeat performance of my last attempt at escape. I was able to return home the next day, but the fear of hospitals, illness, and what that brought with it remained fresh in my mind. I craved to be accepted and to feel loved, wanted, and protected. What I received was ridicule and rejection. In my attempts to be accepted, I often let my siblings trick me into doing something foolish. I added a promise to God to my nightly prayer, "Please God, if you help me, I promise when I grow up, I will never make any kid feel the way I do. I don't want to cry anymore. Please help me not cry tomorrow. Amen."

One summer day when I was about six or so, I had something in my eye and couldn't get it out. I was outside on the patio by the pool. Something flew into my eye and I started calling out, "Something's in my eye! It hurts!"

My sister, Debby, who was with her friends, came out of the pool. She said, "I know what we should do. The only way to get it out of your eye is to make you cry so that the tears will wash away whatever's in there."

"Are you sure? Why can't I splash water on my eye from the pool?"

"The pool has chemicals in it and that isn't good for your eye."

"How are you going to make me cry?"

"Simple. You stand here; we'll make a line. You start at the front of the line and let each one of us tap your cheek. By the time you get to the end of the line, the thing should be out of your eye."

"I don't like this idea."

"We're not going to hurt you; we want to help you get that out of your eye so that you don't scratch your eye and have to go to the hospital. You don't want to go to the hospital, do you?"

"No way!" I said, shaking my head.

"Well, this is the only other way, and we can't take all day. If we don't do it now, I'll have to tell Mommy and she'll take you to the hospital."

And so, my sister and her friends made a line, and I went to each person and let each one slap my face until my cheek was red and the tears were streaming down my face. Louis came out to see what the commotion was all about. The entire line of my sister and her friends were laughing, and I was crying.

Louis was furious, not so much with them, but with me for being such an idiot. He didn't yell at them for being mean. He yelled at me for allowing them to do such a thing. "God, you are so stupid!" he yelled. How could I tell him that all I wanted was to have my sister help me, and I thought this was her way of caring about me?

I was also teased mercilessly about my "operation ear." I was hesitant to get in the family pool, since I might hurt my eardrum. All the other kids would either dive or cannonball in, but I needed to use the ladder. This was a prime opportunity for them to splash me with water until I left the pool in tears yet again. I have some memories of actually getting in the pool, but not many happy ones with my siblings in there with me.

When I went to my mother for help, she'd send me away without even an attempt to comfort me. The song "Lori-ellen" became a number one hit in my household, as everyone sang it to me as I cried. After a while of hearing this, I learned that crying to my mother was not helpful. Instead, I took to my room that I shared with Liz, shut the door, and cried alone. My sisters and brother always told me I wasn't wanted, and it sure felt that way.

My hospital experiences also taught me to be fiercely protective of my body. This caused me a lot of problems, as I was not allowed to bathe alone. I dreaded bath time. Before my hospital experience, Louis and I bathed together. I didn't have a problem with it. We had fun playing around in the water. Now, bath time meant exposing myself to not only my brother but also my father, as he thought it his responsibility to see that I was clean. Every time bath time came around, I asked if I could take my bath alone, and the response was always "No, you don't know what you're doing. You can get in and do the best you can, and your father will be in in a few minutes." I got in and used the wash cloth to scrub as hard as I could. I prayed that when my father came in, he'd say, "Okay now you know what to do," and walk right back out.

After a few minutes in the bathwater, I'd hear my father's footsteps as he approached the bathroom carrying a wooden chair with him. It was my signal that I was about to feel violated again, and the thought of this made me shake with fear. I was sick to my stomach and shaking, because I didn't want to make him mad and hit or yell at me. I wanted desperately to get this over with as quickly as possible. My father came in, opened up the wooden folding chair and placed it in front of the tub. He lathered the washcloth up with soap.

He commanded, "Stand up." I stood up. "Face me." I turned to face him. "Arms up." I put my arms up. That's when he took the washcloth and proceeded to rub it all over my body. "Spread your legs." This was the part I hated. If I hesitated, he'd push them apart, and with his hand wrapped around the washcloth, he proceeded to wash my private parts. I squeezed my eyes shut, and prayed for it to stop, but it wasn't over yet. "Turn around." I turned around. Once again, the washcloth was all over my back and my legs. "Spread your legs." I complied, praying that this was going to end soon. And once again, the washcloth was between my legs. "Now rinse off."

He turned the shower on and pushed me into the water. This time he used his bare hands to rinse the soap off my body. His hands traveled to every part of my body, including my private parts. I shivered and shook the entire time, with tears in my eyes, and my mouth clamped shut to stifle the screams. This made hair-washing doubly traumatic as my father shoved me under the shower spray, head first, to rinse the shampoo from my hair. Water ran into my nose, making it hard to breathe, and with my mouth clamped shut, I struggled against his hands to back out of the shower stream. He pushed me under again. I choked and couldn't escape crying out, but that only yielded yells from my father to "knock it off," and more pushing my head under the water until my hair was thoroughly rinsed. This ritual happened every other day, until I was almost nine years old.

Another ritual was the yearly check-up at Dr. Jones's office. I hated doctors. They didn't make you feel better; they made you feel worse. And my yearly check-up ritual with Dr. Jones was no different. For convenience, my mother made a group appointment for all four of us kids.

Part of the exam was giving a urine sample in a small Dixie cup. Debby and Liz were allowed to use the bathroom alone, since they were older, and Louis was allowed because his aim was obviously better. I asked if I could do it by myself, to which my mother replied, "No, you'll just make a mess, and the doctor needs this. We're not coming back again, so I'm going to go in with you."

I cringed as she straddled the toilet in front of me, holding the cup in the "right spot," as I had to straddle the toilet to make room for her hand. She stared at my private parts, waiting for me to pee. She waited and stared for an eternity. I couldn't pee. She got impatient, and said, "Come on, Lori-ellen, we don't have all day. I know you have to go." She was right. I did, but not with her hand between my legs, and her staring at me "down there." I always managed to squeeze a small amount of urine into the cup; just enough to have her say in an exasperated tone, "We'll see if it's enough." The minute she left the bathroom to check with the nurse, I peed like a racehorse. I didn't have a cup, so whatever she got had to be enough.

The worst however was Dr. Jones's style of examining me. I was stripped to my underwear (no undershirt), and ordered to walk up and down the hallway with the door open to the waiting room. "Let me see you walk," he'd say. I was humiliated as everyone in the waiting room saw my half-naked body walking up and down the hallway. I'd scurry quickly into the examining room. He came in, leaving the door open, and say, "Bend over, and touch your toes." I bent at the waist. He pulled down the back of my underwear and slid a tongue depressor down there. When he snapped the elastic band against my skin, it was my cue to stand up and take out the tongue depressor. He threw it in the garbage.

Next came the examining table. "Okay, now jump up here," he said as he tapped on the table. He used his stethoscope to listen to my heart, and made a face. I could feel my own heart pounding against my chest. "Settle down," he'd say. "Take some deep breaths." I did what was asked and prayed for the pounding to stop, but I knew what was coming.

"Lay down."

Oh God, please don't let him do this again. I hate this. He palpated my abdomen, and checked my reflexes. Then he bent my legs at the knees, pulled my underwear to my ankles, spread my knees apart, and examined me in the same way a woman is examined yearly by the "lady doctor." I am as repulsed today as I write this as I was every time he did this. The door was open, people were walking by, and I was splayed out on the examining table being touched and manipulated by a man I detested. My mind raced. *This isn't right. This doesn't feel right. Why is he doing this to me? Why isn't my mother, who was also watching, doing something? Why is she letting this man touch me this way? Why is the door open for everyone to see?*

That was the end of the exam. I dressed myself as quickly as possible and sprinted toward the waiting room. I tried the best I could to hide my face from everyone. I had my coat on long before my siblings. I rushed to put my jacket on and sit on the chair with my knees against my chest, my arms wrapped tightly around them. I buried my head against my knees and cried as quietly as possible.

"What are you doing, stupid?" one of my siblings would ask.

"I'm cold," I managed to squeak out.

"No, you're ugly, stupid, and weird," was the reply. I ignored this taunt and returned to keeping my cries as quiet as possible. The kids scrambled to get lollipops before we left. I ran for the door. I was the first one to the car and didn't care if I got the front seat. As soon as we got home, I rushed to the bathroom, took a washcloth, and tried to scrub off the smell of the doctor's office. These examinations occurred once or more a year until I reached the age of twelve.

The dentist's office was yet another traumatic experience for me. I needed to have many baby teeth removed to make room for my adult teeth. Every appointment was a horror for me and I'm sure, for my mother. I screamed and struggled as they held me down in the chair so they could clamp the ether mask over my face. The smell of ether was awful and made me gag. The minute I saw that black mask coming toward me, I was making a mad dash to the nearest exit. I never made it out of the chair. Arms came from everywhere to hold me down. Hands took hold of my head as I shook it wildly back and forth to escape the approaching mask. Yells of "Stop it, and settle down!" echoed in my ears as the nurse held my mouth closed to prevent me from biting. Once again, I was restrained and forced into submission. Once again, no one came to my rescue. Once again, my body was not my own, but belonged to others who had permission to do whatever they wanted to me. I don't remember how many trips I made to that dentist, but each one was most memorable.

In 1972, at age nine, I finished with my "examination" with Dr. Jones and waited by the office door to get to the car. Debby and Liz no longer went to Dr. Jones. They "graduated" to a different doctor because they were now fourteen and twelve respectively. I pleaded with my mother to let me go to their doctor. "When you turn twelve, you can go to Dr. Davis, and not before," she responded; end of discussion.

My mother, Louis, and I got into the elevator, but instead of getting out on the lobby floor, the elevator stopped on the second floor and my mother told us to get out. She walked over to an office door and pushed it open. I glanced at the sign beside the door. I couldn't make out the name on the sign, but sounded out the word cardiologist under it. I didn't know what a cardiologist was. She told us to sit down while she went to the receptionist's window. When I heard her say my name, I walked up to her.

"Why are we here?" I asked.

"I have to make an appointment," she replied.

"For who?"

"For you."

"Why?"

"Because Dr. Jones said there's something wrong with your heart."

"What?"

"Shhh – just let me make this appointment and I'll explain when we get home. Go sit down and be quiet," she ordered, and I complied. I looked at Louis. He shrugged his shoulders and didn't say anything.

My heart beat furiously inside my chest, echoing in my ears. I knew enough to know that I couldn't live without a heart, and my deeply held fear of dying before I grew up overwhelmed me once again. When we got home, my mother told Louis and me to go upstairs and play. She would call for me after she spoke with my father.

How could I possibly play when I am going to die? How long do I have to live? Will it hurt when I die? Will I die alone? Why do I have to die? Is God mad at me for crying every day? Am I a bad girl? Will I go to heaven?

I sat with Louis in silence at the top of the stairs, trying desperately to hear what my mother was saying. They were in the living room too far away for us to hear anything. Louis waited with me until I was called down. When my mother called for me, Louis came with me. I thought he wanted to hear them say I was going to die.

"What are you doing here? We didn't call for you," my father said to Louis.

"She's my twin, and I want to know what's wrong with her," he said bravely.

"Her heart doesn't work right. Are you prepared to give her part of yours?" asked my father. Louis stood with his mouth hanging open. His face went white to match mine. I looked at my mother, who didn't say a word. She was going to let this play out.

"Lori-ellen, aren't you going to ask your brother for a piece of his heart? He's your twin and the only one who can give you the part you need, but if he does, he could die. Well, aren't you going to ask him?" my father spat out.

Now it was my turn to speak. My lips trembled, my knees knocked together, and I wasn't sure what fainting felt like, but thought I just might collapse to the floor. "Why does he have to give me a piece of his heart? What's wrong with my heart?"

"When Dr. Jones listened to your heart, it wasn't beating the way it should. We don't know why, so that's why I made the appointment with a doctor who works only on the heart. You may need an operation to fix it. Your appointment is next week. And no, Louis, you don't have to give Lori-ellen a piece of your heart. Your father was only teasing," my mother said.

The color slowly returned to Louis's face as he walked away, but I could see that this little "joke" my father played had upset him deeply. I walked away from my parents, feeling as though my life was over.

I was frightened to my very core. I went to my room and closed the door. I huddled under the covers with my silky blanket. I cried and prayed at the same time. Louis opened the door. His face was its natural color once again, and he seemed to have calmed down. He said simply and with conviction, "I would have given you part of my heart if you needed it," and shut the door again. I cried harder and pulled the covers over my head in the hope that I would simply disappear.

My only comfort was that for the first time in my entire life, I felt as though Louis loved me. My twin was willing to give his life to save mine. I loved him more than anyone else at that moment, and with that simple yet profound statement, he let me know that he loved me too. From that moment, to this day, I have a bond with him that can never be broken. He may lead his own life and have a family of his own, but I would lay down my life for him without hesitation.

The following week, my mother took me to the cardiologist for my appointment. When the nurse called my name, my mother gave me "the look" that said, "Behave or you'll really have something to cry about." Silently I got up and followed the nurse into a room. She told me to take everything off except my underwear, gave me a gown to cover myself, and left the room for a moment. *Here we go again.*

I had no idea what to expect. My mother waited outside in the waiting room. *Did she not want to see the blood and guts that were going to be splattered all over the walls? Were they going to cut me open right there and see for themselves that my heart was still beating? I was sure that it was, since I could feel it pumping furiously inside my chest. I thought, no wonder it doesn't beat right. There's hardly a day that goes by that it's not pounding due to my crying or fear. It probably wore itself out and that's why I may need a new one.* The nurse came back into the room rolling a big machine with lots of wires attached to it.

"Did anyone tell you what we're going to do today?"

"No."

"I promise it doesn't hurt. This is a machine that records your heartbeat on a strip of paper. We can see how your heart is working using this machine. I'll show you how it works. I promise, you're not going to be hurt, and it will only take a few minutes. I will be with you while we do the test. Is that okay?"

"You're not going to cut me open to see my heart?" I asked.

"Absolutely not. I'm so sorry that no one explained this to you. I promise you again. This doesn't hurt at all and will only take a few minutes. The only things that will touch you are these pads, this little suction cup, and the wires that are attached to the pads. All you have to do is lie back, relax, and breathe as normally as you can. Is that alright?

"Yes. You're really nice," I said genuinely.

"Thank you. Okay. We're going to get started."

She explained that the reason I had to take my clothes off was so that she could put the little pads on different parts of my body from my chest to my legs. My breathing immediately settled as I became confident she wasn't going to hurt me or touch me in the same places Dr. Jones always did. She gained my trust and the test proceeded without difficulty. When she took off the pads and suction cup, I asked, "Am I okay?"

"By the looks of things, you're just fine. I'm going to have the doctor see this paper, and he will speak with your mother and Dr. Jones. You did a great job. You can get dressed now and go to your mom."

"Can you be my doctor?" I asked, desperately hoping she would say yes.

"I'm sorry, but I can't. I'm a nurse. I'm sure Dr. Jones will take great care of you."

Wanna bet? I thought to myself. I dressed quickly and went out to meet my mother. I had to wait a few minutes, since she was in the doctor's office talking to him. On our way home, I asked, "Do I need another operation?"

"No, you have what's called a heart murmur," she answered. "It's nothing serious. It makes your heart beat a little funny sometimes. We just have to watch it, that's all." I wasn't sure if my mother heard the words, "Thank you, God" I whispered as I let out a sigh of relief. No hospital, no operation, and I wasn't dying. Now I just needed to get through each day as I used to, hoping that there would be no need for me to cry, be teased, or fear for my life.

CHAPTER 7

THE SPIRAL STAIRCASE

In my mind there's a spiral staircase,
Where it leads is hard to tell
For when life becomes too difficult
The stairs lead straight to hell

Falling down the stairs is fast
I no longer see the top
I cannot seem to turn around
To force my feet to stop

I need to reach the bottom
To feel the depths of my despair
Before I can travel up again
Begin the process of repair

The climb upstairs is painful
A fight each step I take
I push past feelings and my thoughts
Relish the progress that I make

I am standing at the top again
Breathing hard from my hard-fought fight
I await the next painful experience
That will force me down the flight.

Lori-ellen Pisani

TALKING ABOUT MY past with Dr. Mintz each week brought both pain and relief. It was not unusual for me to leave his office in tears, but also with a sense of relief that finally I was telling my story. Keeping these memories locked inside my mind was certainly a major cause of my depression. Dr. Mintz was the first person in my life to listen to me without judgment. I had fifty minutes to pour out my heart to him without fear. The anti-depressant I was taking helped me to acknowledge my pain, push through it, and keep moving forward.

During one session, Dr. Mintz said to me, "Lori-ellen, it is very clear to me that your early life experiences and memories were traumatic and can be attributed to your depressive state. You spent many hours alone in your room in tears. What I'm curious about is what other ways you managed to cope on a daily basis. It's hard to believe that you spent every waking moment in tears."

"Well, when I wasn't in tears I escaped into a fantasy world. In that world, I was a famous actress and singer. I was beautiful, talented, admired, and adored. Everyone wanted my autograph. In my fantasy world, people filled arenas just to see me perform. I won lots of awards for my acting and singing and dancing. I watched TV, and chose from the programs I saw that day who I would be in my dreams when I went to sleep. I replayed what I saw on TV in my mind over and over so that I didn't have to think. I also listened to the radio and spent hours in the evenings locked in my room, hairbrush in hand, lip-synching and putting on some very impressive dance performances to songs by any artist playing on the radio."

"Okay, I get how you coped when you were alone in the house, but what about friends you had in school?"

"When Louis and I entered kindergarten, we were put into separate classrooms. This gave me the chance to be with other children who were not family members for the first time in my life. I never went to nursery school, so I took this opportunity as a chance to see if I could make friends that wouldn't reject me or call me names. Trust me, I was scared to my core, but I wanted friends more than I can say, so I pushed through the fear."

"And how did that work out?"

"My first day in kindergarten, I looked at all the faces of the children in my class. I tried to guess who would be receptive to me. I practiced in my head what I'd say. 'Hi, my name is Lori-ellen, what's your name?' If they responded with anything other than, 'Get away from me,' I thought I just might have a chance to make a friend. As it turned out, I saw one girl who was crying, and was immediately drawn to her. The other children were laughing at her, and since I knew all too well how that felt, I made it my mission to go over and see if I could comfort her. The teacher was busy at her desk and didn't see her crying. I went over and, forgetting my practiced opening line, said, "Hi, I feel bad that you are crying. Come with me, and we will sit over here."

As I continued the story, that day came back to my mind vividly. I brought her to a table and sat down with her. "My name is Lori-ellen," I said, introducing myself.

"I'm Samantha."

"Why are you crying?" I asked.

"Some of the kids called me fat," she said through her tears.

"That's mean, and you're not fat."

"I hate this school, and I want to go home."

"I'll stay with you if you want me to. I don't think we can go home yet."

"Okay."

"Do you want to play in the housekeeping corner? There's no one in there."

"Okay."

And that's how our seven-year friendship started. We played together almost every day after school in kindergarten, and on weekends when I wasn't doing chores. She was my best friend. She wasn't always in my class throughout the years, but we spent a great deal of time together. We understood each other without saying much. We never fought or made each other cry.

Samantha was overweight all through grade school. She was highly sensitive to her classmates' teasing and cried almost every day.

I became her protector. When I saw her cry, I found my courage to tell the other children to stop, or I'd tell the teacher. I must have said it with some degree of force, because often they would stop for the rest of the day. The next day, however, it started all over again. I hated to see her cry. I knew her pain, and I wanted it to stop as much as I wanted my own pain to end.

My teachers always commented that I was very helpful to the other children in the class. They also wrote that I enjoyed school and worked hard on all assigned tasks. I wasn't a stellar student by any means. However, school became my "safe place." I was away from my family, and had friends, especially Samantha, who liked me. I had great teachers whom I grew to admire, and made up my mind very early in my educational career that I was going to be a teacher when I grew up. It was my chance to keep my promise to God. Every child would be safe in my classroom.

When I wasn't busy performing in my room at night, I spent many hours playing school. It felt right to me. I was comfortable playing the role of "teacher" in front of my class of stuffed animals. I kept old workbooks and re-corrected pages I had already done, gave spelling tests, and wrote math problems on a small green chalkboard. My lessons were repeats of what my teacher taught that day. Standing in front of my "class" gave me a sense of importance and power. My "students" were very attentive, and my "lessons" were flawless. Even today, I can name every teacher I had in grammar school. They had a tremendous impact on my life. They encouraged me, supported me, and inspired me.

My third-grade teacher, Mrs. Sidebottom, was my all-time favorite. She was a middle-aged British woman with a soft voice and a kind heart. She introduced me to classical music, which I love to this day. She taught me cursive writing and helped me as I struggled with reading comprehension and math. As the Christmas break approached, she taught the class ***The Twelve Days of Christmas***. She split the class into groups for each day in the song. My group had "five golden rings," and when it was our turn, I belted it out with all I had. I was right on pitch. Mrs. Sidebottom stopped the song, and said to everyone, "I think we have someone here who is going to be a star in the chorus. You have a beautiful singing voice, Lori-ellen," and she winked at me. I was elated. I was going to be famous after all. I had talent. Mrs. Sidebottom said so herself. Maybe this was going to be the way my family accepted me. If they knew I could sing, maybe they'd stop teasing and taunting me.

My mistake was telling my family that I wanted to perform for them. I stood in front of the piano and started to sing the song. I didn't make it to "three French hens" before my family burst into fits of laughter, which sent me scurrying to my room in tears. I kept my fantasy of becoming a famous singer/actress, but never again made the mistake of asking to perform for my family. That didn't include being forced to perform by my father, however.

Samantha's parents divorced just before we entered middle school. She moved away to California. I was devastated. I felt lost and alone. Yes, I had friends who were going to the same middle school as I was, but they weren't my best friends, and we were going to be mixed in with kids from all over our town. I desperately wanted to stay in my grammar school. I was known there by most of the kids and teachers. It was so close to home that I walked home every day for lunch. *Would I be able to make new friends? Would I have a new best friend? Would my teachers like me?* My safe place was no longer there for me.

"What do you mean by forced to perform by your father?" Dr. Mintz asked.

"Do you remember when I described him as a cross between Ralph Cramden and Archie Bunker?"

"Yeah."

"He reminded me of Ralph, because he was always coming up with the next greatest idea for a business and to get rich, just like Ralph, and his ideas always included the family in one way or another."

"What about this performing business? How old were you when this was going on?"

"The first time I 'performed,' I was about seven."

I told Dr. Mintz the story. My father had the grand idea of managing a band called Sound Farm. He was convinced he could get them a record deal. He had them over to the house one day for a meeting. There were about six members of the band gathered in the living room. They had just finished their demo, and my dad was playing it to see if it could be marketed as a dance record. I was upstairs, in my own little world, when I heard him call me downstairs to the living room.

"Lori-ellen, come down here!" he yelled.

"Coming!" I yelled back.

When I got to the living room, my father said that he was going to play a record and he wanted me to dance.

"Umm, what?" I asked.

"When I play the music, dance," he said with an edge to his voice.

"I can't dance in front of people."

"Yes, you can," he said through clenched teeth.

"No, I can't," I said, remembering my last attempt at performing for the family.

"Excuse me for a minute," he said to the group.

He took me firmly by the arm and escorted me into the breakfast room, closing the door behind him. Before I knew it, he grabbed me under both arms, lifted me off the floor, and slammed my back against the wall. He leaned in so close to me that our noses touched. Through clenched teeth, he spoke as he shook me back and forth against the wall.

"When I tell you to do something, you do it – understand? – Now get out there and dance, goddamn it!" He gave me one more shake for good measure and let go. I dropped to the floor. "And put a smile on your face!" he seethed. Once again, I was escorted in front the group, and stood there, knees clearly shaking as he turned the record player on and the music played. I danced as best I could given that my whole body was shaking. I wasn't even listening to the music. I liked to dance and was good at it in my private performances alone in my room. But dancing on command was a different story. My father's reaction to my plea not to dance was so extreme. It scared the hell out of me. I wanted to get it over with as soon as possible. As soon as my performance was over, I ran up to my room, slammed the door, and hid in the closet.

I told Dr. Mintz, "I can't remember what happened with the band after that, and I didn't care. I was humiliated and never wanted to see them again."

"Were there any other times you had to perform?" Dr. Mintz asked.

"I remember my parents having a very important guest to dinner when I was about ten. I have no idea what he did or why he was there, but he was a musician who played the piano. The baby grand in the living room was tuned for his visit. Since I was taking flute lessons in school, my father thought it would be a good idea for me to accompany this guest on the flute while he played the piano. The guest seemed very good natured about having a ten-year-old accompany him. He asked me what I'd like to play. I chose a piece I was practicing and asked if it was alright. He was very gracious and agreed. I counted out beats to the first measure and we began to play together.

I was so nervous that I must have made a mistake every other measure of music, but I made it through to the end. My family sat in stunned silence, but the guest offered words of praise. "Thank you, Lori-ellen, you played very well."

"Thank you, sir," I replied, and gathered the music as quickly as I could before running up the stairs to my room.

"Were there more times your father forced you to dance, play the flute, or perform in other ways for people?"

"As far as I can remember, those were the only performances I put on. Shortly after that, my father's interests in business turned from music to off-track betting, and I became a bookie."

"Excuse me?" Dr. Mintz said, shocked.

"Yup, I was a bookie at the age of twelve."

"I have no idea what in the hell that means," Dr. Mintz replied.

It was 1975. My father went to Bermuda several times over the past year, but he didn't share with us kids what he was doing. He only shared, "I'm going on a business trip," and left it at that. My mother didn't bother to explain anything, and since we got a bit of a break from his tyranny when he was away, we didn't bother to ask.

My father returned from one of his business trips, walked into the living room where we were all watching TV and announced, "We're in business!"

"What? What kind of business?" Debby asked.

"The company's name is Top Turf Limited. It's an off-track betting parlor in Bermuda. It's the only one of its kind and it's going to make us big money. You're going to be very busy working."

"Are we moving to Bermuda?" she continued.

"No, we're going to set up the business in the basement. I'm having machines delivered in three weeks. Don't make any plans for the weekends. On Saturday we need to take care of the house, and on Sundays you'll be working for Top Turf. The time for 'play play' is over. This is serious business."

"What are we supposed to do?" Liz asked.

"You're going to have to learn how to use the machines to get the harness racing information from New York to Bermuda."

"What kind of machines, and what information?" Debby kept on.

"Telex and telegraph machines rented from Western Union, and the information is about harness horse racing and race results. You girls are going to be very busy typing up the race entries and results from race tracks from New York to Pennsylvania on the Telex machines. As you type, it spits out the information on a coded yellow paper tape. The tape then goes through the telegraph machine and the information is transmitted to the shop we set up in Bermuda. It will show up on the boards like the news does in Times Square. Keep your mouths shut, 'cause this isn't exactly legal. Don't tell anyone what we're doing. Do you understand? Starting tomorrow after school, you are to go straight to the basement and help me get it ready for the machines."

We all nodded in silence.

"Who's going to do the typing? Where do we get the information? How is this supposed to work? What if we're caught?" Debby asked.

"Don't worry about that. That's my job. You all just need to make sure you keep your mouths shut. You can't see the basement from the road, and we already have the blinds up to make sure no one can see inside the windows. Just do what I say, and we won't get caught. If we do, you're in a hell of a lot of trouble. You can kiss this house goodbye, kiss your friends goodbye, kiss school goodbye, kiss the cats goodbye, and say hello to the inside of a jail cell. I don't care if Jesus Christ himself asks you what you're doing on the weekends, just say you have chores to do, understand?"

For the next three weeks, we worked every day after school cleaning out the basement, making shelves and countertops, putting red cork board up around the entire perimeter of the room, putting in phone lines, setting up and testing the Western Union machines, and making signs for all the race tracks from New York to Philadelphia. Louis did most of the construction work with my father. By the time we finished, it looked like a scene straight out of *The Sting*.

Every evening after dinner, my mother taught Liz, Debby, and me how to type on the Telex machines. I have to say, at twelve years old, I was typing sixty words a minute. Debby's job was also to impersonate a secretary from ***Sports Eye*** magazine and call about eight race tracks every day and ask for "scratches" (when horses were pulled from races due to injury), and driver changes. Louis went with my father to JFK airport every two weeks on Saturday nights at midnight to drop off cartons of coffee and betting slips to be shipped to Bermuda. My mother prepared the invoices to send to Bermuda for payment of these items, and typed with Liz, Debby, and me every night for a few hours and on Sundays.

Every Friday night, my father drove me into the city, dropped me off at the corner of 79th Street and Broadway to pick up the ***Racing Form, Sports Eye,*** and ***Armstrong*** newspapers. While I made my purchases, he circled the block. When he circled back to me again, I jumped in the car, and we set off for home. There were usually a few men hanging around the newsstand, and after a while of watching a twelve-year-old girl ask for and flip through these papers, they grew rather bold and asked for my predictions for winners. A girl who could talk about harness racing like a pro fascinated them. Once I was familiar with the horses and drivers, odds, and track conditions, I was able to give them my best predictions.

As I typed the results of the races, I gave a silent cheer when one or more of my predictions came true. The guys hanging out at the newsstand began to take my predictions more seriously as time went on. On Sundays, Liz, my mother, Debby, and I used these papers to type the race entries for each track scheduled for the week. This took hours. We started at 8:00 in the morning and finished around 1:00 in the afternoon. Our fingers cramped, and we were exhausted by the time we finished. In the evenings, my mother, Liz, Debby, and I rotated typing the racing results. Homework had to be done early so that we could start typing by post time.

I remember one evening especially. I was typing the results for one of the tracks. After the second race there is an "exacta" result. If a person picks the winner of the first and second race, they also win the "exacta" prize money. The purse was $1,000. I was so tired that I accidentally typed the winning amount as $1,000,000. As soon as the race results were typed, the yellow paper that comes out of my machine with the information coded into it was transferred to a large telegraph machine for transmission to Bermuda. The results of the races were then posted simultaneously on the screen for all betters to see and subsequently claim their winnings.

I didn't pick up this error until I heard my father screaming, "Jesus Christ! What the hell are you doing you damn fool! You have the exacta as a million dollars! Type a correction and hurry up!" With my fingers trembling, I retyped the exacta result; only this time the amount I typed was $10,000. "Can't you read? What the hell is the matter with you! Dianne, get on the phone and tell them we have a small technical malfunction and to wait for confirmation of the results. Lori-ellen, you damn fool, sit down down and type one number at a damn time. If you make one more mistake, you will eat the tape that comes out of that damn machine!"

I sat down once again, and started typing with one finger. I put my two hands on the keyboard and prayed silently for help. I finally managed to type the correct exacta result. I checked it three times before my father ripped the tape from the machine himself and sent it through to Bermuda. He lit up a cigarette and watched as the tape re-typed what I had typed on the Telex machine. When he turned his back to walk away, I let out an audible sigh of relief.

"You're fired!" my father yelled as he puffed on one of the many Camel cigarettes he smoked a day. If I had the nerve, I would have lit up a cigarette too. The pressure of doing this work was getting to me. "Take five minutes and get out of here. Then get back here. You have six more races to get through tonight, and you'd better not screw up again, or you'll be in the deepest shit you can imagine!"

"I thought I was fired."

"Forget that. You're gonna keep doing this till you get it right every time. Get outta here, and when you come back, bring me a cup of coffee and another pack of cigarettes."

"How long did you do this work?" Dr. Mintz asked.

"I worked for my father from the time I was twelve until about fourteen. Technology had changed by then, and we didn't have to type the information anymore. We used satellite hook-ups to transmit the information directly to the shop."

"Were you paid?"

"Are you kidding? I was lucky I didn't get shot!"

"Didn't your mother say anything to your father about working like this?"

"No, and I really can't say that I blame her. She was working right alongside us. And she got her fair share of being screamed at and called names too."

"Was the business successful?"

"Yes; for many years, we were the only betting shop in Bermuda.

It was making some money but losing its appeal as competition was making inroads and clients were leaving. We kept the business going, and my father continued to find other enterprises to fulfill his dream of becoming a multi-millionaire, but we ran into a huge problem."

Dr. Mintz took a deep breath. My life's story was more complicated than he had initially thought, and unbeknownst to me at the time, he was thinking that there might be much more to the issue of depression that I was currently being treated for with Dr. Salamon.

CHAPTER **8**

HOUSE OF CARDS

A home is a very special place to live
It's built on a foundation of love, laughter, and unity
The families inside are happy and safe

I live in a house of cards
With people who fight and scream
Who fill me with fear
A house of cards is devoid of love
Its foundation crumbles as those inside quarrel and fight

My house of cards came tumbling down
And my world was forever changed

Lori-ellen Pisani

THE YEAR WAS 1978. Louis and I were about to turn fifteen and in our first year of high school. Debby was twenty years old and had quit college. She was working in a Manhattan hotel as secretary to the General Manager. Liz was almost eighteen and trying to finish high school without either failing out or being expelled. Although Top Turf was still open and running, we didn't have much to do with the day-to-day operations anymore. My father and his partners in Bermuda were able to utilize technology and staff to do the work we previously had been doing in the basement. The machines were removed, and our basement was once again a safe place to be without fear of being raided by the cops.

My father continued his work as a business agent for the union. His primary responsibility was negotiating the labor contracts with management for his union members at various shops from New York to Pennsylvania (interesting – the same territories we covered for Top Turf). He had a reputation as a no nonsense, larger than life figure (partly due to his size and manner of speech) who was highly successful negotiating contracts for the laborers he represented.

In the winter of 1978, however, he had a problem. Negotiations were not going well at one of his larger shops in upstate New York. The members of the union voted to strike. It was a tough decision, and one my father rarely endorsed because his success rate was very high. Management however, took a hard line, and brought in "scabs" to keep the shop open and running. Negotiations broke down.

It was an extremely cold and snowy winter that year, and my father was determined to walk the line with his members. He had us kids prepare the strike signs at home and told us that this was very serious. Despite all his efforts, he was battling not only management, but also an increasingly disgruntled labor force that was eager for retaliation against the scabs who were stealing their livelihood. Management threatened to permanently replace the laborers with the scabs. The members were enraged. Picketing took place in shifts around the clock. The shop was three hours away from us, and my father spent many days leaving at dawn to walk the picket lines with his members and returning well after midnight.

One morning, however, he didn't return. We thought he was delayed due to either the weather or because negotiations were moving forward once again. This was not the case. My mother received a phone call from my father. "I'm in jail," he said.

"What happened!" my mother yelled into the phone.

"Things got out of hand last night."

"What do you mean?" she continued.

"I can't say much. This call is recorded. Just listen, and do what I say. Things got rough last night, and I did what I had to do."

"Well, whatever you 'had to do' landed you in jail!"

"Jesus Christ, I don't need to hear your shit. Shut up and do what I tell you to do. I can't talk on the phone anymore. Call Joe [his brother who was a lawyer] and tell him where I am so I can get the hell out of here." Click--he hung up the phone. We kids could hear the conversation and asked what happened.

"I don't have time to tell you. Your father's in jail, and I've got to get up there and bail him out," she said, clearly upset and highly agitated.

My mother immediately called my uncle, and together they made the three-hour drive up to the jail where my father and other laborers were being held. They bailed him out and traveled back to the house. They dropped Uncle Joe off to start his legal work, and my parents came home well after dark to find their four children seated silently on the living room couch with the TV going for background noise. My father looked tired, Mother looked angry, and all four of us kids were scared stiff. All we knew was what Mother had said to us before she left that morning.

Daddy said, "Come into the dining room. I need to talk to you." We followed him in and sat around the dining room table completely silent, waiting for him to speak.

"We had a problem on the line last night. A few of my members brought weapons and were determined to kill the scabs who were scheduled to report to the shop for the overnight shift. I was able to convince them to do things my way."

"What way?" Debby had the courage to ask.

"Me and four other guys from the line went to the motel where the scabs were staying. We broke into their rooms while they were sleeping, tied them up, and brought them to the site. We tied them to trees and poured molasses on them and then ripped open your mother's pillows and poured the feathers over them as well. Years ago, it was called 'tarring and feathering.' It was the way things were done when scabs were brought into shops to take over for a striking labor force. Management threatened to permanently replace my men with these scabs. The guys got so pissed off that they originally wanted to kill these guys. I was only able to convince them to do it my way because I called the media in to take pictures of the scabs 'tarred and feathered' and tied to trees for publicity."

"So that's why my good pillows are missing? Why'd you have to take my good pillows for your dirty work!" exclaimed my mother.

My father shot her a look and continued, "The cops came and arrested us."

"You got arrested for putting molasses and feathers from Mommy's pillows on some guys? Kids at school do things much worse than that and all they get is suspended," Liz chimed in.

"This isn't school; this is rural upstate New York, and they didn't see it as a prank."

"What are the charges?" asked Louis.

"Kidnapping, weapons possession, unlawful imprisonment, and assault--all felonies."

"What's the worst thing that could happen?" I asked.

"I may be looking at a long time in prison."

With that, we all gasped. Now it was Mother's turn to go off.

"Son-of-a-bitch, Canio! You didn't once think of your family! Everything in this world revolves around you! I don't give a shit what those men wanted to do. You should have thought of your family and told them if anything bad went down, you were outta there and would come home, but no, not 'Dan the Man,' 'Moose,' 'Big Dan.' No, you had to get right in the middle of it, and in the process destroy your family. You are one selfish son-of-a-bitch who never thought of another human being but yourself! And now, I may be left with four children to raise and no money to do it with. Oh my God--Jesus, Mary, and Joseph, what the hell am I going to do? You selfish bastard!" And with that, my mother stormed off to her bedroom and slammed the door.

We all sat in stunned silence for a few minutes. I, of course, started to cry. Louis kicked me under the table to get me to stop, but it didn't work. My father hated it when I cried. It wasn't because he felt sorry for me; it was more agitating than anything else, and my siblings could see that he was highly agitated already. He didn't need a sniveling idiot like me making him more pissed. I took slow, deep breaths and calmed myself as best I could before he spoke again.

"Look. There's going to be a trial. These things take time to get to court. Uncle Joe is working on the case. It could be a year before the trial begins. So, we need to get ready, and you kids are going to have to do all you can to help your mother out. Debby, you're already working. That's one paycheck coming in. Liz, get your shit together and get a part-time job. At this point, I don't care if you have to sell the pot you've been smoking; just do it. Louis, your job is to take care of this house. You are in charge of all maintenance. Lori-ellen, see if you can get some more work with your friend Sue at that club her family owns." I already had an "off the books" job as a coat check girl and part- time waitress for private parties. I was underage but could pass for eighteen with make-up. "All the money you kids bring in goes to your mother, you understand? I'll see what I can do with Bermuda to get a monthly check coming in, but that isn't going to be much. I don't know if the union will keep me on payroll, so we can't count on that. Your main priority is to keep money coming into this house and to help your mother. And of course, you know to keep this in the family. Keep your mouths shut. It shouldn't make the papers down here."

As my father predicted, it was almost a year before the trial started. In the interim, my uncle was able to get the charges reduced to unlawful imprisonment, and a lesser assault charge. During the trial, we kids did what we could to make money. My father kept a blue ledger book to keep track of the monies we brought into the house. No one asked how the trial was going. It was written all over my parents' faces when they came home each night.

In February 1979, my father was found guilty of the charges and sentenced to one to three years in a medium-security prison. With good behavior, he was eligible for parole in April, 1980. He had a few days before he was to surrender to the authorities. In those few days, you could cut the tension in the house with a knife. My father was busy making lists of chores for us kids to do, my mother walked around the house mumbling expletives under her breath, and we kids were as quiet as we could possibly be. It was the only period when I can honestly say there was no fighting. It was eerily silent in the house. We went about our business in slow motion. Dinner around the dining room table was torturous. No one knew what to say or do. All that could be heard was the clanking of forks and knives against our plates.

On the day he surrendered, he puffed out his cheek, and we kissed him goodbye. I ran to their bedroom to look out the window. I was in time to watch as my mother, father, and Uncle Joe left our house and walked to the car. As my father reached the halfway point of the path to the front steps, he turned around, took one last look at the house, put his head down, and walked to the car shaking his head side to side. When they took off toward the prison, I collapsed in a heap on the floor and cried the hardest I had ever cried in my life.

I must confess that my tears were a combination of grief, fear, and relief. I didn't know what to expect from the ordeal we were about to experience, but at least I knew I wouldn't have to fear my father's wrath on a daily basis. This feeling sent me reeling with guilt. *How could I possibly feel relief when my father had just been sent to jail? How horrible a person was I?* There was no way on earth I could ever share this feeling with another human being. I felt like a monster. I wanted to disappear.

Deep depression was now a feeling I recognized and could identify but could do nothing about. I had to live with it, and somehow cope--and most importantly, not let on to anyone at school that anything was wrong. If a school counselor or social worker found out, they'd have Child Protective Services at our house before the end of the day. I needed to make sure that I kept my emotions in check at all times while at school.

"So, how did you deal with this while going to school?" asked Dr. Mintz.

"I did something stupid and impulsive," I answered.

I flirted shamelessly with the most gorgeous guy in school, whom I had a crush on for the whole year. He was the Captain of the varsity football team Louis played on as well. He flirted with me the whole year too, and I thought we just might have something going. I had the impression that he was really interested in me. It just so happened that a few days after my father surrendered to start serving his sentence, he called me. He wanted me to go to his apartment and "hang out." I was still a virgin but had made up my mind that I was going to sleep with him.

I primped as much as I could to make myself as desirable as could be and made my way over there. I don't think we talked for more than five minutes before we were on his bed, and I gave away a part of me – my virginity. I didn't care at the time. Somewhere in my mind I was convinced I needed to grow up fast in order to handle the strain of living without my father, and having the responsibility of bringing money into the house. I had grown-up responsibilities, so why not go all the way to feel like a grown-up? My impulsivity cost me dearly, and it wouldn't be the first time.

The next day, I approached him in the cafeteria. "Hi. How's it goin?" I asked.

"I really don't have time for you now," he said with a nasty tone in his voice.

"Will I see you later?" I asked, trying to ignore the tone.

"I'm busy."

"Will you call me?" I asked, becoming a bit more desperate.

"I've got a lot of things to do."

"I don't understand. Do we have something going, or not?"

"Nah, we're done here. Later." He walked away and didn't give me a second look.

I was devastated. I didn't know what to think or make of his reaction. Why was he acting this way? He seemed so interested in me these past several months. I thought he cared about me. I wasn't delusional enough to think he loved me, but I thought he cared. I was shocked, horrified, humiliated, and hurt. This was my first experience with a guy I was interested in, and it blew up in my face. *What was wrong with me? What the hell was I thinking? How could I do this to myself?* I felt violated once again, but this time it was my own fault. I had no idea what to do, or where to go with my feelings.

To cope with my depression, I started writing letters to myself. I poured my heart out in these letters, addressed the envelopes to myself, and hid them away. My sisters had diaries, and each one knew the other read them, so I found a secret hiding place for my letters in a hollow ceramic church most people used for Christmas decorations. It was the perfect size to hold my letters. I kept the church on the top shelf of my closet, stored in the back with clothes over it. I put other knick-knacks there as well to make it look like a pile of old things long forgotten. Every so often, I read the letters and destroyed them. It was my way of putting an end to the thoughts and feelings that occupied my mind. Once destroyed, these letters and their contents no longer had a hold over me. I was free, or so I thought.

I kept writing letters until I went away to college. I then turned to journaling. It was safer to keep a journal in my dorm room than to have one at home. Before leaving for college, I read and destroyed all the letters I had not destroyed before, to be sure they were never found.

CHAPTER 9

THE STRANGER WITHIN

Who is this person I see in the mirror?
The image is there
But needs to be clearer

The person I thought me to be
Is there in the glass
But not looking at me

Emotions are confused
They ran away with my brain,
And the loss of control
is an awful strain

I am frightened by this sudden change
It is quick and powerful
Unfamiliar and strange

Have I lost all control over what's in my mind?
Will I recover or
Will this loss be the permanent kind?

I rage and I cry
I scream and despair

I pray for help
That God will repair

Strangers are dangerous
They rob and they steal
I've lost emotional stability
I've lost what is real

Lori-ellen Pisani

WE WERE NOT allowed to visit my father for the first two months. He was in Sing Sing prison for processing before finally being moved to another prison for the remainder of his sentence. He allowed only my mother to visit at first. He didn't want his kids going to Sing Sing. It had a reputation for violence amongst the inmates, and the visiting room was not where he wanted us to be. After he was transferred, he agreed to see us. The prison was about an hour away from our house. My mother, who never liked driving on highways and hated going over bridges, learned quickly how to navigate her way back and forth. We visited every other Sunday.

Our first visit was memorable. I remember sitting in the back seat with Louis and Liz. Debby rode in the front seat to assist my mother with directions. My mouth was dry, my stomach hurt, and I tried to control my trembling hands by folding them over my aching stomach. There was almost complete silence for the whole ride, as we didn't want to make my mother more nervous than she obviously was by arguing or making any noise. Debby was the only one she spoke to. I could see her white-knuckle the steering wheel with both hands. She breathed a huge sigh of relief when we passed through the security gate and parked the car.

We got out of the car and went into the main building. My mother went up to the window to present our birth certificates. She told us before we left not to wear anything metal since we had to pass through metal detectors, and if we set off the alarm, they could strip search us. No belts, no jewelry, no barrettes, no pins, no purses, no metal buttons on our shirts, no change in our pockets, and no shoes--only sneakers. If we had sweat pants, we were to wear them, since my mother didn't want to take any chances that jeans might set off the alarm. She wanted no complications on our first visit, and I made sure I followed every direction so I wouldn't be the one to screw things up.

As each one of us passed through the detector, the others held their breath. When it was my turn, I held my breath, put my hands straight down at my side, closed my eyes, and went through. No alarm – thank God, so far, so good. We were told to wait in the main area until we were called. This gave me some time to think of what I was going to say to my father. I hadn't seen him in two months. The waiting area was crowded with families and other kids. My distraction from practicing my opening line came from my mother, who was about to present us with the rules for visiting an inmate.

"Listen carefully, all of you. There are rules you must obey, or they will end our visit and may not let us visit again. First, when you see your father come into the room, you must not shout to him. He will look for us and come over to us. When he does come over, do not approach him all at once. Let him come to each of you. You are allowed to give him a very quick hug and a kiss on the cheek, then step back immediately. He will sit on one side of the table and we will sit on the other. Keep your hands on the table at all times. Do not put them in your lap for any reason. Keep your feet tucked under your chair."

"What if we have to go to the bathroom?" I asked. My stomach was now cramping to the point that I wasn't sure if I was going to throw up or have diarrhea.

"Go now. Once we're called, we're not getting up until we are told our visit is over."

"Pisani family," the guard called out.

"Yes, sir, we're here," Mother answered.

"Follow me."

Mother hen then led her four scared chicks all in a row behind the guard. One door opened automatically and slammed behind us once we were inside. We waited until the next door opened automatically and we entered the visiting room. It was lined with cafeteria-style tables. Some were long and skinny with cafeteria benches on each side, and others were small tables with four chairs, one on each side.

I got the shock of my life when my father walked into the room in his khaki- colored pants, matching shirt, and sneakers. He had a full beard and lost an incredible amount of weight. I can honestly say that I didn't recognize him. Never in my life did I see him with a beard, and certainly not as thin as he was. His skin color was not the olive tone I was used to, but pale. His eyes had dark circles under them. His beard was a mixture of gray and white. His hair had thinned, and those once strong arms were scrawny looking. His big barrel chest was sunken in, and his huge belly was no more. I was horrified and frightened. *Who was this man? Where was my father? What did they do to him?* My mother said nothing to prepare me for what was in front of my eyes.

I was speechless as he approached me. I wanted to throw my arms around him and hold on forever. The pain I experienced at his hands was gone from my mind, and I was overwhelmed with feelings of love and pity I never knew before. I had no fear of him. He was my daddy, and I was his daughter. I wanted to save him from this wretched place. I wanted him to come home immediately so that I could feed him, nurse him back to health, and show him just how much I loved him. I wanted to apologize for every bad thing I ever said or did, beg for forgiveness, and start over. I wanted my daddy desperately.

Without warning, something strange happened. It was as my brain did a back flip. My hands began to tremble, my legs shook, and I had an almost uncontrollable desire to scream. The feelings of love, longing, and pity I had for him instantaneously transformed into extreme rage. *Oh my God, he's going to die in here,* I thought. *They're killing him because he poured molasses and feathers over some scabs?*

Are you kidding me? I could feel my heart pounding as I envisioned punching, kicking, and fighting every guard that stood in the way of my getting my father out of there. I wanted to rip those automatic steel doors off their hinges and run with him to the car. I'd rescue him from this miserable place.

I was frightened by this sudden change. I didn't understand that I had been triggered into an enraged state. I never had an urge to be violent, but at this moment, so much adrenaline was running through my body, I felt as though I could take on anyone who was in the way. My eyes narrowed as I looked around to see how many guards there were. I could see three. They didn't look that large, and I was confident I could take them on. My body felt as though I had the power and strength of ten men. *Should I throw chairs to create a distraction? Or run at them full speed like a football player with my head down, aim for the middle, and knock them over like bowling pins, then knock them out with the chairs? I bet the other inmates in the room would help once they knew what I was doing.* As I plotted, my leg bounced up and down under the table in an attempt to get some of the energy I felt out of my system. I often did that, as did my siblings. Sometimes, at dinner, the dining room table shook since we had so many legs bouncing under it. Since we weren't allowed to get up on our first visit, I had no other choice but to bounce my leg like a maniac under the table.

These urges and intense feelings distracted me from the conversation around the table. "Lori-ellen, did you hear me?" my father asked. My head snapped back, and my eyes refocused their attention "I'm sorry, I didn't hear you. It's kinda noisy in here."

"Forget about the noise. Are you working more at the club your friend owns?"

"Yeah. I work every weekend. On Friday and Saturday nights I work as the coat check girl, and on Sundays as a waitress for private parties. The place is booked for parties every weekend for the next few months."

"Good. Just make sure you keep the money coming in."

"I will." And I did, as did my sisters and brother. In addition to his doing all the maintenance on the house, Louis took a job at an ice cream shop. He never mastered the art of swirling the ice cream into the cones, but it was a job that helped bring in the money.

By the end of the visit, my heart stopped pounding, and my hands stopped trembling. I was breathing normally again. All the way home, I couldn't help but ask myself, *what the hell happened to me in there?* I felt like a caged animal. I was ready to hurt others to get my father out of there. I didn't recognize myself. I changed like the TV character the "Hulk" into a green monster in an instant. *Was this normal? Did every one of the kids I saw in the waiting area feel the same way I did? Would I feel the same way every time I visited, or was this some kind of a fluke incident?* I was overwhelmed by pity and love one moment, but in an instant, it turned into murderous rage.

I could only thank God I didn't attempt my foolish plan. It was ridiculous to think I could escape with my father from that place, and the consequences of my actions would have been horrendous. "Thank you, God, for keeping me under control," I said under my breath. I never forgot how I felt during that visit. It truly frightened me, but I had no one to share these feelings with. I kept quiet and prayed with each visit that it wouldn't happen again. It didn't.

I was never quite sure of how my mother managed the bills during this time, but she did it to the best of her ability. We kids did the best we could to bring money in on a steady basis. Some of my father's acquaintances visited, and I suspected they gave my mother money, but I was never sure. Mother was very creative with the menus. Casseroles of all varieties hit the plates for dinner, and we all refrained from asking for seconds. Leftovers were on the menu every Friday night. Sometimes my mother combined dishes she made during the week into something creative and new to us. I don't remember anyone in the family ever complaining.

Christmas 1979 was approaching. No one felt like celebrating, but my mother insisted on having a tree, and using some of the money we brought in to buy gifts for each other. We planned to save the gifts we bought for Daddy for his hopeful release the following April.

He was a model prisoner, taking classes and keeping out of trouble. We all hoped he would be let out for good behavior. He would spend a little over a year in prison.

I guess my mother thought the oil left in the tank was sufficient to heat the house, but it wasn't. We woke on Christmas morning to a freezing cold house and a blizzard outside. We quickly exchanged gifts and used the wrapping paper and boxes as fuel in the fireplace. We huddled together in silence for a while. My mother got up and went into the small office we had on the first floor and closed the door. We heard her speaking in a low voice on the phone but didn't dare get up to eavesdrop. We made it through Christmas, cold and depressed, and woke the next morning to the sound of oil being pumped into our tank. It must have killed my mother, who clearly made a phone call in desperation to one of my father's acquaintances for money to fill the tank.

My father was released from prison in April 1980. We showered him with affection upon his return, but it was soon evident that he wasn't interested in our feelings. He was, once again, a man on a mission. He was released from the union, and had only his dreams as prospects for making money. We soon learned how his new mission would turn our house upside down.

CHAPTER **10**

WHAT WORLD IS THIS?

What world is this that I live in now?
It is foreign to me
I am a stranger in my own house
Nothing is familiar or as it once was
And I don't know my place

I am my father's employee
Expected to work to the bone
His jailhouse letters were a cruel hoax
Written with false love and promises of a new family life

His focus now is to make money at any expense
The blue ledger book determines our worth
Our value to him is based upon the numbers inscribed
next to our names each week.

Lori-ellen Pisani

"WHAT HAPPENED WHEN your father was released from prison?" asked Dr. Mintz.

"He was out of a job and desperate for money."

"What did he do?"

"The first thing he did was sit us down at the dining room table for yet another family meeting. He made it clear that whatever he wrote to us that was at all affectionate was bullshit. He needed something to do to pass the time and to keep us motivated to bring in money. We were expected to continue giving him our paychecks from whatever job we had in the community. He continued to use the blue ledger book to document our weekly payments to him," I responded.

"And how did you feel after he made those statements?" Dr. Mintz asked.

"I immediately went upstairs, and took all the letters I saved from him, and burned them," I answered.

"And how did it make you feel about your father?"

"I felt the past year and a half was a lie. I felt that my father knew the words to write or say but refused to mean what he said. I wasn't his daughter; I was his employee. I basically shut down emotionally," I answered.

I stopped working at the club and took a job at a local pharmacy as a clerk. The money was better. The club I was working at had new competition, and attendance was slowing down. My job at the pharmacy was to stock shelves, take inventory, work the cash register, and prepare invoices for account customers. It was part time in the evenings, and I enjoyed it. I made about $50 per week. Every Friday, instead of going into the city to pick up the racing papers, I'd come home from work and hand over my check to my father.

I knew my father wasn't rolling in dough as each month; he'd take the bills that piled up under the cast-iron dog paperweight on the front hall shelf and lay them out on the dining room table in categories: mortgages, utility bills, taxes, and credit card bills. I was also used to lying to bill collectors on the phone. I knew to say that my father was not home every time the telephone rang, and most of the time the callers were bill collectors.

"I'm sorry, my father isn't home at this time. May I take a message?" I'd say.

"Yes, this is 'so and so' from some bank."

"What is this pertaining to exactly?"

"The mortgage on the property on Vaughn Avenue is two months overdue."

"What number can you be reached at, and what time is best to call?" The caller gave me the information.

"Thank you. I will see that my father gets this message and will return your call at his earliest convenience. Have a nice day."

My father never returned the phone calls, but the information was used to determine which bills to select for payment each month. My father had his own unique way of accounting. This caused huge arguments between him and my mother. My mother called my father "crazy" for overextending himself in so many directions, and my father called my mother a "damn fool," for not understanding his need to build his empire.

To avoid these confrontations, my father waited until my mother was out of the house running errands. He called me into the dining room and had me practice my mother's signature so that I could forge her name on checks and documents. This didn't feel right to me, but I was too scared to argue with him. When he yelled, he often punched walls or slammed his fists down on tables. I didn't want his fist to slam into my face, so I didn't question him, although I did wonder if my mother knew just how much I was forging her name. I was too scared to tell her as well, since I risked the wrath of both parents if I did. I was stuck. What I was doing was wrong, but I was too frightened to say anything. I also knew that we were in a financial mess. My father spent money he didn't have, and the bills were mounting, as were the many lies I was telling to the dozens of callers asking for my father on a daily basis.

"How did you all survive? Your father was out of a job, and with the exception of the money you kids were bringing in, what did your father do to make money?" Dr. Mintz questioned.

I explained that once again, we had a family meeting. It felt a lot like the meeting we had before he went off to prison. We sat around and waited for him to speak.

"You know that I don't have a job with the union anymore, so I have to find another way. You need to continue to work and bring in the money until I can make something happen. Your contributions will be added to the blue book. I met someone while at university [our name for prison] who will be out in a few months and will be coming to live with us."

"Who is this man, and why does he have to live with us?" Debby asked.

"His name is Alan, and he has connections to start a business, and that's the way it's going to be. He doesn't have a family to go home to, and I need him close to me if this is going to work. He's going to need a room to sleep in, so Debby and Liz, I want you to start looking for an affordable apartment. I'm sure there's something you can find locally. Alan is getting out in a couple of months, so you have a little bit of time, but get on it quickly. I need to get his room ready."

"What did your mother and other family members say?" asked Dr. Mintz.

"We couldn't say anything. My father made it clear to us that he needed this man to make a living, and we were all going to have to deal with it."

"And what became of this arrangement?"

"Alan stayed for a few months and then disappeared. He was a con man, and my father, of all people, fell for it out of desperation. We supported him until he found another victim to prey upon. There was no business deal. He needed a place to stay and made all kinds of promises to my father. When they didn't come to pass, he up and left. Debby and Liz kept their apartment until the lease was up. Then they moved back home."

"What happened next?"

"My father's interests turned to real estate and professional boxing. He used his connections in Bermuda to help finance his new venture as a professional boxing manager. He brought two boxers up from Bermuda: Mike, a promising middleweight, and Nick, an Olympic gold-medal winner in the heavyweight class. They moved in with us, and once again, pushed Debby and Liz out of the house and into an apartment."

"And what about the real estate venture?"

"My grandfather had an empty lot behind his house that had room for another house to be built on it. He took out another mortgage to finance this project and used us kids as his laborers for anything and everything that didn't require a licensed sub-contractor. I learned a great deal about building houses through this process. Weekends were consumed by slinging hammers, clearing debris from the site, laying tile, painting, cleaning the rooms, washing windows, and anything else my father needed done. The house took about two years to build, and my father rented it out for income. In another venture, he asked his longtime friend to invest with him on an apartment house deal he found in a nearby town. At the closing, his friend backed out, and instead of walking away from the deal, my father went ahead with it. Louis became his partner. The building had nine apartments that required some renovation. Louis and my father worked all hours of the day and night to get the building ready for tenants."

"And what about the Bermuda betting shop?"

"It was barely holding its own but was still open."

"Were these real estate deals and boxing ventures successful?"

"I can't really say that they were. The house was rented, but it barely covered the mortgage, the building was struggling to stay above water, and the boxing venture required a great deal of money that he borrowed from his partners in Bermuda as well as his credit cards to finance. The boxers required special diets, trainers, facilities to train in, promotion, fight venues, travel, and staff to see to their needs. Mike was much more successful. He held the record for the fastest knockout by a middleweight in Madison Square Garden history. He was on par with the champions in his class, and had his shot at a title, but lost. Nick had a few good fights but didn't rise as high as Mike. He quit and went home to Bermuda."

"How was it living in the house with two strangers?"

"We were told to make their stay with us as comfortable as possible. I didn't realize at the time that it also meant letting Mike have his way with me."

"What are you talking about?"

"I was coming out of the shower one morning and opened the locked bathroom door. I had a towel on my head and a bathrobe on.

As soon as I stepped out of the doorway, Mike grabbed me, took me into his room, threw me on his bed, and jumped on top of me. I was so shocked I didn't scream, but I did manage to get him off me just in time and run from his room into mine. I blocked the door with a chair. I waited until I heard him leave the house. I looked out my window to see him riding away on his bicycle. I took the chair away from the door and went downstairs."

"Was anyone home at the time?"

"My mother, but she was too busy making red beans and rice, one of Mike's favorite foods, and managing the kitchen, which operated more like a hotel kitchen than a family one. She didn't like to be interrupted when cooking the various meals he required, so I kept quiet."

"Did you tell anyone?"

"I waited until my father got home and told him what happened."

"What did he do?"

He looked at me and said, "Look, Mike has a shot at being a champion. He's got a big fight coming up against one of the best in the world. If he beats him, he moves on to the middleweight championship. Nothing is to distract him. Do you understand? You need to apologize to him."

"I what! He attacked me! I followed your rules and had myself totally covered up after taking my shower. He grabbed me – he jumped on me- if I didn't get him off me, he would have raped me!" I responded in disbelief.

"You don't seem to understand what I'm saying. Mike is on track to be a champion, which will bring in big money. I won't have anything ruin that. I'm telling you to apologize for putting yourself in his way. I'm not so sure you didn't do anything to let him think you wanted him. And I'm not going to get in his face and distract him over something that isn't that important. I need to have his head clear to train until this fight. Don't you understand? You were able to get away from him. He didn't rape you, so just make sure you stay out of his way. Don't make this more than it is. He's a champion, and there's nothing more important than that."

"How did you feel about what your father said?" Dr. Mintz asked.

"I was stunned. He brings these strangers into the house, turns the whole house upside down as he finagles and plots to make them champions, has us all catering to their every whim, and when one of them attacks me, I'm forced to apologize."

"Did you apologize?"

"Oh yes, he called Mike down from upstairs that evening and said, 'I think Lori-ellen may have given you the wrong impression this morning. Lori-ellen, what do you have to say to Mike?"

"I struggled for words, but came up with, I'm sorry if I gave you the impression that I was interested in having sex with you. I didn't mean to, and I will be much more careful in the future."

"And did Mike respond?"

"Yes. He said, you did give me that impression, now just make sure you keep out of my way."

"What were you thinking after this episode?"

"I was counting the months in my head until I graduated high school and would be going away to college."

"How did your parents afford college with all this going on?"

"At that time, we qualified for financial aid, so both Louis and I applied for and received student loans. I was headed for Fairleigh Dickinson University in New Jersey, and Louis was headed for a university in Connecticut."

CHAPTER **11**

TICKET TO FREEDOM

I got my ticket to freedom
At eighteen years of age
Education was my ticket out
To make the world my stage

I packed my things for college
And prayed with all my might
That God would see me through these years
And with my wings take flight

The rules I made to stay on course
Were to study and focus each day
At night I lay down in my bed
And closed my eyes to pray

Dear God, don't leave me, I am scared
The future is yet unknown
But with Your help I will succeed
And show them all I've grown

I'll prove them wrong
And they will see
You gave me strength
To be the best I can be

Lori-ellen Pisani

IN 1981, LOUIS and I were preparing for high school graduation. My father said he was too busy to attend, so we didn't count on him being there. Since there were over one thousand students graduating, they held the ceremony on the football field. My mother took a seat in the stands. We couldn't find her in the sea of faces. But halfway through the ceremony, I glanced over to the sidelines. There, leaning against a pole, was my father. I tapped Louis on the shoulder and told him to take a look. He did, and returned my gaze with a half-smile. We never said anything to him. If we did, we would get a snide, sarcastic retort, so we just smiled inside that our father did come to see us graduate.

The next challenge was preparing to leave home for college. My parents felt it was their responsibility to send us to school, as they had done for Debby and Liz. Unfortunately for Debby and Liz, college was not a place where they found success. Debby continued to work for a major hotel in Manhattan, and Liz was also working as a secretary. I truly believe my parents thought the same fate would befall Louis and me, so they entered into this process with half-baked enthusiasm.

I had great concerns and fears about being away from home for the first time in my life, and mostly, being away from Louis. We never attended day camp, let alone summer sleepaway camp. We had been together all our lives, and this separation meant a severing of my emotional ties to him. I was connected to Louis more than any other member of my family. Even though we fought horribly as we grew up, there was an unmistakable bond that started with his offering a piece of his heart to me to save my life.

I remember one incident in high school that made quite the splash and made me realize how much I needed Louis. Donald, a guy who I was not interested in dating, spread a rumor around the high school about my "being easy." The rumor got back to Louis, and while sitting in history class, I was startled by this announcement over the PA. It was a voice that I recognized, Louis's voice. "Excuse us, but Donald has something to say."

There was scuffling and then a voice that sounded as if it was being choked out of him came over the loudspeaker. "Ummm, my name is Donald, and I am the idiot who spread the rumor about Lori-ellen Pisani. I want to tell everyone that I am an asshole who is really sorry for doing such a stupid thing. The rumor is not true. I made it up because I am a loser who couldn't get a girl to go out with me. It will never happen again."

Louis came back on the announcements to let everyone know that Donald could be found stuffed in his locker if anyone wanted to look for him.

When we got home from school, I asked Louis why he did that. "He pissed me off," was his reply. "No one is going to spread rumors about you while I'm around."

It made me wonder if there was going to be anyone who would protect me while I was away at school in New Jersey, and he was away in Connecticut. The thought of losing him was deeply upsetting, as was my parents' less-than-confident belief that we would make anything of our college experiences. I knew deep in my heart and soul that I had one chance to change their minds about me, so I had to suppress my feelings about not having Louis around and turn my attention to my next greatest challenge in life.

Going away to college was my ticket out of the madhouse I grew up in. I wasn't a stellar student at the time—average, yes, but stellar, no. My grades were good enough to be accepted into FDU as an education major. If I was ever going to escape my house of horrors, this was the way to do it. I resolved to make it my mission to succeed.

I had orientation in May. My father took me. He stayed with me as my student advisor set up my class schedule. Once that was done, we had a bit of time before the tour of the campus, so we set off up the main street in town to find a bank. My father helped me open a checking account. He put $150 in it and told me that was all the money I would have until the end of the semester, so don't bother asking for more. I signed up for my meal card and waited for the tour. The student guide showed us all the buildings, and I made mental notes as to how to get to each one for my classes.

In late August, I packed my things and headed off to Fairleigh. My parents drove me to my new home, a small cottage-style building with two floors and two bedrooms on each floor. The cottage was called University Court 8. Each room had three beds in it, a dresser and desk for each person, and a walk-in closet. There was a shared bathroom on each floor, a pay phone, and a room for the Resident Assistant on the first floor. There was also a small sitting room with a couch, two chairs, and a coffee table.

I checked in with the resident assistant, Mary Ann, and headed for my room on the first floor. My father brought in my bags, and my mother helped me make my bed. There were no real goodbyes, except for my father's comment, "We'll see if you don't fail out."

"Thanks, Dad," I said.

My mother's advice was to "be careful." And with that, they got into the car and drove off.

I was alone in the room for a while, unpacking my things, and putting up Smurf posters on the wall around my bed. We had a small refrigerator, and I had a small plug-in hot pot. They didn't allow microwaves and hot plates in the dorms. The only other appliances I had were my wind-up alarm clock, and my blow dryer. Computers and cell phones were a thing of the future at that time.

After setting up my side of the room, I sat down on the bed and prayed, *Dear God, please help me. I am frightened and alone. I know that this is my ticket out of my miserable life, and I want desperately to succeed. I can't do it by myself. I need your help. Please help me. Please be with me every step of the way. Please let my roommates be nice. Please help me make friends. Please help me study and not fail out like my parents expect. Please don't leave me. Amen.*

I spent the time sitting on my bed, studying my schedule of classes, and preparing my notebooks. I wound my alarm clock and set it for 7:00 a.m. to give me plenty of time to get ready for my first 9:00 class the next morning. I sat down again to wait for the girls that would soon be my roommates. *What should I say? Will they be nice? Will I be able to be friends with them? Will they reject me?* I was so nervous my palms were sweating, and my stomach churned.

The door flung open, and in walked Susan.

"Hi, my name is Lori-ellen," I said.

"Hi, I'm Susan," she said and we shook hands.

"Can I help you with your things?" I asked.

"Thanks."

We set about unpacking her things and chatting along the way. I learned that she was from a town not too far from where I lived. That was a comfort to me. It made me feel as though we already had something in common. She was a larger-sized girl, with long brown hair and huge brown eyes. She was also a Bruce Springsteen fanatic, and soon her side of the room was filled with all kinds of Springsteen memorabilia, a stark contrast to my Smurf posters. She told me that our other expected roommate was also from the same town. Her name was Mariana. She had a twin brother, Domenico, who was also attending Fairleigh.

Not long after Susan arrived, Mariana walked in with her twin. She was outgoing and friendly. She knew Susan already, which made me a bit nervous. Would they let me into their already established group? As we helped her set up, it was clear she had a penchant for the Bohemian style. She filled her side of the room with beads and tie-dyed scarves. Three very different styles for one very small room, but it worked in its own weird way.

We started talking, and I learned that Susan was a political science major, Mariana was studying liberal arts. All during the afternoon, more housemates arrived. Sara, from Pennsylvania, Eve from Cherry Hill, New Jersey, both communications majors, and Mary from Leonia, New Jersey who was studying business and marketing all made their way into their rooms. These girls were to be my primary friends. There were others, but they didn't form my core group of friends. As the years passed, we stayed together as roommates. Sara, Mary, Susan and I moved from University Court as freshmen to a suite in Linden 8 our sophomore and junior years, and finally, as seniors, to an apartment on campus in Wilshire Court.

The excitement started almost immediately. We heard some commotion in our little sitting area and found that two guys were carrying out our orange sofa. We asked them what they were doing and were told that they needed it. Our RA, MaryAnn, quickly turned them around, and they replaced the sofa. I was attracted to one of the attempted thieves, Jimmy, and made small talk. He had the look of a popular movie star, and that caught my eye. He was a sophomore and lived in a different dorm, Linden 7, not far from where I was. He introduced me to his co-conspirator, Tommy. I walked over with them to their dorm to meet the others who shared their dorm room, Dave, and Steve. It turned out that Steve was a cousin of Mariana and Domenico. These guys would join my primary group of friends during three of my four years at Fairleigh.

That first evening, we all gathered in MaryAnn's room to hear the rules of the dorm and get to know each other a bit better. I was immensely relieved to see that all the girls in my little cottage were as nervous as I was. The rules were basic: no cooking in the rooms, respect each other's property, make a schedule for the use of the bathrooms, and communicate with each other to work out any issues that may arise. Before the meeting ended, we agreed that we would all support each other the best way we could. I made a promise to myself to make the most of this opportunity by being flexible and accommodating. I didn't want to rock the boat in any way.

My mission was to do everything I could not to follow the pattern of my sisters before me. I knew in my heart that this was my one and only chance to break free from the house of cards I lived in, and to make something of myself. The ultimate goal was to become self-sufficient as soon after graduation as possible. In order to do this, I put my studies above all other things on my list of how I'd live the college life. My career was being a student. Since I didn't graduate anywhere close to the top of my class in high school, I was very fearful of the workload and what the classes would be like. I didn't know if I could do the work successfully and pass the exams. The title "Professor" scared the daylights out of me. *Was this all a big mistake? Do I really belong here? Can I show my parents that I'm really worth something or am I really the Bimbo, Damn Fool, Shit for Brains my father always said I was?* These questions brought me to a place in my heart I had relied on all my life--hope and faith in God.

When we settled down for the night, I brought out my silky, and rubbed it furiously in order to settle myself down. I could hear the ticking of my alarm clock. It was comforting. It provided the beat to which I rocked myself back and forth. Not too long into my attempt to get some sleep, I heard a loud cry from the hallway. I bolted upright to hear one of the girls on the phone crying to her parents to come and get her. She didn't want to stay and pleaded for her parents to come get her immediately.

I couldn't tell which one of the girls it was, but her cries frightened me. I turned to prayer for the second time that day. *Dear God, please give me the strength to get through this night and tomorrow, without falling apart and calling home. Please stay with me, and help me succeed. I have one chance to make it, and I can't do it without you. I promise to work hard and do whatever I have to do to succeed. Please don't let me fail. Amen.* After my prayer, I put my pillow over my head to muffle the cries from the hall and fell into a fitful sleep.

At 7:00, the alarm sounded and I woke with a start. I took my turn in the bathroom, dressed, and prepared my books for my classes. My roommates went to breakfast, but I was too nervous to eat. In fact, I didn't go to the cafeteria for almost a week. I was so wound up and charged with energy that I couldn't think of eating. I made do with my hot pot and tea. I picked up my books and headed for class, praying to God the entire way, asking Him to be with me. I can't truly explain it, but I felt His presence with me. I found my classes without difficulty and made every effort to make some kind of connection with my professors. I looked for traits in them that reminded me of someone in my life that I liked. This became a pattern for me all through college and beyond. If I could make any connection, I was more apt to like them, and want to please them with a good performance. I can't say this was a strategy, but it helped me immensely, especially my first term.

Since I didn't have my parents there to make rules for me, I adopted the habit of making them for myself. The primary rule I made was to immediately complete all assignments before anything else at the end of each day. I didn't join my friends at many parties or hang out too much. I was hell bent on completing my work to the best of my ability and studying every night for quizzes or exams, which came pretty frequently. Everyone soon learned that I wasn't going anywhere until my work was done to my satisfaction.

Since Fairleigh was known as a "commuter school," Thursday nights were the usual party nights. Once I got into the groove of classes, studying, and exams, I allowed myself to participate in some of these parties. Linden 7--where Jimmy, Steve, Dave, and Tommy lived--was party central after the University Pub on campus. On Thursday nights, my roommates and I dressed up and headed for the pub (eighteen was the legal drinking age at the time, so I didn't have to worry about proof). I wasn't a drinker, but I did love to dance. After all, I had been performing in front of the mirror at home for so many years, now I had the chance to show my stuff on the dance floor in the pub.

We danced to the hits of the early eighties and hung out with the guys in Linden 7. I enjoyed myself but didn't stay out too long, since I had one class on Fridays. By the middle of the semester, it was clear that Jimmy was attracted to me, and I was attracted to him. Our relationship, however, was rocky and dysfunctional. Not having much experience with guys, I didn't know what a "normal" relationship was, so I didn't realize how dysfunctional it was until it was over and I was once again in a deep depression.

CHAPTER **12**

REPEATING PATTERNS

Repeating patterns are easy to follow
Children learn them with ease
But when these patterns skip once then twice
I lose count and I am displeased

My patterns in life run wild and crazy
Success and failure confound
I try hard to change the outcome
But my failures are too profound

This leaves me both confused and fearful
Will failure cause me to fall?
Or can I break this crazy pattern
And end up standing tall

Lori-ellen Pisani

DR. MINTZ ASKED, "How did you feel being away from home?"

"In the beginning, I went home frequently, but I gradually spent more and more weekends at school. There was also a huge change in my father's behavior that I found pretty remarkable."

"What change?"

"He came to see me pretty often. The university was only thirty minutes from the house, so it wasn't a long drive. Long enough to be away from home, but close enough to get home in case of an emergency. That was a requirement my parents had."

"Why do you think he came to visit you?" Dr. Mintz asked.

"I never did figure that out. All I knew was that when he came, he was funny, sweet, and generous. He always took me out to eat. While we ate, he asked how I was doing, if I needed anything, and sometimes, he spoke about how he was doing with all his business ventures. Before he left, he brought groceries to stock our little fridge. The girls loved it when he came to visit. Often, he'd take us all out to lunch. It was a side of him that I never experienced before as it related to my relationship with him. He behaved like a dad, not at all like the father I had always known. I loved when he came to visit. He was interested in me, for the first time in my life. He was getting to know me, and he cared. I felt close to him and wanted to make him proud of me."

"Did your mother ever visit?"

"No, she never did. I was too afraid to ask why, since I wasn't emotionally prepared to hear her say she didn't have time."

"Did that bother you?"

"No. I was so taken aback by this new relationship with my father that I didn't spend too much time on my relationship with my mother. She wasn't ever emotionally expressive or supportive. Although my father didn't say he loved me, he showed it by coming to visit. It was the closest to feeling love from my father I had ever felt, and I reveled in it."

"Looking back at the history you completed when you first came here, it's apparent that you did succeed," Dr. Mintz commented.

I'll never forget the look on my father's face when my first semester grades were mailed to the house. I was sitting on the bench in the living room as my father went through the mail. He saw the envelope from Fairleigh and said, "Hmmm, what do we have here? Looks like your grades. Let's see how bad it is." He opened the envelope, and I could actually see his eyes widen and his jaw drop. He saw straight A's for all my classes. He looked over at me, smiled, and said, "Don't they give A+s in that school?"

"I just laughed. 'Sorry, but that's the highest grade they give.' He didn't say anything more. He handed me the paper and went to make himself a cup of coffee. That look was all I needed to make another rule. I was to get as many A's as humanly possible."

"And what happened to Louis? How did he do?"

"As it turned out, Louis came down with mono during his first semester away and was unable to complete the term. He returned home and set his sights on going to a local college to study business and accounting. I felt horrible for him. But he didn't seem to mind too much. As it turned out, Louis's college career went the same route as my sisters'. He found that his style of learning is much more hands-on than sitting in classes. He took a job with my sister at the same hotel she worked in. I continued at Fairleigh, even more determined to succeed since now we were three for four as it related to not finishing school."

My achievements afforded me the opportunity to compete for merit scholarships. These scholarships paid for my classes and books. I competed and won these scholarships throughout the rest of my college career and was also inducted into two honor societies. In addition, I received the *Dean's Award* for Scholarship and Leadership, became Editor of the School of Education's newspaper, *Chalkdust,* and represented Fairleigh Dickinson at the teachers' convention in Atlantic City. My 4.0 grade point average was brought down by a C+ in piano. That horrified me. I needed a fine arts class as an elective and chose piano. I love the piano and can play by ear, but when I sat down to play, my hand coordination was painfully absent. I'd start to play the chords with my left hand, but almost immediately, my left hand was playing along with my right hand. I couldn't understand it. I played the flute successfully throughout grade school and middle school, and now I couldn't get my hands to cooperate on the keyboard. The C+ lowered my final cumulative average to 3.89, well enough for Salutatorian. I just missed Valedictorian by .07 of a point. I graduated Summa Cum Laude.

"Graduation must have been very special for you."

"I didn't go to graduation."

"Why not?"

"Because even though I was awarded merit scholarships for tuition from my sophomore year until I graduated, my father had me take out student loans anyway. Instead of using that money to pay my room and board fees, he used it for his business ventures. He fell behind on payments, and did not pay the past due amount on time for graduation. I was told I could walk across the stage, but I would not receive my diploma. I was so embarrassed that I didn't bother to attend. I envisioned myself walking across the stage, shaking hands with the professors, only to be left empty-handed at the end. I didn't know at the time that they would have handed me an empty diploma case, so I decided not to go."

"What did you do instead?"

"My parents took us all out to dinner, and then I went to Mary's graduation party."

"Was that good enough?"

"I convinced myself that it was. I had accomplished more than I ever thought I could or would, and that's what mattered. I made a name for myself as a scholar, and I was no longer called "Bimbo" or "Shit for Brains." My father took all my awards and certificates and had them framed. He hung them on the wall of my bedroom. He called it the "Brain Wall."

"It sounds as though you were also a girl with a mission at college," Dr. Mintz said.

"I was highly motivated, perseverant, dedicated, and successful in everything I attempted, with the exception of that damn piano class. It was like being on speed. I was the Energizer Bunny on speed. I studied hard, prayed every day, went to church on Sundays, and kept my eyes focused on the prize. I was going to make it come hell or high water."

"Did you require a lot of sleep?"

"Come to think of it, no, I didn't. I woke up before the alarm every day and worked until late at night. If I went out on Thursday nights, I could stay out late, and still be fresh for my classes on Fridays."

"What about relationships? Whatever happened with Jimmy?"

"I dated Jimmy during the first two and a half years of school. He was what I consider now to be a 'tough guy.' He drove the latest model sports car, walked with a swagger, was flirtatious, and could drive me crazy. He acted as though I didn't exist sometimes, even when I was in the same room. He ignored me while he flirted with other girls. It made me jealous as hell."

"After spring break in my junior year, I went over to his apartment to see him, only to find him coming out of his bedroom with another girl who was adjusting her shirt. He didn't say a word. Steve, Dave, and Tommy just stared at me to see what I was going to do. I was too humiliated to do anything but leave. The light was out in the stairway leading down from the second floor, and I tripped on a stair and thought I broke my ankle.

"I limped back to my dorm and watched as my ankle swelled to the size of a large softball and turned all sorts of colors. I knew I was in trouble. I called my sister Debby, and she came to take me to the hospital. I didn't call my parents because I didn't want to worry them or explain how it happened in the first place. It turned out that I had severely sprained the ankle and torn ligaments. I was put into a walking cast for six weeks."

"Did Jimmy ever say anything to you?"

"No, he avoided me like the plague."

"How did you deal with it?"

"I was very depressed. I couldn't figure out what I did to deserve that kind of treatment. I put up with all his flirtatious behaviors and nasty comments and teasing when he was drunk. Thursday nights could be rough. He was a nasty drunk, who teased and thought it was funny when we had 'play fights' which entailed his punching me on the arms and legs, often leaving bruises."

"Did you punch back?"

"No, I didn't want him to get mad and break up with me, so I just took it. Looking back, it was beyond stupid on my part. I didn't think of it as abusive, since he wasn't my father or sibling. I realize now that he was not only physically but emotionally abusive. I never made the connection between the way he treated me and the way my siblings treated me as a kid. The bottom line was that I was alone once again. It was just like my first time all over again. Once again, I was humiliated and rejected. I didn't go over to his place anymore. I didn't need to be publicly rejected again. So, I stayed away. I had trouble sleeping, eating, and finding anything that made me laugh."

With Dr. Mintz's encouragement, I continued to tell my story.

I have to say that Dave and Steve were sweet, but honest. They came to visit me in my dorm. They told me that Jimmy was an idiot, and that I was an idiot for putting up with his behavior over the past two and a half years. Dave came more often than Steve, and as we continued to talk, my relationship with him grew into a romantic one. We were together for the rest of the spring semester. He treated me really well, and I fell in love with him. I even met his parents, and he met my father in Atlantic City. Mike was fighting at one of the hotels, and my father met us there. My father liked him, so in my mind, I had succeeded on two fronts: finding someone I loved and thought I might marry one day, and succeeding in my studies. I imagined moving to New Jersey once I graduated to be with him. I thought he was different. He treated me like no other had before. He was kind, sensitive, and considerate. I had no idea what was coming.

Jimmy, Dave, Tommy, and Steve were scheduled to graduate in May 1984, as they were a year ahead of me. Dave and I spent time together over the summer break and talked on the phone a lot. We hooked up again when we got back to school in September. In December 1983, just after finals, I was walking into the pub and saw Dave ahead of me in line to pay the cover charge with his arm around another girl. He turned around, looked at me, and shrugged his shoulders. He had a look on his face that said "whatever," and I instantly knew our relationship was over. I was shocked. It came out of nowhere. He never said anything to me. It was certainly a pattern I recognized with the guys in my life, but I never expected it from him.

"What did you do?" Dr. Mintz asked.

"I instantly became enraged. I was so pissed off that I went into the parking lot looking for his car, so I could slash his tires. I couldn't find the car, so I settled on throwing metal trash cans around the parking lot."

"Did you speak to him again?"

"No, not about that. I'd see him on campus and wave a quick hello. But I didn't approach him. I learned that talking about relationship issues was a dead end and a no- win situation. Guys lie or tell you things that aren't close to the truth just to get you off their backs. It wasn't worth further pain to attempt to have an honest conversation with him. My rage turned into a deep depression. I was grateful for the fact that both he and Jimmy were scheduled to graduate in May. I wouldn't have to see either of them again."

Somewhere in the back of my mind, I made another rule. *The next guy I got involved with was not going to get the best of me. I was going to be in control and protect myself at all costs.* The pain of rejection was too much for me, and it took me away from my most important job, so I was determined to keep my focus on my studies. I had another semester of classes, and summer classes to take before my senior year started. I wanted to focus solely on my student teaching experience without the distraction of courses, so I needed to take additional classes during the summer.

"I had a huge National Teacher's Exam coming up in December 1984, and my student teaching requirement was scheduled to start in January 1985. I was assigned to teach a fourth-grade class in a school close to campus. These were the last two requirements I had before I graduated, and I set my sights on that. My plan however, took a detour."

"What do you mean?" asked Dr. Mintz.

"During the summer, I roomed with a fellow education major, Danielle. We stayed in an apartment type dorm called Wilshire Court while we took our courses. Danielle had a boyfriend at the time and spent a lot of her free time with him. I met John, a security guard on campus, and spent my free time with him. He was older than I was, and different from all the other guys I dated."

"Tell me about him."

"He was a big and tall man, standing six feet four inches, and weighing just over two hundred pounds. He had reddish brown hair and huge blue eyes. I can't say that he was my type, but he was very nice and sweet. He took me to lunch and left me sweet notes in my notebook and around the apartment. He was very sensitive and spoke often of his very large family. His size made me feel safe with him, but I made up my mind that I wasn't going to fall in love with him. He was very religious and often spoke of having dreams about God sending him into the battle of Armageddon as His soldier. Since I too was a faithful person, this commonality of faith gave me the impression that he was heaven sent, and that being 'in love' was not all that important."

"He was a good person, and that was enough for me. He was in love with me, and that helped make me feel emotionally safe. My thinking was, that if he were to break up with me, I wouldn't be as emotionally devastated as I was in the past. I was determined not to feel the pain of rejection again, so I pursued the relationship with him."

"What about love?" asked Dr. Mintz

"I gave up on that. It wasn't worth the pain of losing the relationship, and I wasn't confident enough to believe that anyone I was attracted to would stay with me. There would always be the threat of rejection, and I didn't think I could deal with that, so I pushed it out of my mind."

"So did everything run smoothly from that point on?"

"I had someone in my life who loved me, and I figured what the hell, I might as well go along with it. So, on that front, it was Okay. I passed the National Teacher's Exam in both New York and New Jersey in December, and returned in January to start my last semester before graduation. I didn't know that I was about to have a breakdown. It scared the daylights out of me."

In January 1985, and I was scheduled to start student teaching in a week's time. I woke up one morning from a fitful sleep, paralyzed with fear, clutching my pillow to my chest with my back against the wall, and my comforter tucked under my chin. At first, I thought I had had a nightmare, but I couldn't remember what it was. I was confused, sweating, and frightened. Tears streamed down my face. *What in the hell was happening?*

My roommates were already out of the apartment for the day, so I was left alone with my thoughts and fears. *Were these four years of study and success all a dream? Was I really the most successful elementary teacher candidate of my graduating class? Could I put into practice everything I had learned? Was I really as smart and capable as everyone at school thought I was, or was it really a cruel hoax, like those I experienced as a child? Was I as crazy as Danielle, my friend from last summer whom I roomed with?*

Since she spent most of her time with her boyfriend, it was bound to happen. She was pregnant. She came from a strict and very religious family, so abortion was out of the question. She wanted this baby, but her parents would never accept its father who was African-American. That wasn't the plan they had for her. She was going to marry a man of their choosing and of their faith. She had no choice. She hid her pregnancy from everyone by wearing baggy clothes and by holding her purse and other objects in front of her at all times.

She gave birth in January, just about two weeks before we were to start student teaching together. As a security guard on campus, John found out first, and came to tell us what happened. She delivered the baby by herself in her dorm room, wrapped him in a blanket, put him in a trash bag, and then put him in a dumpster. She studied with me in many of my classes these past four years. I knew how much time she spent with her boyfriend and suspected she might be pregnant. I never in my wildest nightmares thought she was capable of such a drastic action.

She was caught because she inadvertently, or maybe not, had a piece of paper left in the trash bag with her name on it. She was now in a hospital's psych ward, awaiting charges. The baby survived, but Danielle left school, and the baby was put into foster care. She was charged with child endangerment and some other charges but pled to lesser crimes and went home. *Was I having a delayed reaction to this terrible incident?*

I had excelled as a student throughout my four years of college. I was a merit scholar whose professors thought I had the makings of an excellent teacher. As I completed each course with A's as my grades, I grew in confidence that I would indeed succeed and meet my ultimate goal. I looked forward to my crowning achievement for my efforts. I would graduate with honors and begin my career as a teacher. I could finally get out of reach of my family. All of that was now in jeopardy.

While huddled up tight on my bed, visions of entering the classroom and opening my mouth to introduce myself to the students--only to have nothing come out--filled my mind. I was terrified that my true identity as a wounded, broken little girl would be discovered, and they'd show me the door after the first day of student teaching. As I walked away from the school, all the children were laughing, like my siblings did long ago. It was all a set-up, another practical joke at my expense. I was convinced that I had forgotten everything I'd learned in the past four years, and that my true place was to sit behind one of the desks in the classroom rather than stand in front of the class as their teacher. Oh my God, it was true. These past four years were a dream, and the truth was that I was still a little girl, fearful of everything, lacking in wit and intelligence, an unnecessary addition to the family and now to my new profession, and unable to do anything right.

One week before the semester started, and I here I was stuck in my youth again. *How did this happen? Why now? What in the world would I to do?* In seven days, I was either going to be standing in front of a classroom of students, or be in a rubber room somewhere, and all would be lost.

Fortunately for me, I had roommates I could trust. We had been through so much together and were close. Susan came home to find me on the bed. She talked to me for a while. I didn't want to come out of my room. She told me how concerned Sara and Mary were, and that I needed to come to the dinner table to talk to all of them.

When we sat down to dinner, it was clear that something was terribly wrong. I looked awful, with red swollen eyes from crying, raw and bleeding lips from my biting them to shreds, wild bed-head hair, and wrapped up in my comforter. I sat at the table, and the girls put dinner on my plate. I sat there staring at the plate, eyes cast down, not speaking.

Sara spoke first. "Lori-ellen, what's wrong with you? I hate to say it, but you look like hell."

As Susan and Mary nodded their agreement to Sara's comment, I poured out my heart to them.

"I can't do it," I began.

"Do what?" they all chimed in unison.

"I can't be a teacher. I don't have what it takes. I can't remember anything I've learned. I'm going to be tossed out before I even begin."

"You've got to be kidding," Susan said. "You're an A student. You aced all your classes and have been preparing for this for four years. Of course you can do it."

"I just don't feel like I will make it, and I don't know what to do. Should I quit now before I'm humiliated and tossed out on my first day? I think I'm having a breakdown, like they said Danielle had."

Mary responded, "No you're not. You're just nervous as hell. Everyone is when they go into their first job. It's your first job, and you're feeling the way everyone does. Just relax, and everything will be fine after your first day."

"This feels different from just nerves. I feel like I'm four again and can't even tie my own shoes."

Sara suggested, "If you're feeling really bad, then go to the Health Center. They have counseling there, and that should help you get over your nerves, which is all it is. You've come way too far for it to end for no good reason. We'd all be hurt and disappointed if you quit and went home. You're not Danielle. You haven't lost your mind and done anything as horrible as she did. I know you two were close and were supposed to start your student teaching together. But that's not going to happen, and you've got to accept it, and move on. We've all come this far, and it wasn't easy for any of us. You wouldn't only be letting yourself down, but the rest of us as well. If we can't convince you, then for God's sake get to the Health Center tomorrow. They can help."

"Okay. We've been through so much, and we're about to start our lives and careers. I've wanted to be a teacher since I was a kid. I can't let this happen. I can't fall apart now. It would only prove my family right. I'll go to the Health Center to see if they can put me back together before I start next week."

Susan chimed in, "Good – now put some food in your mouth before it gets cold. And while you're at it have some wine. You could use a drink"

The next day, I went to the Student Health Center on campus for help. I asked desperately for any kind of help that would see me through the most important test of my college career. I went every day until just before I started student teaching. I call it counseling because their version of help was to have me take a test to see if teaching was what I really wanted to do or was suited for. The test revealed that I was best suited to be a farmer or a speech pathologist. Since I had no desire to milk cows and didn't know what a speech pathologist was at the time, I figured I was in the wrong place with the wrong type of counseling. They had mistaken my pleas for psychological help with pleas from a person in need of career counseling, not serious therapy. Perhaps they weren't equipped to offer this service. I will never know. After the test results came back and they offered me the two choices it revealed, I knew I needed to continue my journey on my own.

I had only the weekend left before I started student teaching. I reverted to my faith for help. I vowed to face this obstacle head on, and through prayer and God as my defender and protector, I would fight and crawl my way over it, around it, or through it if I had to. My faith, Roman Catholic at the time, was paramount to me during my years away from home. I attended mass each week and tried my best to live according to its creed. At this time of utter desperation and fear, I turned again to God for help, and since I felt His presence in my life throughout my undergraduate experience, I put my entire life into His hands to help me. He did. I completed my student teaching experience with an A as my grade, and prepared to begin my life as a teacher and possibly a wife. I triumphed over my fears, depression, anxiety, abuse, and a near total breakdown. I was a functioning, undiagnosed bipolar and didn't have a clue that I needed help.

CHAPTER **13**

CAN YOU HEAR ME, GOD?

Can You hear me, God?
I'm calling for You
I'm in deep trouble and pain
I need You now for I'm scared and confused
And feel I might be insane

Can You hear me, God?
I need to know
Are you listening to my pleas?
My faith is shaken to its core
I'm begging on my knees

Can You hear me, God?
Please come and stay
For I cannot take much more
I'm about to do something horrible
I'm prostrate on the floor

It's too late, God
I've done the deed
I did it all alone
I tried to keep my faith in You
But Your heart has turned to stone

Lori-ellen Pisani

AFTER GRADUATION, I returned home to New York to find work. I thought it would be easy, given the success I had in college and all the talk from my professors who said, the world was my oyster. It didn't turn out that way. I couldn't find a job and ended up working as a teaching assistant at a private pre-kindergarten program in Rye, New York.

In 1986, I still couldn't land a teaching job, but signed on as a substitute in my home town's school district. I waited every morning from 5:30 a.m. until 8:00 a.m. for a phone call from the substitute hotline. In the beginning, I was terrified. I substituted for everyone from gym teachers to fifth-grade science teachers. It was difficult to prepare each day. I hated it, but it was the only way to get into the District and put a face to the resumés I kept sending out without receiving a reply.

I made sure that I introduced myself to the Principal in every school I was assigned. I left the classroom in neat order and wrote a full report to the teacher upon his/her return as to what was accomplished during his/her absence. It wasn't too long before teachers requested me as their substitute, and my calendar was full. In the spring of 1986, I was chosen as a long-term substitute for a kindergarten teacher who was out on medical leave. This assignment lasted until the end of the year.

In April 1986, during my long-term assignment, John proposed. It wasn't all that romantic. It was a weekday night, and I was just about to go to bed. I had old pajamas on and my hair up in curlers. My father called up to me, "Lori-ellen, get dressed. John is coming over, and he's going to propose. You don't want to look like crap, so change your clothes, put some make-up on, take your curlers out, and hurry up and get down here."

A few minutes after I went downstairs, John entered the house with a bunch of balloons that said, "Lori-ellen, I love you, will you marry me?" The ring was in a box hanging from the bottom of the bundle of balloons. I smiled, said "Yes," kissed my future husband, and let him put the ring on my finger. A few pictures later, and I went back to bed. I had to work the next morning. We set a wedding date--September 18, 1987.

I spent most weekends staying with John, who now lived on the top floor of his sister's house in Putnam County. He left Fairleigh Dickinson and enrolled in the NYPD Academy. One weekend, we were just about to go to sleep when he said something that made my hair stand on end. I just asked him how he'd spent the last weekend. His answer was, "I had some wine, women, and song."

This was totally out of character, and it surprised me. I asked, "What does that mean?"

"It means what it means," he replied.

"John, this isn't like you; what do you mean by wine, women and song?"

"I went out to a club?"

"What kind of club? You don't dance."

"It was more like a pub."

"With who?"

"A few guys from the academy."

"And did something happen that I need to know about?"

"It really didn't mean anything."

"What didn't mean anything?"

"I met a girl and we hung out."

"At the bar?"

"Yeah, but then I went back to her place."

With that, I sat straight up in bed. "What happened at her place?" I demanded.

"We slept together."

"WHAT!" I yelled a little louder than I meant to.

"Shh. You'll wake up the whole house. It didn't really mean anything. I had a few too many, and that's what happened."

"If you think that cheating on me doesn't mean anything, you are out of your fucking mind!" I jumped out of bed, put my clothes on, and got into my car at midnight to drive back home. Before I stormed out, I left John with these words: "Here's your ring. Go give it to your new girlfriend."

For the next two weeks, I refused to speak to him. My father finally approached me and said, "Look, Lori-ellen, you're never gonna find another guy like John. Every man screws up. You have to accept it. Here's a man who loves you and has a good career ahead of him. Get over it, and call him back."

I thought about it for a few days. It wasn't that I was jealous. I was more shocked that he picked up another girl and went to bed with her. He wasn't that type of guy. He had a very strong faith in God. That was one of the things that made me feel safe emotionally. Why would he do such a thing? Did he know that deep down, I wasn't in love with him, and he wanted to see if I could be jealous? I hoped I made him feel loved, and I did care for him deeply. I just couldn't bring myself to fall in love with him. It was for my own protection, not because he didn't deserve it. *John, if you are reading this book, I sincerely and deeply apologize to you. Please understand that I was undiagnosed at the time of our marriage. My thoughts, feelings and behavior were compromised by mental illness. I take full responsibility, and I'm profoundly grateful that you have a family and life filled with love and success.*

We met for dinner. He apologized profusely. I told him how I felt about the issue and what my expectations were. Of course, he agreed, and we continued to make wedding plans. The wedding plans were apropos for the late eighties. The preparation, however, didn't go as I had planned, and I didn't pick up on what the next event actually meant for our future.

John and I agreed to save five thousand dollars each to put into our new joint bank accounts. The plan was to use it to buy furniture and necessary items for our apartment on the third floor of my grandfather's house. My parents had lived there when they were married, and it seemed fitting for us to start our married life there as well. The rent was very modest, and that helped make the decision for us.

I slaved for months and months to save the money. A few weeks before the wedding, we went to open our joint accounts at the bank.

John didn't say a word to me as we walked into the bank. Once inside, we met with a manager and started the paperwork for the accounts. I was going to put my money in checking, and John was to deposit his share in savings. The manager took my money, and when it came time for John to give his, he whispered that he didn't have it with him. I took him aside and asked John where his share of the money was, he told me that he didn't have it at all.

"I don't understand," I whispered. "You're getting paid a regular salary while you're in the academy, and I'm saving every bit of my substitute teaching money to make sure I meet my obligation. Why haven't you been saving?"

"I thought I'd sell my Mustang to get the money."

"And when will that be?"

"It needs a lot of work before I can sell it."

"So what you're telling me is that you don't have the money at all and have no idea when you will. I feel like you lied to me. Now I've got to go over there and make up some stupid excuse and have the manager split my money so that half can go into each account. I had no idea you sucked with finances."

"It's no big deal."

"Yeah, lots of things are no big deal or don't mean anything to you. I get that now."

It just so happened that the wedding took place two weeks into the new school year, September 18, 1987. I had just been hired as a kindergarten teacher in one of the schools in the district. I couldn't believe the timing. The district knew of my plans, and accepted that I would have to be absent for a few days. My students and their families were also very understanding. I took three days off, since the wedding and Jewish holidays fell in the same week.

The wedding was the usual fare for the late 1980s. I was a devoted fan of Princess Diana, and my gown reflected that. Its train was so long it got stuck in the door as I was walking down the aisle, and one of my guests had to free it from its trap so I could continue walking. Candles were on every pew and lit the church in a warm glow as the sun set outside. The organist played our chosen hymns while the priest, who had known John since he was an infant, conducted the mass.

We were married in New Jersey because John had many more family members coming than I did. Most of mine were fighting with each other and let me know that if I invited one, the other would not attend. I invited all whom I thought should be there and let them duke it out for themselves. The result was that of one hundred eighty-six guests, thirty of them were mine.

During the reception, I remember thinking it odd that my sister Liz's boyfriend, Michael, was awfully demanding of the maître d'. He might have been in the party- planning business, but I didn't hire him to plan the wedding. He was a little too high- strung for me. Years later, I found out that it was because my father borrowed the money from him to pay for the reception, and he wanted to take charge of all that went on. He must have driven the poor maître d' nuts the whole night.

Instead of a romantic honeymoon in Hawaii, John planned a few days' stay at a cottage on the water in Bar Harbor, Maine. We spent the time deep sea fishing, sailing on a schooner, walking around the town, feeding ducks, shopping, and eating seafood. This was not my idea of a honeymoon, but it made him happy, so I went along. The only saving grace of the honeymoon was that I caught the second-largest fish on our deep-sea fishing voyage. At first, John thought I'd snagged something, but the Captain came over and disagreed. Then John wanted my pole.

"No way, Buster; now you can watch the way it's done," I said. I struggled with that fish for more than a half hour to get it on board. They filleted the fish, and we brought it back to our host in the main house where we were staying.

After the honeymoon, we settled into married life in our little apartment. The ceilings were so low that John had to duck to get in and out of the small rooms. We had to send back our first set of living room furniture because it wouldn't fit through the door. The next time, we were smart enough to measure before we bought the second set.

John graduated from the police academy later that fall and started working the four o'clock to midnight shift in the South Bronx. Everyone kept asking if I missed him and if it put a strain on the marriage having opposite schedules. I said that I did, but the truth of the matter was that I didn't mind at all. I enjoyed my alone time. I honed my cooking skills, worked on lesson plans, and watched the TV shows I wanted to watch without interruption.

Since John was the man of the house, I let him take care of most things. He insisted on paying the bills and fixing things around the house. In time, I became so co-dependent that I couldn't even pump my own gas. My responsibilities included all the cooking, cleaning the apartment, grocery shopping, running errands, and laundry. We went on in this way until January 1988. That's when my brain did another back flip. I truly have to say that I lost my mind, and broke with reality.

In late December 1987, I started feeling very ill. Abdominal cramps sent me to the floor, and I was losing weight at a rapid weight. Something was wrong. I didn't feel well at all, and I didn't get my period. The rapid weight loss had me almost convinced that I had some kind of serious illness. Since my younger years were not exactly healthy, I always had a fear of dying young of some horrible illness. I planned to see my internist, since I had already lost about eight pounds in two weeks. I never guessed that I was pregnant, since my symptoms were nothing like morning sickness, and the cramps were so horrendous, I found myself on the floor of my classroom on more than one occasion. I pretended I fell over, and the kids got used to helping me off the floor. I had a bathroom in my classroom, and when I went in, I was convinced I'd feel my uterus fall out of me with the next cramp.

One night, John was off from work and suggested I take a pregnancy test. I'd bought one a while ago. I took the test. It couldn't be positive. I was sick, and my illness caused my period to stop. The test strip turned blue in half the time it was supposed to take to get a reading. I looked at the blue stick and my mind went into free-fall.

Something snapped inside my brain. The blue stick was my death sentence. Instead of saying, "Oh my God, I'm pregnant," I said, "Oh my God, I'm dying." My mind did not compute that I was carrying a child. The pain I was in, and the way I was feeling, all indicated to me that something was wrong, not that something was right. This "thing" inside me was killing me, and I wanted no part of it. I thought, *this can't be a baby, this is a tumor masquerading itself as a baby that has invaded my body*. I showed John the stick and said, "This can't be right. Something is horribly wrong with me. This can't be a baby inside me making me this sick."

"I have seven sisters. There's lots of ways pregnancy can show itself," he replied.

"Well, this isn't one of them. I'm losing too much weight too quickly, I'm having pains that send me to the floor, I'm not nauseous, and I'm not throwing up. This isn't normal. Something's very wrong." I couldn't say what I was really thinking.

"Let's go for a test at the clinic up the street."

"Okay."

As we drove to the clinic I silently prayed, *Oh God, please help me. This isn't right. This doesn't feel right. Something is very wrong with me. This can't be a baby. A baby wouldn't make me feel as if I'm going to die. Please don't make this be true.*

The nurse said, "Congratulations."

John replied, "Thank you."

I didn't believe her. I continued to pray, *Dear God – this can't be a child inside me. This is a tumor, and it's going to take my life. I can't let this happen. Please help me get rid of it. Make it go away. I don't want to die.*

A few days later, I was still praying, still falling to the floor in pain, and still losing weight. I hadn't slept well at all, I couldn't eat a thing, my face was as pale as a sheet, my shoulders slumped over with my hands ready to hold on to my abdomen that was convulsing in cramps every hour or so. By the following week, I had lost almost twelve pounds. *This is cancer, I convinced myself. I know some women lose weight in the very beginning of pregnancy, but this is more than it should be. This isn't a baby; it's cancer that's showing up as a positive pregnancy test. I've got to get rid of it before it kills me.* I was functioning, but barely. Every pain that sent me to the floor was a reminder of this thing inside me that I had to get rid of. I was in another world, one that terrified me, and reminded me all too clearly of my mini-breakdown in my senior year at Fairleigh. *What was I going to do?*

I can tell you what I didn't do. I didn't make an appointment with my gynecologist. I didn't want to hear the words pregnancy, baby, or child. I couldn't tolerate them. I didn't want to talk about it with anyone, especially John. There was no way he could understand where I was emotionally, and he was even more religious than I was. I knew one thing, however; I was going to save my life, and the only way to do that was to make an appointment at a clinic for an abortion, and I did. I told John I had made the appointment. He said, "You do what you feel you have to do," and walked away from me. I didn't respond.

It was a cold Saturday in January, 1988. John drove me to the clinic in New Jersey. He didn't go inside with me. I filled out the forms while I waited to see the counselor. When my name was called, I stepped inside her small office and sat down.

"Are you sure you want to terminate this pregnancy?" she asked.

"Yes."

"Can you tell me why?"

I couldn't tell her what I really felt or thought, so I said, "It's not the right time in my life. I'm also in a great deal of pain on a daily basis and have lost a lot of weight in a short amount of time. I believe I may be miscarrying but have not started to bleed yet. My husband and I are eager to end this and begin again at a better time in our lives."

"Is he here with you today?"

"Yes, he's waiting outside. This is very stressful for him."

"I understand. It is very stressful for both of you. I do have to tell you, however, that you may not be far enough along to have this procedure today."

"You need to know, that if I can't have the procedure done today, I will have to take care of this myself. I cannot go another day in this kind of pain. I would prefer to be under a doctor's care."

"Excuse me a moment, would you?" she said as she left the office. I don't know whom she spoke to, but when she came back she said, "We will take you back to the operating room, and the doctor will determine what is going on for you and if he can do the procedure. We must stress to you, however, that your statement has concerned us. We strongly recommend that you see a therapist to discuss this situation and enter into counseling with your husband."

"Thank you. I will take your advice under serious consideration and speak with my husband about it when we have both settled down."

"Okay. Have a seat in the waiting room. We should be with you shortly."

As I sat in the waiting room, the reality and horror of my situation hit me like a ton of bricks. I was about to murder an innocent human being because I couldn't tolerate the thought or physical aspects of pregnancy. This was the lowest point I had ever reached, and it was all my own doing. I was choosing my own life over a child's. I wasn't fighting to keep the unborn safe or to preserve its life; I was fighting to end it. I was more than disgusted with myself. I hated myself, and I deserved whatever punishment God had in store for me. I prayed for Him to release me from the pain, but it was not in His plan for me. So, I stopped praying and took matters into my own hands.

As I lay on the operating room table, I said one last prayer. *God, if you choose to take my life as a result of my actions, I deserve it.* Then the anesthesiologist put the needle in my arm, and I went to sleep.

I woke up in the recovery area alone. John waited in the car outside the building the entire time. The nurse came to check my vital signs and went over the post-operative care instructions with me. I got dressed and headed for the car. For most of the ride home, we didn't speak. At a red light, John turned to me and said, "While you were in there, I was out here praying. Mary came to me holding a child in her arms. It was our child, and it was a boy. I just wanted you to know that."

All I could manage to get out through the very large lump in my throat was, "I'm very sorry."

When we arrived home, I went immediately to the bedroom to lie down while John headed for the living room to watch TV. I could hear the television, but was lost in my own thoughts and feelings. Part of me felt relief that the ordeal was over, but the greater part of me was profoundly disgusted, horrified, and guilt-ridden. I was snapped back into reality, and it was crushing me. I had just killed my unborn child. I didn't wait for God to take it away by spontaneous miscarriage. I decided I was going to do God's job and get rid of it myself. I had committed the ultimate sin, for which one is not forgiven. I would spend the rest of my life being punished for my crime, and I deserved every bit of it. God had spared my life, but I was no longer welcome in His world.

Success, happiness, and a good life were no longer mine to be had. I was to live the rest of my life in penitence for my crime against God and nature. As these thoughts swirled around in my head, I began to think of ending my own life as a means of penitence. John kept his service revolver in the top drawer of his dresser. It would be easy enough for me to load it, put it to my head, and pull the trigger. It would be over in an instant. I didn't deserve to go to Heaven, so my straight gait to hell was not an issue, nor were my feelings for John. I had, in his eyes as well, committed the ultimate sin against God, and deprived him of his son. I knew that our marriage was irreparably damaged and changed forever. *Would he ever speak to me again? Could I explain why I aborted his child? Would this be the end of my marriage? Would he say that my actions were so heinous that he couldn't forgive me?* I wouldn't have to know, if I ended my life that evening.

I took the .38-caliber handgun from the dresser and loaded it with bullets. I closed the dresser drawer in case John came in before I was ready to do the deed. The gun was heavy in my hand. I sat down on the bed with my back against the wall and my legs stretched out in front of me. If I put the pillows behind my head, the mess might be easier to clean up, so I piled the pillows high behind my head. I held the gun in my lap and contemplated whether or not I was going to put it in my mouth and pull the trigger. In the living room, I could hear the laughter of the TV audience. John was watching a sitcom.

I must have been there for about an hour or so. I could hear the TV programs changing in the other room. Then I heard footsteps coming toward the bedroom. I slid the gun under the covers and waited. John came to the bedroom door.

"Do you want some tea or something to eat?" he asked in a gentle tone.

"No, thank you," I replied with my head down.

"We need to talk about this, but I don't think either one of us is ready today. Let's go to church like we usually do tomorrow, and we'll go to lunch after and talk."

"Thank you, yes, we need to talk," I managed to get out.

"I'm gonna sleep in the living room tonight," he said.

"I understand."

After he left the doorway, I unloaded the gun, put the bullets back in their case, and put the gun back in the top drawer, just as I had found it. I went into the bathroom to wash up, changed into pajamas, and returned to the bed. This time, I lay down and pulled the covers over my chin. I closed my eyes to pray:

Dear God, I know I have committed the most grievous sin against You, and I hate myself for it. I pray that one day You can forgive me. From tomorrow on, I promise that I will be a better person, and I will NEVER AGAIN do Your work for you. I will accept whatever happens to me as Your decision, and I will make every child I teach feel special, important, wanted, and needed. That is my solemn vow. I made this promise to You as a child for different reasons, and now, as an adult with children who count on me to be their teacher and helper, I swear to You that I will NEVER repeat this horrible mistake. In Jesus's name I pray, Amen.

With that said, I tried as much as I could to get some sleep. It didn't come easily.

I felt like the worst human being on the planet walking into church the next morning. John and I usually sat toward the front, directly in front of the pulpit. I let him lead me to the same pew we always sat in and didn't ask to sit farther away. I was not going to make any demands or ask for any special favors. I didn't deserve any. During the sign of peace, John kissed my cheek, which was wet from my tears. He didn't say anything. I sat through the rest of the service but did not go up to receive Holy Communion as I usually did. John excused himself, and I watched as he received the sacrament. I didn't think I would ever receive it again, and that was something I was going to have to live with as part of my punishment.

After church, we went to a local diner for lunch. I couldn't even think of eating, but I ordered scrambled eggs, toast, and coffee. John ordered a cheeseburger deluxe. I waited to see if he was going to start talking. I waited to hear if he was going to tell me to go straight to hell and get out of his life, both of which I would have deserved. I waited to hear that he could never forgive me. But all I heard was silence. I didn't know what to do with that, but I knew I had to explain in the best way possible why I did what I did.

"John, what I did is an unforgivable sin against God, and you. I have no excuse, but I have a reason, which I can only hope you can understand," I began.

"I'm listening."

I cleared my throat. "You know that for a few weeks before I took that pregnancy test I was feeling horrible. The pain in my abdomen, John, was so horrendously bad that I thought I was going to hemorrhage all over the place. I was losing weight instead of gaining it, and I wasn't having any morning sickness or nausea. I know you said that pregnancy is different in everyone, but what I was going through didn't resemble pregnancy in the slightest. You also know that I didn't grow up the healthiest of kids, and that I grew up having a fear of doctors and hospitals. I was convinced that with my medical history,

I wouldn't see old age. I somehow had it in my head that this was not a pregnancy, but a tumor that was trying to kill me, and I needed to get rid of it. I didn't let God take care of me. I took care of me, without regard for you or God, and for that I will never forgive myself, nor can I ever expect that you can understand and forgive me. I guess what I need to know is where we go from here."

"I cannot say that I will ever forget what you did. As for my forgiving you, I think it would help me if you asked God for forgiveness in a formal way."

"You mean go to confession?"

"That's a part of it. There is a sacrament called Reconciliation. It's for those people who have committed horrific sins and seek God's forgiveness. There is a special mass for this sacrament."

"I've never heard of this, but I will do whatever you need me to in order to put this behind us as best we can and move forward."

"Good. There is a mass on Wednesday night. I looked it up and found one."

"Where is this service?"

"At St. Theresa's church in the Bronx."

"Do you know how to get there?"

"Yes."

"Then that's what we'll do."

So, on Wednesday night of the following week, John and I traveled to the Bronx for this Reconciliation mass. My knees literally shook as I entered the church. I had no idea what this service entailed, and I was as scared as I had ever been in my life. Soft organ music played while we waited for the service to start. Then a priest came to the altar and asked all those seeking forgiveness for their sins to raise their hands. I raised my hand. He instructed us to make a line in front of the confessional, so that we could confess our sins to God. I did as instructed, and when my turn came, I told the priest that I had an abortion, and that I knew it was a horrible sin, and that I begged God for His forgiveness. He told me to say twelve Hail Mary's and twelve Our Fathers and wait for the service to continue.

I came out of the confessional feeling as though I would make it once again in life. God had heard my confession, and although He was angry with me, He would not condemn my soul to hell. What I didn't expect was the next part of the service.

"All those gathered here who have committed the sin of abortion, please step forward to the altar," announced the presiding priest. "And those who are with you may approach the altar as well." I wasn't prepared for this. Now, I had to stand up in front of the others gathered there and publicly acknowledge my sin. I looked at John. He was already on his feet, so I jumped up and followed him with my eyes staring at the floor. I couldn't look at anyone around me, let alone a priest, face to face.

"We have come to the part of the service where the children you have taken away from God and yourselves by your own hand will be baptized into the Catholic faith and be drawn to Heaven to be with God."

I began to go weak in the knees. The priest began the baptismal service. I can't remember how many others were standing beside us. I couldn't see anything. My eyes were overflowing with tears. The priest continued with the service and we answered the questions that are asked of parents and godparents. The priest then asked for the name of our child. John and I had previously spoken of names we would give our children. If we had a boy, his name would be Joshua Matthew, and if we had a girl, we would name her Katherine Dianne.

When the priest asked us for the name, John said in his deepest most solemn voice, "Joshua Matthew." The priest handed me a daisy and John a candle to symbolize Joshua and baptized them with holy water and oil. I had to hold on with both hands since I was trembling to the point of losing my balance. I wasn't sure if I was going to pass out or throw up. I prayed for control.

"Go in peace," were the last words I heard from the priest. At that point, I dropped to my knees and cried hysterically. John stood beside me but didn't put his hand on my shoulder or try to help me up. I guess he figured my falling to floor in a heap was exactly what I needed.

After the mass, I spent a few more minutes on my knees in front of the altar, crying. John waited at the doors in the back of the church. I managed to get up and went over to light a candle at the feet of the Virgin Mary. I prayed again for salvation, and for Joshua Matthew. The child that I murdered now had a name and was with God. My sin was "officially" forgiven but would remain with me for the rest of my life.

When we returned home, the daisy and candle were put into the Bible to be forever preserved, and I put myself into bed, exhausted in every possible way. John continued to sleep on the couch for the next week. I didn't ask him to return to the bedroom. I figured he would, if ever, when he wanted to and on his terms.

I had my follow-up appointment with the doctor who performed the abortion the following week. Physically, I had recovered, but emotionally, I was a complete wreck. The doctor told me after he examined me that he determined during the procedure that I was bleeding internally and would have lost the baby through miscarriage. The bleeding caused the severe cramping, but I circumvented the process by having the abortion before my body could release the contents of my uterus on its own. To this day, I'm not sure whether he told me that in an effort to make me feel better, or if that indeed was the case. Either way, it didn't matter. I didn't let God do His job. I did it for Him and vowed that I would never do that again. I did, however, immediately get a prescription for birth control pills. I wasn't taking any more chances, even though birth control was also a sin.

When I got home, I told John what the doctor had said and offered him the phone number to call and speak with him if he wanted to. John didn't say much, but did say that he understood we would have lost the child anyway. We never spoke of it again--ever.

CHAPTER **14**

RAGE

There's a trigger inside my head
When pulled I lose my mind
I change to a person I do not know
A person who's dangerous, not kind

I use my words like weapons
Striking down the enemy I see
My hands restrained so I cannot fight
My goal is to make them flee

I lose control of my actions
I want to hurt and scare
The effect rage has overwhelms me
The consequence I do not care

I need to stop my raging ways
The cost is far too much
I risk the loss of love and respect
My heart too cold to touch

Lori-ellen Pisani

FROM THAT POINT on, I concentrated all my efforts on my teaching and did not share my thoughts or feelings about the abortion with John.

I had enough to worry about as a new teacher. My principal, Kathy, disliked me, and made my first year of teaching kindergarten a living hell. At the end of the year, I seriously wondered whether I should consider farming as my new profession. Luckily for me, she retired in June of 1988. Our new principal, Don, started in September of 1988. I developed a very positive working relationship with him. Don and I were on the same page as it related to teaching and learning, and we liked each other as individuals. He was a major improvement over the last principal, and I started to feel more comfortable in the role of a teacher.

In the spring of 1989, however, I had my very first episode of rage in school that would test our relationship. One of my students, Jennifer, was a foster child. Her foster mother was quite old, I thought, to be parenting this child, let alone the four other children in her home. Jennifer was a very challenging student to teach. She was difficult to manage behaviorally and was not making progress academically. I had several conferences with her foster mother and provided her with games and materials to help Jennifer learn early literacy skills and number concepts. Nothing seemed to be working.

Her foster mother shared her own frustrations with Jennifer at home, so I suggested we speak with the school's social worker for additional support. She agreed that a meeting should be held not only with the social worker, but also with Jennifer's therapist. I wasn't aware that Jennifer was seeing a therapist and asked why she was in therapy. She told me that Jennifer's life before she came to her home and my class was very difficult and tumultuous, and that Jennifer was in counseling at the local center. There were no HIPPA laws in place at that time, so information could be shared without consent forms on file.

The meeting took place after school in my classroom. I met with Jennifer's therapist, her foster mother, and our school's social worker. During the meeting, it was revealed that Jennifer suffered sexual abuse before being placed in foster care, and that while with her present family, had both molested her foster brother, and arsoned her home on three separate occasions. Jennifer sprayed paper towels with bug spray and put them on the hot radiator. This caused a two-alarm fire. Luckily, all escaped the fire without injury. I was horrified and shocked beyond my comprehension. Tears sprang from my eyes. I tried desperately to compose myself.

"Please forgive me. I am so sorry to hear this," I began.

"We don't usually share this information," the social worker responded. "It appears that Jennifer is not making the progress in school that we had hoped she would."

"Now that I know what this little five-year-old has endured and what she has done, I wouldn't think she could make much progress at all," I continued.

"We thought she was cured of her abuse by now, and she hasn't had any more incidents relating to the fires. This is why we thought she'd be successful in a general education setting," her therapist replied.

"What!" I exclaimed in a louder voice than I anticipated. In an instant, rage flooded my entire body. My eyes narrowed and focused directly on the therapist, and I could feel my cheeks burning red, and my entire body tense. I had a lump in my throat, and I was pissed beyond measure. I got up from my seat and leaned over the table two inches from the therapist's face. "I don't know what cereal box you got your license out of, but any fool can tell you that you don't cure anyone from sexual abuse!" I shouted at her.

She pushed her seat back away from me, clearly frightened by my aggression toward her. The social worker jumped in and said, "Lori-ellen, you need to sit back down and get a hold of yourself. You are out of control."

"This woman is a disgrace to her profession! She shouldn't be anywhere near Jennifer--or any other child, for that matter. Are you fucking for real? Who in their right mind would ever dare to think that anyone is cured of abuse! No wonder Jennifer continued to molest her foster siblings and set fires in her home. She's screaming for help, and you don't have a clue as to what to do! This is disgusting!" I spat out.

I tried to lean even closer to the counselor, but someone was behind me, pulling me away from the table. I had no idea that Don was nearby, saw and heard what was happening, and entered the room from behind me. I felt his hands around my waist, pulling me backwards. As he pulled, I kept yelling, "This is an outrage! I hope you never get a good night's sleep for the rest of your life!" And with that, he pulled me out of my classroom and into his office.

"Have you completely lost your mind?" Don yelled.

"Did you hear what they said? They said they thought Jennifer was 'cured' from her abuse! You don't cure a person who's suffered sexual abuse. No wonder she's a mess in my room and I can't teach her a thing. Good God, what in the hell is happening?" I yelled back.

"I can tell you what's going to happen." His voice lowered but had anger and power in it. "You are going to go back in that room and apologize profusely for your own behavior. Do you realize you may lose your career over what you just did? I can never and will never justify your behavior. You'll be damn lucky if she doesn't press assault charges against you. You're a good teacher, Lori-ellen, and I can see that you care, but you crossed way over the line here, and you need to fix it – NOW!"

"But what about Jennifer?" I asked, clearly recognizing that both she and I were now in trouble.

"We'll call an emergency meeting of the Committee on Special Education and see if she can be placed in a therapeutic setting. If you were more experienced, you would know that there are places for children like her, and we can help them. You took it upon yourself to play Superman, and it just may cost you your entire career. Now we're going back in there, and you're going to get this straightened out. Do you understand me?"

"Yes. I'm sorry. I just lost it."

"Don't tell me, tell them."

I went back into my classroom and sat down at the table. Don stood behind me with his arms folded. There was complete silence, and I could see shocked and angry faces around the table. My head was down, and my voice trembled with both emotion and fear as I began to address the therapist. "Mrs. Graves, there is no excuse for my inappropriate, aggressive, disrespectful, and outrageous behavior. I am ashamed, horrified, and mortified by my own lack of professionalism, and loss of control. My actions are unforgivable. I can only hope that perhaps you can understand that I am an abuse survivor, and clearly I have never fully recovered. When I learned that Jennifer was also abused, I left all rational thinking behind and lashed out at the very people who are trying to help her. I apologize most sincerely for my actions and can only hope that you will accept my apology," I rambled.

"I must say, that I found your behavior toward me shocking, insulting, frightening, and unjustified. I have worked very hard with Jennifer and her family, and to be attacked by you is unacceptable in every way. I have to wonder whether some sanctions should be brought against you for this outrageous conduct, and moreover whether the classroom is the right place for you," she responded.

"You have my word, Mrs. Graves that I will follow through with the necessary steps to ensure that this never happens again and impose the appropriate sanctions against Mrs. Pisani," Don said in a very stern tone. "Her behavior is an embarrassment to the entire school and will not be dealt with lightly," he continued. "We value our working relationship with your agency and hope that this incident does not have repercussions as it relates to our future work together," he continued. "Mrs. Pisani is a new teacher, who lacks experience and understanding of the many ways we can support children in need. I will ensure that our Child Study Team sits with her to instruct her in all the myriad ways our school and district serve our students. You also have my word that Mrs. Pisani's behavior will never be repeated in this school against any staff member or colleague," he finished.

"With those assurances, I will accept Mrs. Pisani's apology, and expect that it never occurs again. I am gravely disappointed in you, Mrs. Pisani," said Mrs. Graves.

"And I am also disappointed, and sincerely apologize again for my disgraceful behavior. I can tell you, this incident has given me serious pause to reflect on what happened and seek help." I figured I'd throw that in for good measure.

With that all said, everyone got up from the table, shook hands, and left. I followed Don into his office. He closed the door and plopped himself in his chair with a great big sigh. I sat across from him. I was scared this was the end of my career.

"Well, that was a load of crap you spread around. You're lucky they bought it," he said, staring straight into my eyes. "I know you're still pissed and didn't mean a word of it."

"In all honesty, I didn't. It just came rambling out of my mouth. What I really wanted to do was beat the hell out of her," I said, relieved that he understood me, but still scared as to what was going to happen to me. "I am truly sorry to you for losing it. I can't explain what came over me. It was like a switch or a trigger being pulled. All of a sudden, I became an animal. I've had this happen before, but never to this extent. I can promise you that it will never happen again. What sanctions are you going to impose?"

"This conversation is your sanction. But I can promise you this. If you ever lose control like that again, I will have you suspended, and since you are not tenured yet, I cannot promise that you will be. This is extremely serious, Lori-ellen. You need to know that you came all too close to losing everything and possibly being charged with assault. Your gift of gab saved you this time. It won't the next time. You are very young and inexperienced. You have a lot to learn, and I'm here to help you. I like you as a person and think you show great promise as a teacher. Don't let me down."

"Thank you, Don. I'm deeply grateful for this second chance, and I promise I won't let you down." I was silent for a moment. "What about Jennifer? What do we do to help her?"

"Just what I said we'd do. I'll work with the Child Study Team to set up an emergency CSE. She will be placed in a therapeutic setting and receive instruction there. It will take several weeks to set this up, but she will get the help she needs. You are not to have any further contact with her foster mother. The team will handle that. Keep your head on straight, and finish the year strong. Are we clear?"

"Yes, sir; we're clear. And again, I am deeply grateful to you for understanding, and helping both me and Jennifer," I said.

I stood up, and as I shook Don's hand, he asked one last question. "Lori-ellen, you don't have to answer, but what you said about being an abuse survivor, was that true?"

"Yes," I replied.

"I'm sorry to hear that, but use what you've learned to help and not hurt others, okay?"

"That's what I was hoping to do today, but it didn't work out that way. I've got a lot of thinking to do," I said with my head down, unable to look him in the eye. I left his office and went back to my room. I sat down to think and collect myself.

What in the hell was wrong with me? How did I lose control like that? I not only scared the hell out of a complete stranger, but I almost lost my career as well. What scared me the most was that while I was screaming at the poor woman, I felt a huge sense of power. I actually liked the feeling of being a threat. It was a tremendous release of adrenaline. That couldn't be normal. My whole life, it seemed, was spent being the abused, not the abuser. Now, here I was, threatening others with my words and if not restrained, possibly my hands. Something was definitely wrong with me. Maybe I should go to therapy myself, but John would tell my family, and they'd think I was crazy. I'd never hear the end of it. I couldn't tolerate that.

I knew this much. I needed to keep my emotions under control, and if I got that pissed off again, I needed to find another way to deal with it. Exhausted from this whole experience, I picked up my purse, drove home, and threw myself into bed. John was working his four to midnight shift, so I was alone, thank God. I wouldn't have to speak to him. I needed time to try and figure out my life.

CHAPTER **15**

MY LIFE IN SHAMBLES

How will I tell my parents?
What will they think of me?
I've lost everything I've worked for
There's nothing left, but me

My marriage is in shambles
My husband and I are done
My teaching career is over
The demons inside have won

I'm free from him, and I must go back
To the house I knew when small
I'll do what's needed to start again
And pray that I don't fall

Lori-ellen Pisani

FROM 1989-1992, JOHN and I slowly returned to life as it was before the "incident." I continued my teaching career as a kindergarten teacher, and John thought seriously about making a move and joining the FBI. We talked about it for a few months. We agreed that joining the FBI had its advantages. The biggest advantage was it would enable us to move to New Jersey where I went to school and was permanently certified to teach, and John's entire family lived. Since we spent a great deal of time in Jersey, the whole idea made sense. I didn't have to pursue a master's degree as required in New York to continue my career, and that could save us a lot of money. We started the application process for the FBI in 1990.

In another move to make more money, John and I built a second home in a gated community in Pennsylvania in 1990. We were getting hit hard with taxes and were advised to do this by our accountant. John found land that he liked and took me down to see the property. He was very excited about this project, and since I didn't want to disappoint him again, I went along with it, despite my reservations. We bought the land and contracted with the community's builder to have a custom "A-frame" home built on the site. The prices in Pennsylvania were much cheaper than if we built the same house in New York. We thought we were getting an amazing deal. We would also become landlords, which was a prospect I wasn't thrilled about, since my father had all kinds of issues with the tenants he had in the apartment building he bought and the house we built.

After many headaches and delays, the house was finally built, and John and I now had a mortgage of $140,000 and taxes to pay in addition to the rent and expenses related to our New York apartment. We searched for tenants and found a nice couple to rent the house. The rent covered the mortgage payments. The income was going to come from the tax breaks we had as investment property owners. This investment required money management skills that John unfortunately did not possess. He wouldn't allow me, however, to manage the house. It was his job, and he wasn't giving it up to me. I was allowed to make deposits.

From 1990-1991, John continued with his application with the FBI. It was an arduous process. The application was almost one hundred pages with all the documentation required. We had background checks (which I was positive would toss us out of the process, since my father was a convicted felon), and John had many interviews and preliminary exams to complete.

Time was ticking on my teaching certification. New York requires that a teacher obtain a master's degree within five years of beginning steady employment. Since John and I were determined to be in New Jersey shortly, I did not pursue this degree. Nor did John and I pursue trying to have another child. We agreed that we would wait until we were settled in New Jersey. I was secretly grateful, since the thought of being pregnant again scared the daylights out of me and actually made me nauseous. I couldn't look at a pregnant woman for a very long time after the "incident." In effect, I was pregnancy phobic. I figured when the time came, I'd go to hypnosis or therapy to deal with it. And with that, I put it out of my mind.

From late 1991-1992, my marriage started to crumble. Alarms went off in my mind, and this time, I listened. The first red flag was when I returned home from making a deposit at the bank enraged because nine thousand dollars was missing from our savings. This money, I thought, was to be used to pay the expenses for both New York and Pennsylvania. We lost our renters in the Pennsylvania house, and couldn't find another, so we were on the hook for the monthly mortgage payments in addition to our other expenses each month. I returned home from the bank to find John sitting at the kitchen table, papers in hand. I needed to calm myself down before speaking to him, so I started to prepare dinner.

After a few minutes, I said, "John, I went to the bank to make a deposit, and asked for the balance on the account. Nine thousand dollars is missing. I told the teller that there must be a huge error, but she assured me that you made the withdrawal. She showed me the withdrawal slip. It's in your handwriting. What's going on?" I asked.

"I needed the money to finish restoring my Mustang. The parts had to be specially ordered and the paint job is also custom. So, I took the money from the account," he replied flatly.

"John," I continued, "that money was to be used for our expenses. You can't fool around with mortgage, insurance, and tax payments. These need to be paid on time and they're all due in a few days."

"I put the tax payment on a credit card, and I borrowed twenty thousand dollars from my future pension, so don't worry about it," he said as he held up the papers he had in his hands.

"Holy crap; you did what?"

"Just what I said. I'm not going to deny myself the things I want in life. I lived with eight brothers and sisters. There were plenty of things I went without, and I am not going to sacrifice anymore. If I want it, I will have it."

"I see, and what about our responsibilities?"

"I borrowed the money. We have the money to pay our bills."

"Yes, and on top of that, we now have another loan payment to make. What about selling the Mustang that you told me you were going to sell before we got married?"

"I haven't decided. It's a classic car, and I might put it in shows. The prize money will bring in extra cash. That's my plan."

"I guess what's not going to happen is your selling it as we agreed."

"No, I'm not going to sell it now. I want to enjoy it."

"I see." This conversation took place while I had a meat cleaver in my hand and was busy hacking up a chicken. I was so enraged I wanted to hack off his head, but instead, made mincemeat out of the poor chicken.

The second and third incidents that continued to break down our marriage were an attempted assault, battery and robbery, and an attempted carjacking, all with me as the intended victim. John was now a detective with the NYPD, working undercover with the narcotics squad. He was working his usual four o'clock to midnight shift. I came home late one evening from work. As I exited my car, a man approached me. "Hey lady, gotta match?" he asked.

"No, sorry," I replied. I tried to move around him, but he blocked my way.

"You gotta lighter?"

"No, please move, I'm late and my husband is waiting," I lied. I could feel my heart pounding inside my chest.

"You got some money?" he asked as he pushed me against the car with his body pressed against mine and held one arm down at my side. With his other hand, he groped me and started to grab for my purse.

"Get away from me!" I yelled. I head-butted him and pushed him off me with all my might. I ran as fast as I could up the side door stairs to our apartment and slammed the door shut. I bolted it tight.

Since my rule was to never call John at work unless it was an emergency, I waited until early the next morning to tell him what happened. John asked me to describe the guy. I did. John replied, "I know that guy; he's a crack dealer who lives a few houses down on this block."

"You know him?"

"Yeah, I've seen him around a few times."

"And he lives on our street?"

"Yeah, so you need to be careful if you come home late. Just make sure you run up the stairs and close the door as fast as you can. It's metal, so you should be okay."

"Aren't you going to go over there and tell him who you are, and that I'm your wife, and if he ever approaches me again, he'll be sorry?"

"Nah, just stay away from him."

"I didn't approach him; he came after me."

"Look, I deal with this every day at work. Just run away if you see him on the street."

"Somehow that doesn't make me feel any safer, Detective," I said with sarcasm.

"It should. We have a metal door, and since there have been threats made against you after some major drug busts, I'm glad we have it."

"WHAT! And when were you going to tell me this?"

"You don't need to know what goes on at work. They can't get through the door."

"That may be true, but you failed to tell me there have been threats made against me. What am I supposed to do with that?"

"Run faster."

"I'll be sure to do that." I couldn't believe it. My own husband, a police undercover narcotics detective, wouldn't even protect me against a crack head who lives down the block and tried to attack me, and God knows who else out there that wants me dead to make a point to the cops to stay away. Somehow, I didn't feel any safer having a cop for a husband.

The only time I ever called John at work was to tell him that I was the victim of an attempted carjacking. Once again, I was coming home late from work. I took my usual route, which brought me through the seedier side of town. I stopped at a light. There was one car in front of mine. From out of the blue, a group of about six guys, with bandanas covering their faces, approached the car in front of mine and tried to open the doors. Failing that, they rocked the car back and forth, trying to tip it over. Horrified, I was able to reach the button to lock my doors (they didn't automatically lock in my car).

Since they were having no luck with the car in front of mine, they came over to my car. I looked behind me and saw that there was no one. As they approached my car, I threw it into reverse and hit the gas. They jumped off my car and screamed threats that they were going to "get me." They jumped on the car again, rocking it back and forth and pounding on the windows. I put it in drive, swung the wheel to the left to get around the car that was still in front of me, and put the pedal to the floor. The guys jumped away in every direction. I had a look on my face that said, "Whoever is in the way is going to get hurt, and that's just the way it's gonna be." I turned right at the light and put the gas pedal to the floor again. I clocked myself at ninety miles per hour, and honked the horn as I approached lights, stop signs, and other cars, in the hope that I would attract a cop. I didn't.

When I got to my street, I parked half on and half off the sidewalk, jumped out of the car, and ran as fast as I could up to our apartment. I was breathing heavily, sweating and crying. It took three tries to dial John's work number. I was screaming into the telephone, trying to communicate to John what had just happened.

"What do you want me to do about it?" he asked.

"I want you to come home. I'm scared out of my mind. First I get accosted on my own street, then you tell me that I'm a fucking target, and now not two weeks later, I am almost the victim of a carjacking or kidnapping, or worse. I need you to come home," I cried into the phone.

"Did you lock the door?"

"Of course I locked the door! I'm now a prisoner in my own home, thanks to the drug addict who lives down the street and the thugs who want me dead!"

"There's nothing I can do. You got away, and that's what matters. Is the car alright?"

"What?"

"Is there any damage to the car?"

"How the hell should I know! How about the damage to me?"

"You're fine. Have a cup of tea and calm down."

"Shouldn't we be calling the police or something?"

"Can you identify these guys?"

"No, they had bandanas on their faces."

"Then there's not a whole lot we can do. I'll call over to our local precinct and ask if they can put a car on that street. You shouldn't be driving in that area at night."

"So you're not coming home?"

"I've got a lot of paperwork to catch up on. There's no emergency. Stay inside and get some sleep. Just remember to stay away from that area next time."

"Fine; sorry I bothered you," I said in my most sarcastic tone.

"I've gottta go now. I'll see you when I get home."

I slammed the phone down and sat for a while with my cup of tea and a cigarette. Here I was, married to a big, brawny undercover NYPD detective, and he wouldn't even help his own wife. What was the use of being married to a police officer if I didn't feel safe with him?

The next incident was scary. I came home from work one evening with a terrible pain in my leg. The pain got so bad that I couldn't stand on it, so I hopped to the bedroom. I took my pants off to see if I could find a bruise or something that would account for such pain. There was no bruise, but the leg felt hot. I had no idea what that meant. I put ice on it, thinking that might help. Over the past couple of days,

I had also developed a severe cough and was having trouble breathing. I was a pack a day smoker at the time and thought I was coming down with bronchitis. When John came home, I told him how I was feeling, and he suggested I sleep half sitting up to see if that helped. It didn't. About 11:00 the next morning, one of my coughing fits brought up blood, and my leg was on fire. That's when I got scared. I told John that I needed to go to the hospital. Something was very wrong.

Instead of carrying me, John took me by the arm and had me hop down three flights of stairs and into the car. He drove casually to the hospital. Instead of pulling up directly in front of the emergency room and calling for a gurney, he pulled into the parking lot, and made me hop, cough, and gasp for air into the emergency room. By the time I got through the ER doors, I collapsed in a heap. I guess I was lucky that the security guard on duty caught me, or I would have had a head injury to go along with whatever else was happening.

The security guard called for the gurney and I was wheeled directly into the treatment room. I explained the best way I could what was happening and for how long. I saw a look of concern come over the nurse's face, and when she left, I looked at John. Doctors and nurses entered the room and tests began. I asked what was happening. They explained that I might have had a blood clot in my leg that broke off and traveled to my lung, and they needed to find out rather quickly if that was the case. "You mean I might have an embolism?" I asked.

"Yes, and you'll need aggressive treatment if that is the case," answered the nurse, who was doing the Doppler test to see if I had a deep vein thrombosis. The next test required me to be injected with radioactive dye and have X-rays of my lungs taken to see what was happening. This test takes time. It was more difficult than usual due to my incessant coughing. I could see John pacing outside the room. I thought he was terribly worried.

"Please tell my husband what's happening so he doesn't worry too much," I asked the nurse.

I saw the nurse go out the door and speak to John. John has a deep, rather loud voice. I could hear him say, "I'm not worried about her, I'm going to be late for work." The nurse came in and came over to the bed. I had tears in my eyes.

She grabbed my hand. "I'm sorry," she said.

"Thanks, could I ask another favor? Please tell my husband that I insist he go to work. Can someone call my parents? Maybe one of them will come."

"Of course I will," she said. "And I'll stay with you until someone comes."

"Nurse, am I going to die?"

"We're doing everything we possibly can. You hang on and be strong. I'm not going to leave you. Just let me get your parents over here."

John left for work and my mother came to the hospital. She was shocked, and I was feeling rejected and abandoned. "What in the hell is wrong with him?" she exclaimed.

"There's a lot you don't know, and I don't want to talk about it. It's better that he's at work. Thanks for coming."

She didn't add to her comment, but rather, let it go.

As it turned out, I did not have an embolism. They couldn't find a clot in my leg. They couldn't explain the leg pain, except to say that it might be potassium depletion causing severe cramping. They did find, however, that I had double pneumonia. I have never had a respiratory illness come upon me so fast in all my life. My doctor's instructions were to take strong antibiotics and total bed rest for two weeks. My mother took me to fill the prescription and then home.

I called the substitute hotline to let them know I'd be out for two weeks and crawled into bed. My mother made me some tea and soup. I thanked her and let her know I'd call if I needed anything. When John came home, he woke me up and asked what I had made for dinner. It was clear that he expected me to get up and make him something, and for some reason that I still can't explain, I did. I hopped around the kitchen making him pasta. But in my mind, I thought, *I'm done. He won't protect me when I'm accosted, and he won't take care of me when I'm ill. What the hell am I married for? I don't feel safe in any way. I left my house of horrors because I thought I would be protected. Obviously, I'm not. I'm better off alone.*

The final incident that destroyed my marriage came in December 1992. I had, quite frankly, resolved in my mind that this marriage was over. I didn't feel emotionally or physically safe with John. The incidents that took place over the past year made me realize that I was last on his list of priorities, and perhaps he never truly forgave me for taking away his child. I was miserable.

Our finances were in shambles, and John, despite going to a financial planner with me to help us with a budget, refused to abide by her suggestions to cut back on spending. I started to open the bills and noticed some peculiar charges for restaurants I'd never been to. His gas bills for his car were in the hundreds of dollars a month, despite the fact he drove an unmarked police car on duty. He applied for more and more credit without my knowledge. He maxed our credit cards to their limits. Once again, I was back in my father's house, robbing Peter to pay Paul, and the feeling of insecurity was growing more and more powerful.

On December 22, 1992, John and I were driving to finish Christmas shopping. In my head, I was planning on asking for a separation after the holidays. I didn't want to ruin the holidays for him. On the way to the mall, John, who was driving, stated, "I want you to know that I'm not going to pursue the FBI anymore. I decided to stay in New York. I'm not interested in joining them. In fact, I have a second interview with another police department after the holidays. It looks like I'm going to be asked to join their force, which will get me out of the city."

I instantly became blind with rage. I saw my entire future disappear. My dreams and career vanished in a flash. This was it. I was done. I was better off alone than in this loveless marriage. I looked at him with utter disbelief and contempt. "What! First of all, we have been preparing for you to join the FBI for the past two years. You had only one step left, and that was your physical agility test, which I noticed you kept putting off. Now you are telling me that you are going to blow that off and join another police department without even having one conversation with me? Have you completely forgotten that I am not permanently certified to teach in New York, but I am in New Jersey, *and* that I purposely didn't pursue my master's degree as required in New York, because it would over qualify me for a starting position in Jersey? What in the hell am I supposed to do about that?"

"You'll figure it out," was his answer. "Oh, by the way, what do you want for Christmas?"

I looked him in the face and said, "A divorce!" I couldn't believe those words flew out of my mouth. Even I was horrified by the rage that accompanied those words. If he hadn't been driving, I would have hit him with all my might. With that, John swung the car around, and without a word, started to blow the speed limit to get us home. When we got there, he got out of the car, slammed the door, and went inside. Not wanting to follow, I stayed in the car for a while, shocked at my own brazen outburst, and stared out of the window.

After about half an hour, I knocked on my neighbor's door and called my sister, Debby, to see if she could come and get me to take me to her house. I was terrified to walk into the apartment. Debby came to pick me up. Months prior, I confided in her all that I was feeling and thinking of doing. She was supportive and understanding. She was the only one I could think of in that moment that I could talk to. She was married, with kids, and we had developed a good relationship over the passing years.

We got back to her house where we sat down and all my anger and hurt poured out. In the middle of telling my story, the phone rang. I jumped. It was my father, wanting to know if she had seen me. She told him I was with her. My father told her that John had already called him to report what I said, and that he thought I was having a nervous breakdown. Debby simply stated that I was upset about the situation at home, but that I was not having nervous breakdown. She went on to say that she'd bring me to their house after I settled down.

About two hours later, Debby brought me over to my parents' house. I walked in to find my mother and father sitting on the couch with scowls on their faces.

"Do you know that John called here very upset?" my father said angrily.

"I can imagine," I responded

"What the hell is wrong with you?" my father demanded.

"There's a lot of things you don't know, Daddy."

"Like what?"

"John and I have been having problems for a while, and he just told me out of the blue that he no longer plans to go into the FBI as we had agreed, but that he plans to stay in New York, which costs me my career, since I don't have my master's degree."

"Well that's your own fault," my mother chimed in. "You should have completed your requirements for New York, and not left it so that you'd end up without a job. You have no one to blame but yourself for that."

"I was told by many people not to get my master's because it would over qualify me for an entry-level teaching job, and New Jersey wouldn't want to pay a starting teacher a master's level salary," I said defensively.

I don't believe that for a second! You were lazy, and that's the truth," Mother continued.

"You're not in the field. I did what I was told was best," I retorted.

"John thinks you've lost your mind, and I think he's right!" my father exclaimed. "You're never going to find another man like him, and you've hurt him badly. You're a damn fool, and should go home, beg for forgiveness and fix this now! You have no clue about what you've done."

Mother chimed in, "And I need you to know something. John is a like a son to us, and he is welcome here in this home at any time."

I exploded with emotion. "You both have no idea what's been happening in my home for the past year. You have no idea, because I haven't told you. I kept it all to myself. John presents himself one way to you, and I get to see the other side. We're financially ruined! Our house faces foreclosure because he's taken thousands of dollars from our account and squandered it on his precious Mustang. He spends money like he's Rockefeller, and in case you've forgotten, he abandoned me in the hospital trauma room with a possible blood clot that could have killed me. Doesn't that count for something?"

"You need to understand that John has a very stressful and dangerous job. He needs to focus on what he's doing, and you should allow him to relax when he comes home. He doesn't need to hear your crap," my father barked.

"So what you're saying is that I ruined my marriage, and he did nothing wrong?"

"Yes," my father responded.

"So do I take this to mean that if I separate from John, he is to come live with you instead of me coming home to get myself together and figure out my future?"

"If you can't fix this thing, John will stay in the apartment, because he needs to be there for his job, and I'm not forcing him out. You can pack your stuff, come back here, and figure out your screwed up life. But know this: He will be welcome here, and you will have nothing to say about it. You really screwed up this time. I can't believe you did this!" my father shot back. With that, the conversation ended, and I went back to Debby's to spend the night. Debby called John to let him know where I was.

I returned to our apartment after John left for work the next day. I had no school the following week, as we usually recessed for the winter holidays at this time. I walked around the apartment in circles for the longest time. I couldn't believe my own parents were taking John's side. I felt rejected and misunderstood again. I established a good relationship with them when I was in college, and throughout my marriage, and this return to scorn and ridicule hit me hard. It had been many years since I lived in that house on a permanent basis, and my mind conveniently, or by necessity, forgot all the pain and hurt I suffered there.

I was in shock, and unprepared for my next steps. I suppose I was grateful that they didn't throw me out onto the street. There was another part of me, however, that was immensely relieved that I finally said to John what I needed to say. I wanted a divorce, and I didn't regret for one moment what I said. I regretted the timing, but not the words.

John returned to the apartment after his shift. I was petrified he would hit me, but he didn't. His speech was controlled but devoid of emotion. He spoke with his family, told them I was ill and wouldn't be joining them for Christmas. He went alone. He told me that he also spoke with my father who, believe it or not, thought we should see a counselor to help me in this situation, since it was all my fault.

John and I met with a marriage counselor, who immediately decided I needed "fixing" and that after I was "fixed," all would be well again. I felt as though the whole thing was a set-up and was determined to "fix" them both. I was unyielding in my conviction that the marriage could not be saved. It soon became apparent to John and the therapist that the idea of counseling was a huge waste of time and money. I don't mean to say that I don't believe in marriage counseling. On the contrary, I believe strongly in getting help when relationships are in trouble. I have learned that marriage counseling should be sought for one of two purposes: a) if each person in the relationship is willing to work on his/her issues, therapy can provide excellent strategies for communication and problem solving, and b) if one person wants to end the relationship, therapy can provide support for the one who is left with feelings of abandonment, betrayal, anger, embarrassment, shame, and loss. We stopped therapy and started looking for lawyers.

After John announced that we were not leaving New York, I rushed to enroll in a master's degree program at Long Island University with the hope that Albany would agree to extend my provisional certification. I traveled to Albany to appeal for the extension in person to anyone who would listen. I cried my way from the receptionist in the lobby all the way to the Deputy Secretary of Education in New York. I explained my situation through my tears. He listened with elbows on his desk and hands clutched together under his chin. His facial expression was not at all compassionate. I finished my appeal, and after what seemed like an eternity, he said, "You had five years to at least begin your master's training, and you expect me to grant an extension at the eleventh hour? You have not demonstrated your commitment to the teaching profession, and therefore, I will not extend your certification. Good luck in your future, and goodbye."

I was beyond inconsolable. My dream of being a teacher and making a difference in children's lives was over, all because I trusted my husband to keep his word and I didn't follow the requirements for New York's permanent teaching certificate. I was supposed to be living in New Jersey where I was permanently certified to teach. Now, I was headed off to my parents' house, a failure in marriage and in life. All my accomplishments in college were erased in the eyes of my parents and to tell the truth, my own. I was once again a Bimbo, Damn Fool, and Shit for Brains, and I deserved it.

CHAPTER **16**

STARTING OVER

I'm a big girl now, all grown up
But living back home in shame
I stay once more in the room I had
As a child in constant pain

Life has a way of circling 'round
I'm big, but yet I'm little
I keep away from the fights and feuds
I can't get stuck in the middle

I study each night and work all day
To scrimp and save my money
I'll plot and plan each breath I take
If not pathetic, it'd be funny

I can't go back to the olden days
When I'd cry each day and pout
I need to gather both courage and strength
I'll need them when I get out

Lori-ellen Pisani

I PACKED MY things and prepared to return to my parents' home the first weekend in January 1993. As I was coming out of the shower that

Friday morning, John was awake. He grabbed me by the arm, threw me down on the bed and had his way with me one last time. I didn't struggle as I was so shocked by this behavior that was totally out of character for him! I dressed quickly to get out of the house as fast as I could. As I got to the door, he took one last parting shot.

"God forgive you, for you know not what you do," he said. A chill ran down my spine. I found it incredible that he would quote Jesus Christ after assaulting me. *Was that normal? Had he become fanatical? Would he kill me to rid the world of a sinner in Jesus' name?* Over the past two years, he had turned our apartment into a mini chapel with crosses everywhere and a lectern in the living room. He often spoke of his role in Armageddon and told me that he was dreaming about it more frequently. *Was he planning my destruction?*

My hands shook as I tried to unlock the car door. I managed to get in the car and start it, and peeled away from the curb. I was so distracted and frightened by what just happened at home that I rear-ended the car in front of me when the light turned green. I hit the gas not realizing the other driver hadn't even taken her foot off the brake. We both got out of the car, and I immediately apologized for my carelessness. She took one look at me, and one look at her car, and said graciously, "I think you need to go home and pull yourself together. It's only a scratch and my car is old, but you don't look well at all."

"You're so kind, and I am deeply grateful. I am not feeling well but need to go to work. I have students who are not prepared for a substitute. I promise to drive much more carefully, and again, thank you for your generosity and understanding," I managed to get out through my swollen lips and bloodshot eyes.

"Are you sure you want to do that? Is there someone I can call for you?"

"No thank you, there's no one to call. I will stop in the deli and get myself a cup of tea. I'll wait until I can calm down before getting back behind the wheel. I take driving very seriously, and although this accident is very unfortunate, I'm lucky to have bumped into such a kind person as you. It's a wake-up call for me, and I will not repeat this mistake."

"Okay, only if you're sure," she said,

"Thank you, I'm sure."

I never got her name, but she returned to her car and drove off. I went into the deli across the street, got myself a cup of tea, and came back to my car. I sat behind the wheel for about fifteen minutes sipping tea and smoking cigarettes. I was dazed by what had happened with John and was afraid to go home to him. I knew I had to get out quickly, which was why I waited until I was sure he was at work that night, went into the apartment, grabbed the things I could carry in one trip, and closed the door behind me.

Holy God, help me," I prayed. "I'm going back to the house of horrors I fled from six years ago. Am I strong enough to endure my father's wrath, my mother's indifference, and my siblings' harsh remarks? I am not a little girl anymore. I have a voice. I need to express my gratitude to my parents for allowing me to come home, but I also must stand my ground on issues I know more about than they do. Help me, Lord, to get back on my feet and move forward. I've lost so much. My career is over. My marriage is over. I'm feeling lost and hopeless. I need Your help. In Jesus's name I pray, Amen.

When I got to my parents' house, I went immediately to my room and closed the door. I unpacked the green garbage bags that held the only things I took from the apartment, my clothes and toiletries. My childhood bedroom was once again mine, and it didn't feel good to be back in it. I left all the furnishings and decorative things for John. *Where and how did I fit into this new family configuration? Should I shop for groceries for myself, make my own dinner, do my own laundry, and pay rent? I hadn't discussed this with my parents. They had made it clear where they stood with respect to John, and I felt like the outsider who was trespassing on their property. How long would they allow me to stay before they kicked me out?*

After unpacking, I spent some time sitting on the bed, looking into the mirror. "Well, you've really done it this time," I said out loud to the pathetic face looking back at me. Even though I made the right decision leaving John, I made the wrong decision regarding my life. I should have never trusted in a dream of moving to New Jersey, but completed the requirements for New York. *What was the real reason I didn't pursue the master's degree before the deadline?* The answer was hard to face.

The truth of the matter was that I was afraid of failing. I was afraid that my success as an undergraduate was all some kind of miracle that could never be repeated, and it was a secret relief to me that New Jersey did not require a master's degree to be certified. How convenient it was to tell myself that I would be overqualified trying to pursue a career when an advanced degree wasn't required. My father was right. I was a damn fool. My mother was right. It had been my responsibility to fulfill the requirements for New York regardless of what plans I had. I deserved my punishment. Looking in the mirror, I saw a thirteen-year-old girl staring in the face of a thirty-year-old stranger. It was time to face my parents.

I walked downstairs to find them sitting in the living room watching TV. I sat down on the ottoman, facing both of them. "I know you have strong feelings about my divorcing John. You've told me how you feel about him, and that he's welcome here at any time, since you consider him your son. I won't argue with you about that. This is your house, and it's your rules I must live by. What I need to know is--what are the rules regarding my staying here?"

"What do you mean?" asked my mother.

"Well, I need to know if you would like me to pay rent, buy my own food, do chores around the house, and things like that," I replied with my head down.

"You are responsible for your own bills, you can contribute to food bills, and do your own laundry as well as help keep the house clean and help with outside chores, but you do not have to pay rent.

You can save your money so that once you're on your feet, you can find an apartment," my father said.

"Thank you for letting me come back. This is not the plan I had for my life, but this is what my life is. I will continue to study for my master's degree, and I've been offered a position as the school's secretary since ours is retiring. It's contingent upon passing the Civil Service exam. I plan to reapply for my certification as soon as I can, and if I'm lucky enough to find another position as a teacher, I will make sure to complete the requirements for permanent certification in New York," I replied.

"Then that's the plan for your career. What's the plan for your divorce?" asked my mother.

"I need to find a lawyer, and hopefully things will go smoothly. I'm not going to ask for alimony or any money. I just want to end it and move on."

"Uncle Joe can help with finding you a lawyer, and I don't want this to get ugly. Remember, you left John, he didn't leave you," my father reminded me.

Back in my room, I sat down on the bed again, put my head in my hands, and cried. It was clear that my parents were not pleased with me and still had feelings for John. I was lucky to have a roof over my head and made the decision not to speak ill of John or complain about the divorce process to them. My biggest fear was being kicked out, without the means to afford an apartment of my own. So, the best thing to do was keep my mouth shut, work hard, study hard, pass the exam, get the job as the school's secretary, and save money. I could only hope the divorce would go smoothly. It didn't.

John was angry. He sent boxes to the house with knickknacks and other miscellaneous items in them. He always included a 'Mass Card.' I wasn't sure if I should take it as a threat, but it sure felt that way. My mother was there for one of these deliveries. She wanted to see what he was sending. She saw the card and thought it was strange. I didn't say a word. I collected them, and believe that to this day, masses are still being said for my soul.

John also attempted to have the marriage annulled. I received the papers from the Archdiocese of Connecticut. For the life of me, I couldn't understand why he would apply in Connecticut since we were married in New Jersey and lived in New York, but I didn't question it. I completed the forms, taking full responsibility for the breakdown of my marriage. I wrote how immature I was and how I didn't understand my role as a wife and my responsibilities, and that I wasn't emotionally or psychologically prepared to be married. After mailing back the forms, I took the wedding album John had sent in one of his packages and threw it in the trash. Strangely enough, I never heard back from anyone. I guess the Tribunal decided they would not hear the case, and John decided not to pursue it again. I never asked.

John and I had a few meetings with our lawyers, which didn't go well. He tried to sue me for expenses such as all the flowers he ever bought me, changing the locks on the apartment door, his lawyer's fees, court fees, and emotional distress. My lawyer fired back with charges of emotional abuse and physical abuse. This was getting ugly, and the only people getting anything out of it were our lawyers. I spoke to mine and told him how I wanted him to handle the case. He disagreed, so I fired him. I found another lawyer who agreed that he worked for me, and I went ahead with my plans to end the marriage without the process becoming a war, and to move on. The one sticking point we had was the house we built in Pennsylvania.

We were horribly in debt. We owed over $140,000 and couldn't sell it. We had paid more than the house was actually worth. I was so pissed off with myself for not doing my homework before purchasing the land and building that house. I went along with it because I still had huge guilt over aborting our child. I desperately wanted to do something to make John happy. He really wanted this house, so I didn't ask any questions, and let things roll. We rolled craps. As a result, we ended up filing Chapter 11 bankruptcy, which ruined our credit for the next ten years of our lives.

The annulment was never pursued. Three years, two lawyers, and several thousand dollars later, I received my divorce in 1995. John and I did not speak for years afterwards. There were the occasional boxes with Mass cards, but for the most part, we let each other go.

CHAPTER **17**

A LETTER TO LONELINESS

Dear Loneliness,
Why have you come to visit me?
Of all the emotions I know, you are the one I had hoped not to meet
Yet here you are

I fear you, and do not want you here
You make me feel insecure, frightened, and unworthy
You take away my reason for living, and my motivation
You leave me empty and exhausted

Why have you intruded upon my life?
You are punishing me for my selfishness and pride
What do I have to do to make you go away?

People surround me, yet I am alone in the world
You make it impossible for me to reach out in troubled times
You make me feel as though I am a burden to others, and unworthy of their love and support
You have turned my heart to stone, unyielding to those who may wish to enter my life

You cause me to seek those who hurt and reject me, for that is what makes you stronger

Leave me now, for you have done your damage
You have broken my spirit, destroyed my self-confidence, and turned my dreams into nightmares

Lori-ellen Pisani

I HAD A lot of time to think while living with my parents. I couldn't believe that I had experienced so much success as an undergraduate student, winning awards and scholarships, and finally landing a job as an elementary school teacher. Now, at age thirty, I was back in the house of horrors I grew up in, separated from my husband, working as a school secretary to support myself, financially ruined, studying for a master's degree in counseling and development, and alone.

I was scared to death that I would fail in my graduate studies. I lost all confidence in my abilities, and feared I could not repeat the success I had at Fairleigh Dickinson. I met with my advisor, Dr. Robert, who was also the Chairperson of the Education Department at Long Island University and a professor.

I remember our first meeting well. I was standing in the offices of his department, waiting for my meeting. I turned around to see a man approaching the office. He was my height, much smaller than John, with salt and pepper hair, olive skin, and a charming smile. I judged his age to be around forty-five. He introduced himself and asked me to come to his office. We sat down across the desk from one another. I thought the purpose of this meeting was to go over my plan of study to matriculate and to select courses for the semester. I didn't expect a personal conversation.

"I see you are a teacher," Dr. Robert began, as he read the T-shirt I was wearing.

"I was a teacher," I explained. "I didn't complete my course requirements in time to receive permanent certification in New York, so I had to resign my position as a teacher. I am now the school's secretary in the same school I taught in for several years."

"What stopped you from completing the requirements?"

"It's a long story. I'm sure you don't have time. Suffice it to say that it was a mistake on my part, and now I am pursuing this degree to reinstate my certification and get back to teaching."

"I've got time."

"To make a long story short, I thought I'd be living in New Jersey by now where I'm permanently certified. Things just didn't work out."

"What didn't work out?" he persisted.

"My soon to be ex-husband and I had plans to move, and at the eleventh hour he changed his mind and my world."

"That shouldn't have stopped you from continuing your studies."

"I thought having a master's degree would over qualify me as a first-year teacher in New Jersey."

"Nice try. Try again," Dr. Robert said looking straight into my eyes.

"Umm. Excuse me?" I stumbled in reply.

"That excuse might fly with most people, but not with me. What's the real reason you didn't complete your requirements?"

I took a deep breath, put my head down, let out a long sigh, and felt the tears sting my eyes. "I was scared," I choked out. The lump in my throat getting larger by the second as I tried to suppress my impending burst into tears.

"Now we're getting somewhere," Dr. Robert continued. "Let me guess. I can see by your transcript that you were an excellent student as an undergrad. You probably never experienced that level of success in your life, and you were afraid that it was all a fluke and you couldn't repeat it again, so you didn't even try. And what's the connection with your soon to be ex-husband?"

"When he told me that he was staying in New York, it was the last straw for me. I felt as though he ruined my life, along with many other things that had happened along the way. I ended the marriage, and I'm in the middle of a divorce."

I couldn't help but ask myself: *Who was this man? He was looking right through me. It was odd, but also a bit comforting. It seemed as though that without even trying, he knew who I was on the inside. Everyone else basically bought my story about being overqualified, but he saw right through me. His intellect attracted me.* Dr. Robert ended the conversation with, "I'm going to make out your schedule. You will have two classes with me, and we'll see how you do with that," he concluded with what felt like a challenge in his voice.

I left his office with a strange feeling in the pit of my stomach. *Did he have these conversations with everyone? Was this his usual practice? Why was he so interested in me? And more importantly, why did I find myself attracted to him?* This was the beginning of a very unusual relationship that would be a roller-coaster ride emotionally for me.

I picked up my textbooks only to see that he was the author of one of them. It was the best-selling textbook relating to the theory and practice of counseling and human development. I was studying with the guy who actually "wrote the book" on the therapy process. When I saw his name I said to myself, *Holy shit; now I really have to perform.* My stomach tightened and my heart raced. *What if I really don't have what it takes? What if I make a complete fool of myself?* The feelings I had as an undergrad just before I started student teaching returned with a vengeance. I was feeling a mixture of severe anxiety coupled with depression.

This time, however, I wasn't paralyzed on my bed. I was energized, super energized. I was manic, but once again, didn't know it. I couldn't sit still. I paced my bedroom floor, trying to figure out a plan. I knew that my "paper bag method" worked well for me, so I started with that. All through my years at Fairleigh, I used cut-up brown paper bags and colored markers to transpose my notes into a color-coded visual outline. This minimized the number of notebook pages I had to study. I took my notes from class and from the text, condensed and combined them, and wrote them on the bags. I studied the bags every night to prepare for exams. I figured if it worked at Fairleigh, it would work at LIU. I went to the grocery store and asked for as many paper bags as they could spare. By the end of my studies, my paper bag collection reached to about three feet tall.

Listening to Dr. Robert's lectures each week only attracted me to him more. His intellect was both intimidating and awe-inspiring.

He never used notes and was at times provocative. For example, he asked the question, "What if your birth certificate had an expiration date on it. How would this affect your life's choices?" The question both disturbed and intrigued me. I thought about my answer for a long time. Quite frankly, I never thought I was going to live as long as I had. The fear of dying young was part of my baggage from childhood. Having had two surgeries before age five, and then having a heart issue at age nine, followed by lung issues, kidney problems, and a host of other ailments along the way, I was convinced I was not long for this world. I was dreadfully fearful of death then. Every trip to the doctor brought fear of bad news. But here I was, at age thirty, starting over. I came to the conclusion that the things I'd change were my entire childhood and marrying John. I would have waited, started my career first, moved into my own place, and be an independent person, and only then find someone to share my life with rather than hurry into a marriage to get out of an abusive household.

I never met anyone as brilliant as Robert. Often, we met for a few minutes before class to talk. We often engaged in a debate about one of his lecture points. Just before the end of the semester, Robert commented, "You look as though a truck ran over you. What's going on?"

"John sent me another box with some pictures of us while on vacation. There was another Mass card in it. I'm not sure if he's planning on killing me."

"Have you gone to the police?" Robert asked.

"John is the police. They stick together. I have to wait for him to actually do something to get a restraining order. He knows exactly what he can get away with in order to keep me fearful, but unable to take action."

"How long until your divorce is final?"

"We're still fighting over bullshit items his lawyer is throwing at me. It's becoming a huge waste of money. I just want out. That's it; I don't want anything from him."

"It's time to change lawyers," Robert suggested.

"I don't even know where to begin. The whole thing is a mess."

"Why don't you come to my house, and we can talk more about it."

"That's very kind of you, but is it appropriate?" I questioned.

"Of course, we are two adults getting together to talk. I think you can use some guidance."

Now let's be real. I knew that this invitation was not for "guidance." I can be foolish, but I'm not a fool. He was waiting for an answer, and I needed to think fast. I made the impulsive decision to accept his invitation.

"I'll need directions to your place."

"I'll give you a call tomorrow. What number can I call you on?"

"Right now, I'm living with my parents, so I don't think that would be a good idea. I'll give you my work number. It's better that way." I gave him my number, and we went into class. My mind was so preoccupied with what just took place that I didn't take a single note during class. *What did get myself into?*

What I got myself into was more than I ever bargained for. Robert and I began an intimate relationship. I was so awestruck by his brilliance that I didn't think about any consequences. He was fifteen years my senior. I supposed that meant his life experience and intellect would bring me a sense of safety. One of my biggest problems with John was his lack of knowledge regarding finances. He had a simplicity about him that I first thought attractive, and subsequently grew to resent. I never considered that Robert's relationship with me would bring me harm, but it did.

Our relationship was what is commonly known as an "open relationship." Robert was not monogamous, and I went along with his thoughts on what relationships really mean. He made reference to how the male of our species has an innate drive to mate with several females. It's in the genes. He showed me many references from his vast library to prove his point.

I went along with the parameters he set for our relationship, thinking that we could be casual, but I soon developed a need and desire to be his only girlfriend. I kept this need to myself. I secretly hoped that he would pick me above all the others and develop a monogamous relationship with me. I thought I was special to him. In the beginning, I didn't complain, I didn't nag, I didn't ask for much. He was free to talk to me about his other relationships and their challenges. I was supportive, hoping that he would see this as a unique quality about me, and once he grew tired of the others, he would choose me to settle down with. I was wrong.

Several months into this relationship, I started developing infections. I never had them before, and now, every month, almost like clockwork, I'd have another one. In addition, I had a golf-ball-sized lump just outside the vaginal wall that swelled up and decreased in size intermittently. My doctor, Dr. Giovanni, performed a pap test every time I went to see him, and the results yielded that my cervical cells were dysplastic (changing to a pre-cancerous state) as well. For three months, we kept an eye on these cells, and managed the infections with medication. After three months of this regime, he asked to speak with me after my exam.

"I need to tell you a couple of things," Dr. Giovanni began. "First, there's a reason for your continued infections, the swelling, and dysplastic cells."

Oh dear God, I thought. *This is it. He's going to tell me I have some terminal illness.* "What's going on?" I managed to ask.

"Let me ask you first. Are you in a monogamous relationship right now?"

"To be honest, no. I am not sleeping with anyone else, but my boyfriend does have other girlfriends," I said ashamed.

"I can't see how this type of relationship could be good for you. But let me tell you, his having relations with these other women and passing their bacteria along with his on to you cause the infections. These recurring infections can be treated, but he also needs to be treated with an oral medication to be truly effective. These infections can cause other more serious viral infections such as HPV, Human Papilloma Virus, which may lead to cervical cancer. Your cervical cells are changing, which leads me to believe you have the virus. We will treat it, for now, with silver nitrate. This is a warning sign. You also have a clogged

Bartholin's gland, which is causing the swelling and the lump. It can only be treated surgically. I will have to remove it."

"Does this gland have the possibility of being cancerous?"

"I don't believe it is, but I will have pathology look at it. Now, is your boyfriend agreeable to being treated?"

"I'll have to talk to him, I replied.

"While you're having a talk with your boyfriend, you should have a serious talk with yourself. You deserve better than to be in this kind of relationship. I can't see how this is helpful to you, and it's certainly not healthy for you. Think seriously about what I'm telling you. You're headed down a dangerous road. We're already talking about one surgery. Do you really want to continue this way?" Dr. Giovanni asked.

Tears rolled down my cheeks. I couldn't believe this was happening. *What was I going to do? I couldn't believe a man as brilliant as Robert wouldn't know that I was getting sick because of his behavior that I enabled, and worse supported, in the hopes that he would "come around" and end them all to be with me. Would he agree to being treated, or would he toss me to the curb?*

"Okay, first and foremost, we have to get this infection cleared up before surgery, and I promise I will speak with him about getting treated. When do you want to do the surgery?"

"We'll schedule it for two weeks. In the meantime, you need to take the medication to clear up the infection, and I strongly advise you refrain from any sexual activity with your boyfriend."

"How do I schedule the surgery?"

"Mary, my nurse and receptionist, will help with that. Go see her, and you'll work with her to get it all scheduled."

"Thank you, Dr. Giovanni," I said with my head down.

"You'll be fine, Lori-ellen. Just think very seriously about our conversation."

"I will."

I got up from the chair, made my arrangements with Mary, and went home. I told my parents that I needed surgery for a clogged gland, but that was all I said. They asked a few questions about the doctor I was using and the hospital where I'd be, but nothing more. I went up to my room to contemplate my life, again.

Once I learned I didn't have cancer and wasn't going to die, I focused my whole attention on how I was going to tell Robert that that he needed to be treated in order for my infections to clear up. I took a shower and lay on my bed. I needed to think of the words to say to explain the situation to Robert. It felt as though a dark cloud had enveloped me. I was more concerned about his leaving me than I was about my own health. *Here I was, facing surgery and having treatments for pre-cancerous cells, and I was freaking out over Robert's reaction to this news.*

The next time I was with Robert, I told him what Dr. Giovanni said. Although he agreed to be treated with antibiotics, he vehemently denied that our sexual relationship was the cause of my getting the infections "If that was the case," he claimed, "then there would be others with the same condition. It's just you." I believed him. That was a mistake.

Two weeks later, I had the surgery to remove my Bartholin's gland. It was a little more complicated than Dr. Giovanni previously thought. He found a cyst beneath it, and therefore, had a lot more cutting to do.

It was a difficult recovery, but I managed. Believe it or not, I was more worried about Robert using my recovery time to bond with one of his other girlfriends. I made sure to look my very best around him, never complained about the pain I was in, and never asked about his other relationships.

When I healed, we resumed our intimate relationship. I wanted to put the surgeries behind me and get back to the routine we shared previously. I noticed, however, that something changed. Robert didn't seem as interested in me as he had been. He started flirting with other women in front of me. He talked about his other girlfriends to me in more flattering ways. He was harder to reach by phone and seemed bothered by my phone calls. These were signs of things to come, and they weren't pretty.

Our renewed relationship brought new rounds of infections. Dr. Giovanni was growing increasingly impatient with me, urging me to get out of my relationship with Robert. I knew he was right, but I was holding on, hoping that Robert would come around. I didn't ask Robert to be treated along with me for these infections again. I knew that would be the end of our relationship. He didn't have these problems with his other girlfriends. *Why keep me around if all I did was complicate his life?* That all changed in what seemed like an instant.

Robert and I had just finished dinner when he told me he was going away.

"Really, where are you going?" I asked.

"I'm going to England," he responded in a flat tone.

"Is this business or pleasure?"

"I'm going with Emily and a few other friends."

"England! The one place I've longed to see and we've talked about visiting, and you've chosen to take Emily and a few other friends?"

"Yes."

I exploded with rage. It came over me in an instant, like a flood. My brain felt like an electrical shock went through it. My eyes became narrow. He was standing in front of me and I moved nose to nose with him.

"I can't believe this! Are you for real? I have sacrificed my dignity by watching you parade your other women in front of me and suffered through countless infections! And now, you tell me you're taking one of your other girls on a trip that we talked about and you knew was my most favorite place to visit on the entire planet! You don't give a shit about anyone else but yourself, and I suffered the consequences of it. You are a selfish bastard, and I'm the idiot to have allowed myself to be any part of this insane relationship!" You bastard!" I pushed him backwards with my hands. I wanted desperately to get into a real knock-down drag-out fight with him, so I kept moving forward, and pushed him again. "You wanna hit me? Come on, let's do this!"

"You need to calm down," Robert said in a steady tone.

"No, I don't. I need to beat the livin' hell out of you for destroying my life!"

"You're out of control and need to settle down so we can talk."

"I'm done talking. I put up with so much unbelievable crap in this relationship. I gave you carte blanche to do what you wanted without ever complaining. And how did I end up? In my doctor's office once a month for infections I got from you and your harem of whores. And the last straw is that you're going away to England with one of them, when you knew that was the one place on earth I longed to see. I don't know what in the world I was thinking. I played your game and lost. I'm done talking and I'm done with you. What an idiot I was. I thought you were different. You're not. You may be a double Ph.D. and brilliant, but you're a selfish bastard when it comes to relationships! You don't have a clue!"

With that said, I grabbed my purse and left. I got to my car, started it, and pulled around the corner. I pulled over to the curb and stopped. The tears and crying made it too difficult to drive. I must have cried for about a half hour before I was able to drive home. Once home, I cried the rest of the night.

It wasn't easy looking at him during class. And it was worse watching him leave the parking lot with other women in his car. I was grateful that, after the semester, I wouldn't have any more classes with him. We never said a formal goodbye; the relationship died its own death, and a piece of me died with it. I graduated from Long Island University, Summa Cum Laude. I didn't attend this graduation, either. Robert was scheduled to receive an award from the University, and I couldn't bear being in the same room with him.

CHAPTER **18**

RESPONSE FROM LONELINESS

Dear Lori-ellen,
I have received your letter, and quite frankly, I am surprised.
Perhaps you are unaware of this, but I did not intrude into your life
You invited me

You are a chameleon, constantly changing yourself to suit others
Your color may not change, but your masks do
You are a phony and deserve my presence in your life

You make people believe what you want them to,
Then berate them for not understanding you
I, however, do understand you, and I know the real person hiding behind the masks

You present yourself as smart, attractive, self-sufficient, and capable
Yet I know that you second-guess your every move, dislike your appearance, and choke under pressure. You're afraid that others will discover this, so you mask yourself in a persona of confidence and ability
I must say, at times, you do it well

Don't forget, my friend, I am there during your "midnight talks" with yourself. You invited me. I feed on your admonishments to keep things under control, and yes, that is what makes me stronger

You are playing a dangerous game, and you are losing. Your invitation to me came in the form of your unforgiving, distrustful, and misleading attitude and demeanor toward others. And for as long as you have those qualities, I will remain with you

-Loneliness
Lori-ellen Pisani

FOR THE NEXT several weeks, I sank into a deep depression. I was broken in more ways than one. A big part of me thought I deserved what happened. I rejected John, and Robert rejected me. Now I knew how John felt. It was God's way of punishing me. The experience also destroyed my faith in God. I truly felt He was very angry with me, thus this punishment and I expected more to come. I stopped going to church. I prayed, but I didn't think He was interested in hearing me. After all, a soon to be divorced person was no longer welcome in the Roman Catholic Church. I was excluded from receiving Holy Communion. I was, in my mind, excommunicated, and tossed out of the church for being a miserable, horrible human being.

The next month, I was back in Dr. Giovanni's office with yet another infection. He shook his head at me. "If I was your father, I'd smack you in the head," he said, exasperated. "I cannot understand for the life of me what you see in this guy when you deserve so much better. You're ruining your health and your life. What the hell are you thinking?"

"I didn't know then, but I can tell you that I know a lot more now. He's taking one of his other girlfriends on my dream trip of a lifetime."

"What does that tell you?"

"It tells me that my relationship is over, and that he doesn't have the feelings for me that I hoped he would," I croaked out as tears rolled down my face.

Dr. Giovanni took another sample of cervical cells, and I walked out of his office with another prescription to treat the infection, my shoulders slumped, and a lump in my throat the size of golf ball – the same size as the gland Dr. Giovanni had to remove. Two days later, I received a call at work. It was from my doctor's office. He got on the phone, "I need to see you," he said solemnly.

"When do you want me to come in?" I asked.

"Yesterday."

"Holy shit. What's wrong?"

"Just get here when you can."

"I'm on my way."

I immediately left work and drove like a maniac to his office. I basically ran from the parking lot into his office and waited until he could see me. *I was confused. I had been in to see him only a few days ago. What in the world could happen in such a short period of time?*

"Come with me," Dr. Giovanni said. I followed him to his inner office.

"What's happening?" I asked as I sat across from him with sweaty palms and trembling legs.

"I've got your latest test results from the pap we did," he began.

"And what did they show?"

"Your dysplasia has turned to Carcinoma-in-Situ stage IV," he continued.

"Carcinoma means cancer, doesn't it?"

"Well, it's more like turning to cancer, but my concern is the very rapid rate that your cells are changing. You can say that yes, it's a cancerous state, but having the cells change from dysplastic to stage 4 in such a short period of time means there is a great risk of becoming more dangerous and spreading. We don't have much time. We need to move quickly."

Once again, the tears rolled unchecked down my cheeks. I asked, "Am I going to die?"

"Certainly not, but we need to be much more aggressive in your treatment."

"Do I need a hysterectomy?"

"I'd rather not, since you may want to have children later in life."

"I don't want to have children."

"You are in no shape right now to make such a major life-changing decision. We can treat this. I will basically remove your cervix. If you decide to have children, you will be able to, but I would have to sew the mouth of your uterus closed in order for you to carry the child, and you would need to be on bed rest for a majority of your pregnancy."

"I can't even think of being pregnant right now. I just want this cancer out of me as soon as possible."

"We will go ahead with the procedure, and the pathology report will determine our next steps. What I want you to clearly understand is this. Your condition was preventable. This didn't have to happen. You have made some poor choices, and the alarm has sounded your wake-up call. You're lucky we caught this when we did. It could be a whole lot worse. I know what our next move is with respect to treating this, but I want to know what your next move is."

"I guess this is the ultimate punishment for my relationship with Robert, and I deserve it," I said crying openly. Dr. Giovanni had become a trusted person in my life. He was old enough to be my father, but always demonstrated a caring attitude toward me. I needed him now more than ever.

"You will get through this, and we will get through this," he said as he came around his desk to give me a hug. I wept in his embrace for about a minute. I had someone in my life who cared. And not only that, he was going to save my life. We broke apart. He told me to work with Mary once again to make arrangements for the surgery. I would go in at the earliest possible date, which was the following week.

I went home and told my parents that I had cervical cancer and would be having my third surgery (including the two for the Bartholin's gland and cyst removals) in two years.

"Jesus Christ! What the hell's wrong with you?" my father shouted.

"Shut up, Dan," my mother retorted. "She just told you what's wrong. Have a little compassion, for Christ's sake. Will you need chemo or radiation?" she asked.

"We won't know until the pathology report comes back. Dr. Giovanni is confident that it is confined, and once removed, I shouldn't need any more treatment."

"When are you going in?" my mother continued.

"I need to get all my pre-op tests done this week. We're looking at next Friday."

"Son-of-a-bitch!" my father grunted.

"I'm sorry," I said with my head down. I felt like such a failure in every respect. I lost my career, my marriage disintegrated, I had to file for bankruptcy, my relationship with Robert was over, and I just learned I had cervical cancer.. Suicidal thoughts were not far from my mind. I had to convince myself to fight this disease, recover, regroup, and move forward. It was, at that point, my most vicious battle. I was as close to dying as I ever thought I'd be....not realizing that years later, I'd face the ultimate life or death decision, and medical issues would not be the enemy.

If there was a bright spot, it was finding an apartment I could afford. After my surgery and recovery, I was headed off to my own apartment. Even that thought, however, scared the hell out of me. I felt unready, unstable, and unable to care for myself. I had lost all confidence in my ability to think straight and make good decisions. I didn't even have God to turn to anymore. Life just didn't seem worth living.

The pathology report determined that further treatment was not necessary to treat the cancer. My cervix was completely removed, and margins were clear. The recovery was awful. I never felt more broken in every way in my entire life. What I needed to do now was heal. Even with the new apartment and an offer to return to teaching at a different school once I completed my master's degree in a few months' time didn't help. In fact, that horrible feeling I had before I started student teaching returned with what felt like a vengeance. I was out of control, and one night in early 1994, I made the call to the suicide prevention hotline.

CHAPTER **19**

THE ANSWER

I finally have the answer
The puzzle has been solved
I am bipolar and in treatment
All my issues resolved

That was my hope and my goal
The pain and rage would end
I'd regain my life and my dreams
The stairs I'd never descend

I learned that's not the way it works
The fight for stability remains
I'll need my meds and therapy
To keep from falling again

This is a lifelong battle
A war – I must prevail
If I want to succeed in life
I must fight each day – not fail

The goal is peace of mind and heart
Will I ever feel relief?
I'll keep fighting – not give in
For that is my belief

Lori-ellen Pisani

AFTER ALMOST TWO years of treatment with Dr. Mintz, it became clear to him that I was not suffering from depression alone. In December 1996, he approached me gently and told me what he was thinking.

"Lori-ellen, I want you to consider something," he began.

"Consider what?"

"From what I've learned so far, it appears that you may have an illness more complex than depression."

"What illness?"

"I believe you may have bipolar disorder."

"What does that mean?"

"Bipolar disorder is difficult to diagnose. People who have it go through periods of mania and severe depression. Without a proper diagnosis, it's hard to say. You have described experiences with suicidal depression and periods of mania during college and graduate school when you were racing around doing many things successfully at once. Mania doesn't always show up the same in everyone. It is quite possible that you were manic for almost your entire college career, until you crashed just before you started student teaching. I'd like to explore this possibility with Dr. Salamon. You will need to be evaluated to confirm the diagnosis."

"How does this work?" I asked with concern in my voice.

"You would see him for several sessions in order for him to evaluate you and make a determination regarding bipolar disorder. If he confirms the diagnosis, he will prescribe additional medications. You'd see me for therapy, and Dr. Salamon for medication follow-ups on a regular basis as you have been for your depression. Dr. Salamon's role is more like managing your medications and how they affect your ability to function in a balanced and controlled way. These episodes of deep depression, rage, creativity, extremely high energy and multi-tasking are symptoms of undiagnosed bipolar disorder. Your brain chemistry is out of balance. The medications are designed to re-establish that balance without swings in your mood that cause you to fall into a deep depression or become enraged or manic. I will call Dr. Salamon to review my notes with him. If he agrees that an evaluation is in order, I will call you to make an appointment with him."

"When will you call?"

"I can call you tomorrow tonight.

"I really don't know how I feel about this. I find this whole thing frightening."

"I understand, but you need to know that although you have merely managed to succeed with only anti-depressant medication, you have had many serious episodes of depression and extended episodes of possible mania. You're still standing, and that's what matters. This is an opportunity for you to enjoy life more rather than endure it. Think of it this way--you wouldn't have come into my office to see me for these past two years if things were going well all the time. All I'm saying is that there may be more to your emotional well- being than being treated for depression. You don't have to worry about going crazy after you leave this office. You are the same person you were when you walked in today. The only difference is that we recognize you are a more complex person, in need of a more complex therapy regime. That's all there is to it."

"Funny you should say the word 'complex.' I was asked to describe myself in an essay for a writing class I took many years ago, and I chose the oxymoron 'simply complex' as my description."

"There's nothing wrong with that. It makes you more interesting."

Early the next evening, I received a call from Dr. Mintz. He told me that he discussed my case with Dr. Salamon, who agreed that a consult was in order. I made the appointment in December 1996. He had also suspected that I was bipolar based upon my descriptions of rage and extreme energy while on the anti-depressant medications. He further evaluated me and confirmed the diagnosis. I started medications for bipolar disorder in February 1997. I was about to embark on a new journey that would last the rest of my life, and a relationship with Dr. Salamon that, at times, would save my life.

I arrived a little early at Dr. Salamon's office, so I parked my car and had a cigarette. I was shaking, and I wasn't all that sure I wouldn't throw up all over myself. *Calm down,* I thought to myself. *You're here to get help. Be honest, so Dr. Salamon can get a good evaluation. Don't try to be something I'm not. Don't pretend there's nothing wrong. There is; I'm miserable and despite what anyone in my family says, I'm going to do something about it. Take a deep breath and get in there.*

I walked into the waiting room, sat down, and prayed for help. *God please let me be alright. I'm scared.*

The doors opened and Dr. Salamon peeked out.

"Come in," Dr. Salamon said

To my immense relief, Dr. Salamon started off the conversation. "As you know, I have spoken with Dr. Mintz, and I have a pretty good sense of what's happening for you, but I'd like to hear from you directly. You've been on anti-depressant medication for a while, but there is more to who you are than clinically depressed." he began.

"Well, there are times in my life when my feelings and thoughts range from suicidal depression, to episodes of high energy, creativity, and the ability to multi-task and succeed. There are also episodes of rage that at times has me thinking of committing violence against another or a few times, becoming aggressive."

"Have you ever attempted suicide?"

"There was a time when I was married, that I was very depressed. My ex-husband was an NYPD detective, and while he sat in the living room, I was in the bedroom with his .38-caliber service revolver loaded and in my hands."

"Any other times?"

"Just before I started with Dr. Mintz, I called the Suicide Prevention Hotline. I was planning on killing myself but didn't have a gun."

"What stopped you from committing suicide?"

"I really don't know what stopped me the first time. I guess I lost my nerve. The second time, I thought about my former students and how they would react to the news that I killed myself."

"And what about the rage you experience--can you tell me about that?"

"When I become enraged, I get this immediate adrenaline rush, and I either start screaming foul language at the person who pissed me off, throw things, or try to instigate a physical fight. There was a time when I instigated a fight between myself and a guy I was seeing. He didn't engage with me, but I was ready and actually wanted to duke it out with him."

"Where on the spectrum between rage, mania, and depression do you feel you are now?"

"Right now, I'm depressed. I'm miserable. I feel totally alone in the world. My family doesn't understand me, my marriage failed, I lost a child, which was my own fault, I lost my career because I trusted my husband and had to start over, and I ended up with cervical cancer as a result of the relationship I had with Robert, who had too many other girlfriends to count."

"Would you say that the majority of the time you are depressed, or angry?"

"Depressed."

"Are you suicidal right now?" he questioned.

"No, I'm nervous as hell, but not suicidal. I'm hoping that working with you and Dr. Mintz will help me."

"Let's talk a bit about mania. Describe for me what happens for you."

"Well, I'm not all that clear on what mania is, but I don't paint the house funky colors and go on shopping sprees. When I'm manic, I feel a surge of energy. Not the same energy I have when I'm angry, more like the energy I would have by drinking twelve cups of coffee. I don't require much sleep, and it is often difficult to sleep. I can do many tasks at once, whereas I'm usually a very linear thinker and a 'one thing at a time' kind of person. I am much more creative in my teaching and problem-solving than I usually am. I'm in a better mood and can laugh much easier. When I was in college, I became like a super student, winning awards and graduating at the top of my class. To be honest, I like the way I feel when I'm like that. I have confidence in my abilities, and I'm successful in whatever it is I'm doing. I feel like I'm high."

"A lot of people feel that way. Mania can manifest itself in different ways. Your mania is exactly what you say it is, a burst of creative energy and confidence. It's a great feeling to have. And then what happens?"

"Well, there is usually some kind of crash."

"What does that mean?"

"Something will happen, and I will fall very quickly out of that state of being high down what I have labeled a 'spiral staircase' to a state of depression, or someone will say or do something to totally piss me off and I want to strangle them. It's very upsetting."

"As it would be; a person cannot maintain a state of mania forever. One can be in one state or another for quite a long period of time, like when you were in school, but there comes a point in time when the brain will attempt to shut down from running on high speed for so long."

"Yeah, like the time I fell apart in school just before I started my student teaching," I offered.

"I believe Dr. Mintz mentioned that as part of our consult. What happened?"

"I found myself huddled in my bed, paralyzed with fear. I'm not sure, but it felt like a nervous breakdown. I was a complete wreck and didn't think I could go forward with student teaching. I went for help on campus, and talking did help, but they didn't have much to offer me except a test that determined I should either be a speech pathologist or a farmer."

"What are your thoughts on being bipolar?" I inquired.

"There are two types of bipolar disorder, Type I and Type II. From your accounts, I'm thinking that you have Type II, but we will need to meet for several more times before I can make an accurate diagnosis."

As I left his office, I was feeling a sense of calm. I was in the right place and with the right doctor. We were taking things slowly. Dr. Salamon clearly knew what he was talking about, and that comforted me. I was finally on a journey that would hopefully lead me to a sense of balance and control over my life and my feelings.

I met with Dr. Salamon for several weeks before he was comfortable enough to confirm the bipolar diagnosis. His sessions with me, along with a thorough review of Dr. Mintz's copious notes, assisted him in making this diagnosis. I grew very comfortable with Dr. Salamon. He was easy to talk to, understanding, highly intelligent, and not at all shocked by my story.

At the end of May 1997, my insurance company decided that my sessions with Dr. Mintz had to come to an end. They would only continue to pay for my sessions with Dr. Salamon and my medication. I was enraged once again. I had been with Dr. Mintz since 1994. And now, some idiot behind a desk had determined that I no longer needed him. I wanted to sue the fool and the insurance company.

I railed against them in my session with Dr. Mintz. "How dare they determine what my needs are? Who in the hell do they think they are? I've just been diagnosed with a serious illness and they think I'm done with therapy? They're the crazy ones, not me."

I appealed the decision but lost. They insisted that my illness could be more than appropriately treated with only Dr. Salamon but agreed to give me four more sessions with Dr. Mintz as part of the termination process. I spent most of those weeks crying, and he spent the time trying to reassure me that I was in good hands with Dr. Salamon, and that he was never more than a phone call away.

Although my family knew I was seeing a therapist. I did not immediately reveal to them that I was diagnosed as bipolar. I knew what it would bring: mean-spirited comments about being crazy, and humiliation. It wasn't my plan to tell my family, but then plans change. My plan changed in late June 1997, as a result of a message left on my answering machine.

CHAPTER **20**

FORGIVEN

Daddy fell down the staircase
He couldn't make the climb
He fell into depression
The suicidal kind

His body went into freefall
His kidneys shutting down
The doctors saved his life
But couldn't erase the frown

He started to see a therapist
In a futile attempt to heal
His children went to a session
But one heart was made of steel

He asked us all to forgive him
He knew what he had done
Three of us gave it freely
All of us but one

We left the room in silence
He said no more to us
My father was now broken
His spirit and heart would rust

Lori-ellen Pisani

I RETURNED HOME one evening after school to find a message from my mother on the answering machine. "It's Mom. I just want you to know that your father is in the hospital." Click, the message ended. I grabbed my keys and drove like a maniac over to my parents' house. In all my life, my father had only been in the hospital once, when he had a gallbladder attack. I always thought he would have a heart attack due to his immense size, but he had lost a lot of weight. That didn't prevent a diagnosis of Diabetes II, but it was manageable. I couldn't believe that could be it. I parked the car and ran into the house.

"What happened?" I asked my mother, almost frantic.

"I took your father to the hospital this morning," my mother answered. "He refused to get out of bed for the past three days, and I found he was both dehydrated and unresponsive."

"What do you mean unresponsive? He wasn't breathing?"

"He was breathing, but he refused to talk to me and tell me what was wrong."

"Did they run tests? What is wrong?"

"His kidneys are not functioning properly, and he didn't want any treatment. He was sullen and depressed. He kept saying that he wanted to be left alone. The doctors had a hard time communicating with him. He was uncooperative in his silence. They believe he might have also had a few mini-strokes, but your father is refusing to have anything more than fluids right now. The doctors approached me and suggested that once stabilized, he should be admitted to the psychiatric ward for an evaluation."

"Did all this happen in just three days?"

"He has been in bed for three days, but things must have started happening a while ago. I received a call from his office the second day he was in bed. They told me that he was having trouble remembering his appointments and managing his business affairs. They were concerned about him. This has been going on for well over a month, but they just decided to let me know now."

"Have you noticed a change in his behavior?"

"All I really noticed was that he wasn't very talkative. I just figured he was tired. Since he doesn't usually take phone calls, I started receiving calls from the banks about the mortgages, the shop down in Bermuda, credit card companies, and utility companies telling me the accounts were months overdue. I thought he was up to his old tricks, you know, robbing Peter to pay Paul, but it's much more serious than that."

"Okay, wait a minute. First, what do they have his condition labeled as now?"

"He's listed in serious condition. They are worried that his kidneys will shut down completely, but he won't allow them to do anything."

"Do you have any authority to do anything about that?"

"Since he is also scheduled to go into the psychiatric ward, he is considered incapable of making these decisions at this time, so I gave my permission for them to do what they have to do to stabilize him and confirm the mini-strokes."

"Does he want to see anyone?"

"No, he doesn't. I'm the only one he will see."

A lump formed in my throat, and it took all the strength I could muster to keep the tears from coming. "Okay. The next thing we need to do is get Debby and Liz over here and figure out what he's been doing these past few months and how bad the situation is."

Within an hour, Liz and Debby were also at the house, and we sat around the dining room table to get a grip on what was happening. Since Louis was living in the house, he came downstairs once all of us were together. We made phone calls to Bermuda only to find out that my father had turned down a $350,000 offer to buy Top Turf several months prior. Competition was cutting into our base and had more sports options to offer. He told my mother that he would run the place into the ground before he'd sell, and that's exactly what happened. The competition's operation was bigger and better than ours, and their marketing plan poached our "loyal" customers. Top Turf couldn't stay in business and would be closing its doors in August. None of us had a clue. We'd had that business since 1975, and now it was gone, over, finished, done, and there wasn't a dime left.

My mother then called Mr. Sachs at the union. My father was rehired as a business agent about six years after he was released from prison. He was promoted to Vice-President of the local in 1996. Mr. Sachs informed my mother that my father's job performance had been slipping badly for the past several months. He had a conversation recently with my father to discuss his concerns and suggested that my father retire. According to Mr. Sachs, the conversation did not go well, and my father failed to report to work several days out of each week. We, his family, thought he was out checking on his shops, but now we were left guessing as to where he was during that time.

We took the bills that were kept under the cast-iron bulldog on the front hall shelf and started to go through them. To our horror, we realized that mortgage payments on the apartment building, their own home, and the retirement home they bought had not been made in several months and foreclosure letters were mixed in with the delinquent notices. Credit card bills and utility bills for these properties stacked up a few inches high.

"Oh my God," was the only thing my mother could say.

"Holy crap," Louis added. Liz started crying, and I sat in stunned silence.

"We've got to figure this out," Debby said in an effort to get us to compose ourselves and move forward. "We need to call the accountant and Uncle Joe to help figure this out."

"It's ten o'clock at night. We can't make any more calls tonight. We'll have to do it in the morning." With nothing left to do for the night, my sisters and I went home.

I didn't sleep at all, but paced the floors of my apartment, drinking coffee and smoking cigarettes. I couldn't reconcile how my father was in the psych ward of the hospital, and I had a secret that could potentially help him. I called to leave a message with Dr. Salamon that I needed to see him before my next scheduled appointment.

"What's happening?" Dr. Salamon asked.

"My father is in the hospital's psych ward, and I'm freaking out."

"What happened?"

"We're still trying to figure it out. He's refusing to talk and is uncooperative, so all we can gather is that for almost a year, all of my father's businesses as well as his full-time job have collapsed. They think he might have had some mini strokes, but it's hard to say. His kidneys are also not functioning well."

"And how are you dealing with this?"

"I'm scared to death that the same thing is going to happen to me that's happening to my father now. We talked about my father over the past couple of months and his behaviors, and I'm realizing that although I don't behave like him, there are similarities."

"Has your father been in treatment?"

"No, the possibility of his having any kind of mental illness was never discussed until now. For all these years, he was just a man on the go, coming up with crazy schemes for business ventures, and doing things his way. My parents thought I was nuts for seeing Dr. Mintz for so long. I didn't tell them about what's happening for me now, and I don't know if I should bring it up now. It might be too much for them to handle, with my father the way he is. On the other hand, by keeping my diagnosis a secret I'm afraid I might be hurting him."

"If your father is in the psychiatric ward, as you say, then he will be properly evaluated. I am aware of his history since you went into it in great detail with Dr. Mintz. My educated guess is that if he is bipolar, then he's been in a manic state for quite a while and has shifted to the depressive side of the spectrum. The doctors will make recommendations for medication and treatment after he is stabilized medically."

"And should I take the chance and say something about my diagnosis?"

"That's up to you. Since your mother is communicating with the doctors, she can relay the information. Remember though, you are not your father and vice-versa. Your mother and your family need to know this. There is no magic bullet here. It's not like an antibiotic you take for infections. Treatment is highly individualized, and what may work for you may not have the same effect for your father."

"I feel like I'm living a nightmare. I can't believe this is happening. They've lost everything, and I have no idea what the future will hold for them."

"Let's talk about you for a minute. How were you feeling before this happened?"

"It's hard to say, given what's just happened. What I can tell you is that before this crisis, I wasn't jumping for joy, but I wasn't as down in the dumps as I usually am, either. I am managing day to day better than I was before the medication, but now I don't know where the hell I am. I'm relieved to know that what happened to my father doesn't predict my future, but I'm completely thrown off by what's happened to him. He has now agreed to let us visit him in the hospital. I'm supposed to go see him tonight and have no idea what to expect. The whole thing scares the hell out of me."

"He'll probably be just as you described, very quiet. Take your cues from him. If he's non-responsive, keep the visit short. As for you, it's a good sign that you are beginning to respond to the medications and that instead of doing anything drastic, you picked up the phone to call for an appointment. You're using your head. You're thinking and not reacting on impulse. That's a positive step. We'll keep you on the same dosage for another couple of weeks, and at our next appointment, decide what our next steps will be. If you need to see me before our next appointment, just call."

"Thank you. If I need to, I will."

I left Dr. Salamon's office with a heavy heart but comforted by his words. Strangely enough, I didn't care at that point what my mother or any other family member would say to me when I revealed that I was being treated for bipolar disorder. My focus was on saying and doing whatever I could to help my father, who was in crisis.

I drove over to my parents' house to meet my family so we could go to the hospital together. I got there first and went into the kitchen to speak to my mother.

"I have something you need to know that may be helpful to Daddy," I began.

"What is it?"

"You already know that I was seeing Dr. Mintz for depression. What you don't know is that he recently referred me to his colleague, Dr. Salamon, a psychiatrist, for further evaluation. I've been diagnosed with bipolar disorder type II. It manifests itself in different ways, depending upon the individual. It is possible, however, that a person can be manic for many years, and then crash into a deep depression."

"What in the hell does that mean?" she asked, getting agitated.

"All I'm saying is, that for all of my life, Daddy has been a man on the move, coming up with crazy schemes to make money, spending money he doesn't have, and making some pretty impulsive decisions. All of these things are characteristic of mania. Now, for whatever reason, he's crashed into a deep depression, which has led us to where he is now. Since you are speaking directly with his doctors, I thought you should know this, as they might want to evaluate Daddy with this information in mind."

"Lori-ellen, I'm too overwhelmed right now trying to fix the mess your father has made to think about what you're saying. Let's see what the doctors say, and we'll take it from there."

"I'm sorry. I didn't mean to make things worse for you. I just thought you should know. I won't bring it up again," I concluded. By that time, Debby, Liz and Louis had come in, and the conversation was dropped. We headed over to the hospital.

We arrived, signed in, got our passes, and headed to the psychiatric floor. We were buzzed in and led to a small room that served as both a dining and meeting room. At that time, a patient could smoke in a designated area, so we waited for my father to finish his cigarette and join us in the meeting room. When he walked through the door, I was grieved to see the vacant expression on his face and how he hung his head so low his chin touched his chest. One by one, we greeted him with a kiss on the cheek. I desperately wanted to stay away from the words "How are you?" so I kept it to "Hi Daddy."

I was overcome with a sense of fear and déjà vu. My mind went right back to the first visit I had when my father was in prison. Once again, my father was unrecognizable. He looked drawn, pale, and had dark circles under his eyes. He wore khaki-style pants, and a pullover shirt, and slip-on shoes with no laces. This time, however, he wasn't giving out orders for each of us to follow when we got home, and I wasn't enraged. I didn't want to escape with him. I wanted him to get help and return to the Daddy I loved and feared.

He sat slumped in his chair and didn't say a word. I had no idea what to say, and neither did anyone else. It was an incredibly uncomfortable silence. My mother finally spoke up after what seemed like an eternity. "Dan, are you eating?" she began. My father shrugged his shoulders in response. "Are you sleeping?" she tried again. Another shrug. "Do you need anything?" Her voice was growing a bit desperate.

"Cigarettes," he replied in a whisper.

He was broken. I knew from that moment on that I'd never again see the man I had known as my father for all of my life. Gone was "Dan the Man" and all the other nicknames he had earned over the years for his outgoing, gregarious demeanor, as well as for being a master planner and schemer. In that chair sat a man without a spirit or soul. He was empty, drained of all of life's energy. He was done with life, and it showed.

A week and a half later, he was physically stabilized and released, but in a deep depression. His outpatient treatment plan included seeing a psychologist and a prescription for anti-depressants. He agreed to both, since he was under threat from my mother that if he didn't comply, she would put him back into the hospital. About a month into his therapy, my mother told us kids that the therapist wanted us to attend one of Daddy's sessions. He had something to tell us.

We all arrived at the therapist's office together. Debby drove. She did her best to crack jokes on the ride over to cut the tension. The rest of us silently speculated on what we were going to be told. I could only guess that we'd hear something about what my father was going through and hoped the therapist would give us suggestions on how to help him. What we got was a shock in more ways than one.

We were escorted into the therapist's office and asked to sit on the couch. My father sat across from us in a chair, and the therapist sat behind him in his office chair. He began by thanking us for coming. Debby was brave enough to say, "We're here because we love our father and want to help." Louis and I nodded our heads in agreement. Liz, who was sitting on the end of the couch, did not nod her head. I noticed this, but did not question it. I was intent on focusing on my father.

"Your father has something he wants to say to you all," the therapist continued. "Dan, your kids are here to listen to what you want to say." Tears rolled down my father's cheeks. He put his head down, chin to chest, and sobbed quietly for a few moments. I had never seen him cry in the whole of my life. As Daddy cried, Debby and I started crying quietly, Louis fidgeted on the couch, clearly uncomfortable, and Liz sat there without a tear, staring at my father.

In what can only be described as a raspy whisper my father said simply, "I'm sorry," and continued crying. "I wasn't a good father to you, and I'm sorry. I hope you can forgive me." We looked at each other in shocked disbelief. What did we just hear? My father always made it quite clear that he would never apologize for anything he said or did. We grew up knowing that we would never hear those words from him. And now, here he was, sobbing and saying he was sorry and asking for our forgiveness. I couldn't figure out whether he felt he was being forced into this, or if he really wanted to share this with us.

It didn't matter if he was coached or not. At that moment, all I wanted to do was run over to him and throw my arms around him. He didn't have to say any more. In my mind, all was forgiven. He said he was sorry and asked for forgiveness. I knew that whatever the source of his apology, it took every ounce of strength he had left to say those words. It was confirmation for me that he would never be the same after this moment. Here was my father, the strongest, most fearless man I ever knew, a man whom I'd feared all my life, but loved dearly, sitting there crumpled up, crying, and broken. I vowed, silently, right then and there to forgive him and do my best to move forward.

Again, there was silence. We looked at each other, not knowing what in the hell to do. A huge lump was in my throat, Louis's leg was bouncing up and down, Debby was crying into her tissues, and Liz had the oddest expression on her face. It looked like anger. I couldn't figure it out but didn't have time to try.

The therapist started talking again. "Your father recognizes how patterns repeat themselves. He sees how his own upbringing has affected the way he parented you. He understands that he wasn't the most supportive or nurturing father he could have been. He knows that he's been hard on you all, sometimes to the point of abuse, and he's asking for forgiveness. Do you forgive him? He needs to hear from each of you."

One by one, we answered. Debby started. "I forgive you, Daddy," she stated as clearly as she could manage through her tears.

"I forgive you, Daddy," I croaked out.

Louis cleared his throat and in his best attempt to hide emotion said, "I forgive you, Daddy."

Then it was Liz's turn. "Well, I don't forgive you, Daddy." We snapped our heads to look at her in shock. Even the therapist's jaw dropped. She continued, "You made my life a living hell and you expect me to forgive you? Well, I don't. I'm sorry if that upsets you, but you have no idea what hell you put me through my whole life, and you can't expect me to forgive and forget in one instant."

Debby, Louis, and I were horrified and sat in disbelief. Here Liz was, bold and arrogant, telling a man who had just lost everything, including his dignity, that she didn't accept his apology. He had, according to her, ruined her life, and she had no intention of forgiving him. The irony was that Liz's acting-out behavior caused most of the huge issues that made my father lose control in our past, and we suffered for it. She should be asking forgiveness of the rest of us kids and my parents, not getting on her high horse and refusing to accept his apology.

The silence that followed was frightening. You could cut the tension with a knife. I was so enraged I wanted to slap her face with all my strength right there and let her know just how much her selfish behavior all of her life screwed up our lives as well. The feeling came over me in a flash. I recognized it and knew I was going to be in trouble if I didn't get hold of myself. I hated her in that moment. I couldn't stop thinking, *Who made you God? And how dare you say what you did! You spent your whole life doing what you wanted to do, shoving it in our faces, breaking all the rules, and causing so much grief. And here you sit with a smug look on your face, telling your father you won't forgive him. How many times did the rest of us end up cleaning the kitchen floor with our toothbrushes because you, Liz, fucked up yet again. How many different schools did you get thrown out of for your disrespectful and inappropriate behavior? How many times did you break curfew to keep the whole house up worrying about where you were. How much pot did you smoke while hangin' out with your friends and running from the cops?*

It took every ounce of restraint not to let loose on her. I took my focus off of Liz to look at my father in order to see his reaction. It was unchanged. He blew his nose in his tissue and continued to weep silently.

His therapist, clearly shocked, had to say something, so he came up with, "Sometimes it takes a little time to get to the point of forgiveness if there is a deep wound that needs to be healed." What else could he say? I bet he didn't expect Liz to go off, and he had to salvage what he could of what should have been the beginning of the healing process for my father and the rest of us, only to have it turn into a bloody shambles. The session ended with all of us, Daddy included, heading out the door. No one said a word. We drove home listening to elevator music on the radio. We dropped my father off at the house. As he walked inside, all of us turned to Liz.

"Are you fucking kidding me, Liz?" I lashed out. "Could you not see the man is broken? It took everything he had to say he was sorry and you had the nerve not to forgive him!"

Debby chimed in, "What the hell were you thinking! Have you conveniently forgotten all the crap you put our parents through all your life! You didn't care about rules or consequences. You lived your life the way you wanted to, and it screwed up everything for the rest of us. While you were out getting high, we were scrubbing floors and picking up broken china Daddy threw at walls while screaming about you!"

"You don't have a clue about what he put me through!" Liz retorted. "And have you forgotten how he abused Mommy all of our lives? What about her? Why do you think I spent my time out of the house? I couldn't take it anymore, and I don't have to forgive him. I said what I said, and I meant it. So deal with it," she countered.

"Forget it. It's done. It's over. I don't want to talk about it anymore."

"I'm outta here," Louis said flatly. He got out of the car and went in the house. That effectively ended the conversation, and we never spoke of it again. My father ended treatment and stopped taking his anti-depressant medication after that session.

CHAPTER **21**

MISTAKES

My mistakes were getting serious
My students triggered me
I had no place to run and hide
I had no place to flee

Medicines weren't helping me
I wanted to stop them all
Since I was to be a Ph.D.
I didn't think I'd fall

This mistake was arrogance
I thought I could heal myself
I stopped my meds and therapy
The meds left closed on the shelf

As soon as my studies were over
And mania came to a halt
I dropped like cement to the bottom
Crashing down was my own fault

I went back to meds and therapy
Head low and heart in hand
I truly understood this time
Getting help was a command

Lori-ellen Pisani

AS TIME PASSED, what I was most fearful of was the loss of concentration. After completing my master's degree in counseling and human development, I immediately enrolled in a doctoral program. My course of study was modern psychoanalysis and psychotherapy. I chose this degree primarily to find out what had happened to me in my early life, and why, out of all my siblings, I appeared to choose a different path. *Why was I so intent on figuring out my life? Why did I choose to seek professional help when my siblings and father did not? Why was my experience of all that happened at home so different than theirs? What made me vow to God at age five that no child would feel unloved, unwanted, forgotten, dismissed, and threatened in my presence? Why did I feel a need to marry John? What caused me to abort our child? Why was I terrified of becoming pregnant again? Why did I basically abandon my faith after my marriage?*

Since all of my graduate credits transferred into the program, I was able to take courses specifically in the areas pertaining to modern psychoanalysis and psychotherapy. I was terribly worried that due to medication changes, I would not be able to focus enough to complete the course requirements. This was when I did something incredibly stupid. I took myself off all medications and stopped treatment. In my warped mind, I thought that since I was studying to be in the field, I could basically heal myself. Since my pattern had always been mania while I was in school, I had no idea what I was doing to myself. What I did sent me spiraling back down the staircase and back into treatment with Dr. Salamon.

When I obtained my degree, I was done with school (or so I thought). I focused again on my teaching. Slowly but surely, however, I began to slide back into a deep depression. My attempt at "doctor heal thyself" was a huge failure, and I was once again miserable. I should have known better. Pride and arrogance caused me to stop treatment. Desperation, depression, and humility caused me to pick up the phone and call Dr. Salamon.

"So, how have you been?" asked Dr. Salamon.

"I feel like I'm all over the place," I answered. "I seem to be running the gamut of emotions. Some days I'm fearful that I'm going to end up like my father, who sits in the house all day blankly staring at the TV screen and not talking to anyone. He is no longer working. He doesn't sit at the table and eat. He nibbles on small snacks while sitting on the couch. He doesn't make any attempt at conversation and answers in one-word utterances. Mostly he spends his time in bed sleeping for upwards of twelve hours a day. He gets up at night when everyone else is asleep and goes downstairs to watch television. He clearly doesn't want to be around people. I have no idea who this man is anymore.

"My parents have lost everything. My mother has taken control over all things financial. She had to sell their retirement home in Maryland, Top Turf is closed, and my father no longer manages professional boxers. The apartment building he bought with my brother was sold at a loss, as was the house we built as a family, and now the house I grew up in is on the market. My mother flew down to Florida with my sister, Liz, and in two days bought a small home so that my parents can leave New York and head down to Florida. It's just as well. The FBI was sniffing around."

"What?" asked Dr. Salamon.

"The very last business my father took a shot at was offshore betting which is illegal. Once again, the basement was turned into a betting parlor. Instead of Telex machines, phone banks were set up for taking bets. I walked into the house one day to find my father sitting around the dining room table with some really scary-looking guys dressed all in black with lots of diamond jewelry. I wanted to laugh, but I was told to make them all coffee and get out of the house quickly.

"The basement became off limits to all of us. Strangers came in and out of the house at all hours. It was really creepy. Anyway, the FBI got wind of it and called my parents in for questioning. They raided the basement and took a whole bunch of boxes, telphones and equipment out of there. All I know is, this coincided with my father's breakdown, and they used his medical records from the hospital during the questioning so that they wouldn't pursue charges. My father was unable to remember or answer any of their questions, so it was difficult for them to prosecute. After that, my mother flew into action, bought the new place in Florida, and is in contract to sell the house I grew up in. It feels as though they're fleeing the country. The whole thing is bizarre."

"I can't say I disagree with that," said Dr. Salamon.

"Welcome to my world," I said and continued with my self-reporting. "Other days, I get enraged at the slightest irritation at school and don't know how to handle it. And then underneath it all is my feeling depressed over where I am and what my life has turned into."

"Let's start with the rage at school. What's happening there?"

"I'm finding it more and more difficult to be in the classroom all day. I have to be on my game from 8:30 a.m. – 3:30 p.m. on a daily basis. My concentration is compromised by all these emotions floating around in my head. If the kids are difficult to manage on a given day, I don't explode, but my tone is harsh, and my words are punitive instead of constructive and helpful. It's not at all how I want to be. And then there was the argument with my assistant principal."

"What argument?" Dr. Salamon asked.

"I honestly can't remember specifically what we were talking about. It was a difference of opinion on best practices for early childhood education. She said something, and my response was 'When you can rub more than two brain cells together to make an intelligent argument, be sure to let me know,' and I walked out of her office."

"You realize you crossed the line with that statement and could have been formally reprimanded, don't you?"

"Yes, I felt that instantaneous rage again, and used my words as weapons. I did apologize the next day, but I'm concerned about my ability to manage my rage with my students and other staff. Being in the classroom all day long feels almost like being trapped in a cage. I can't just get up and leave for ten minutes to regroup. I need to seriously consider my options."

"You may not have many options if you continue to take heads off with your words. Do you ever feel aggressive toward your students or colleagues?"

"I know enough not to use my hands, which is why my words are so hurtful. If I don't get this under control, I just might lose my job."

"You're right about that," Dr. Salamon agreed. "What you said could be construed as insubordination. You were clearly out of line and out of control. Are you ready to recommit to therapy and medication to help manage your emotions and regain control over them?. There are new medications on the market that have had good results with bipolar disorder. As with the anti-depressant, it takes time to get to therapeutic levels."

Dr. Salamon prescribed another new mood stabilizer and I started taking it along with the anti-depressant. I experienced some of the side effects of the new drug, and I consulted with Dr. Salamon. We decided that another drug, also promising, would be more of a match for me. Again, I experienced side effects. Some of these side effects included trembling, loss of focus, loss of concentration, confusion, and an inability to write my lesson plans. Some of these side effects were immediate; others started a few weeks after starting the new medication.

On one occasion, I came to school (driving on automatic pilot), and upon entering the building, I went straight into the auditorium. I couldn't figure out what I was doing there and began to cry in frustration. My colleague, Eve, came in the building a few minutes after I did, and heard crying from the auditorium as she passed it. She walked in to find me crouching on one of the seats. She sat with me for a few minutes, and since I had shared my story with her, she was able to ascertain that something was not right with the medications.

She looked me straight in the eye and said, "I'm going to walk you to the main office and we're going to say that you just threw up and need to go home. When you get there, you are to call your doctor immediately and tell him what happened. Do you understand me?"

"Yes," I replied.

"Good. I'm going to get you some water and crackers and check on you to see if you are able to drive or if someone should take you home," she stated authoritatively.

After we stopped in the main office and a substitute was secured, Eve brought me to the teachers' lounge to settle myself. She brought me crackers and water. I must have sat there for a good half hour. She came in again to check on me. She asked me several questions and determined if it was safe for me to drive. When she was satisfied that I could drive home, I did, and called Dr. Salamon, to make yet another appointment to discuss changing medications.

It was becoming clear to me that one size does not fit all as it relates to effective medications to stabilize mood for bipolar II sufferers, and it takes time to find the right balance and combination of medications to reap the benefits. It was a difficult process and journey for me. At times I felt like a guinea pig and lost hope that there would be a combination that would work for me. I had, however, complete faith and confidence in Dr. Salamon. He was available every time I needed him, and he reassured me that we would find the right combination of medications. We finally hit the right combination in 1999. I stayed on this regime for many years.

The coursework for my degree was challenging and illuminating. Mostly, I was learning more about how my mind, as well as others', was shaped and influenced from early on in my life to present day, and what my responses to each significant event in my life meant. I learned more about why I repeated dysfunctional patterns of behavior even though I knew these behaviors didn't bring me joy, but misery. I understood more fully why my parents continued the cycle of abuse they suffered as children with us. They knew no better.

With understanding, I was able to forgive Mom, Dad and my siblings and let go of the pain I carried with me for so many years. I would never forget what happened, but the need to hold on to the intense feelings of rejection, abandonment, and abuse eased. I learned that life is a series of disappointments, and it's how we cope with these disappointments that will determine whether we are ultimately happy. Achieving happiness and peace were and still are my ultimate goals. I cannot say in all honesty that I've achieved either. However, I have been able to achieve contentment at times, and that is one step further than I have been able to achieve for so many years.

Each session with Dr. Salamon became a challenge for me to analyze my own behaviors and responses to situations and check whether or not he was in agreement. There were times when I was spot on, and others, especially when I was in a mixed state, when I was way off the mark. I knew one thing. I was alone again and wanted love in my life. My relationships with men thus far were not at all functional but served their purpose – only for a while.

CHAPTER **22**

LOVE IS NOT A FAIRYTALE

Once again, I am picking up the pieces of my broken heart.
They're smaller now, and more difficult to put together.

With each failed relationship,
My heart, soul, and spirit are less able to become whole again
Pieces of each are destroyed

Age is coupled with wisdom
But for me, the child within holds on to wishes made long ago
When dreams where of knights in shining armor
Riding to rescue this distressed princess

All that is left of those dreams
Is the armor that now surrounds my heart
This princess is alone to rescue herself

Wisdom requires that one learns from each failure
Age makes it more difficult to accept mistakes

Love is not a fairytale
And dreams are for little girls who slumber in peace each night

Lori-ellen Pisani

I MARRIED JOHN to escape my family home and the abuse I endured for so many years. He was a big, strong cop. I needed protection. I thought he would provide it. He had most of the qualities of a great husband, except for a few. I didn't think I could "have it all" (handsome, intelligent, funny, generous, kind, thoughtful, creative, and sexy). I wasn't in love with him, but he provided the basics, and that was all I thought I could have. When the marriage ended, I thought long and hard about what mattered most to me in a relationship, and after my marriage failed, Robert filled the bill.

My relationship with Robert was an eye-opener as it related to my use of defense mechanisms such as rationalization (finding good reasons for things that we really know are wrong). His high level of intellect convinced me that his relationships with several women was the right way based upon the difference in instinctual patterns of men v. women. It never felt right, but I bought into it for a very long time. I even believed that my jealousy over not being his primary partner was a defect in my brain chemistry. So, I kept my mouth shut until I couldn't take it anymore and exploded in a rage over just how much the relationship cost me in self-esteem, and ultimately my physical health.

It took a while to get over Robert. I felt rejected, alone, misunderstood, and unworthy. I fell into a deep depression, the suicidal kind. I believed I would never find love again, and that there was no "combination" that would work for me. Being alone frightened me, as did being in a relationship. I couldn't reconcile the two extremes. I desperately wanted someone to love and to love me, but I couldn't tolerate the feelings of abandonment and rejection when the relationships ended. So, what did I do? I entered into relationships that had nowhere to go but downhill.

I met Mark while I was teaching first grade. One of my students invited me to her home for dinner. I went, not knowing that her mother had invited her brother, Mark, as a set-up. She thought we would get along, and she was right. I was immediately attracted to him. He was good-looking, creative, had a voice like deep velvet, rode a motorcycle, and was sexy and articulate. He also had a "bad boy" image. He was a risk-taker, once rappelling down my apartment building. He had many tattoos and loved pit bull dogs. He was employed by a moving company and had a tattoo business on the side, but what he really wanted to do was be a fire fighter. It was another challenge to him. I thought it was a good way for him to channel his need for taking risks, so I encouraged him. I helped him study while he was in the academy and celebrated his achievement upon his graduation.

I thought we had a good relationship. I stepped up my cooking skills again and made gourmet meals every night. He kept me interested with his conversation and skills in the bedroom. Six months into the relationship, I was thinking that I just might have found the man I would marry, but I became as co-dependent upon him as I was with John. I didn't let the poor guy sneeze without having a tissue ready, and easily handed over to him the responsibilities I should have maintained. That was a mistake.

Mark must have sensed my need and desire and started to pull away. He'd make plans with me and not show up. I injured my back and needed him to take me to the doctor, and he never showed. I sank into another deep depression. The last straw was when one of my colleagues approached me to let me know she saw Mark at a bar (when he was supposed to be with me), and he asked her out. She told him that she was my friend and asked why he would do such a thing. His answer was, "Why buy the cow when you can get the milk for free?" He gave her his tattoo business card with his number on it and a handwritten "call me" note. She gave me the card and apologized profusely. It wasn't her fault. For me, it was another personal failure and rejection. I broke up with him and was, once again, alone.

In 2003, I did something really stupid and hurtful. I decided I didn't want any attachments to a man, so I pursued an affair with a married man. The opportunity came when an ex-boyfriend called me on a whim. He Googled my name and found out where I lived. I received a phone call one evening, and we spent the next hour on the phone reminiscing about old times (the good times). He told me he was married with kids, and that was fine with me. He asked if we could meet for drinks, and I accepted.

I knew the minute I saw him that we were not going to be "just friends." The attraction we shared years ago was still there. The fact that he was married with two children did not factor into my decision to have an intimate relationship with him. I rationalized that there was no danger of rejection or abandonment. This was simply a relationship with no feelings attached, so no one was really getting hurt. He thought the same thing, so we were on the same page. We continued this affair for almost a year and a half.

My affair with him also ended my relationship with God. *I turned away from Him, partly because I believed He was very angry with me for the abortion and divorce, but mostly because I knew I was actively and deliberately breaking His commandment not to commit adultery, and I couldn't bear confessing it. The affair was wrong, and I knew it, but didn't care. What was I to do? A huge part of me believed that God was an angry deity, always looking to punish me for my sins. Too many Catholic sermons dedicated to our sinful natures over the years convinced me that I needed to fear God rather than be embraced by Him.*

I had plenty to fear. I had committed the mortal sin of murder. I had violated Canon Law by getting a divorce. I didn't honor my mother and father. How many other commandments I broke were too numerous to contemplate. I figured, *what the hell; I'm doomed. God hates me. That's why He gave me cancer and left me with no one to love. I don't deserve it.*

I was miserable in my relationship within a year after it started. Mark was becoming difficult to deal with. He was argumentative and pushy. I was spending way too much time preparing for his visits than it was worth, and the sin I was purposefully committing was beginning to weigh heavily on my mind and heart.

The truth was that I missed my relationship with God and felt a desire to re-establish it. I broke off the affair. I was disgusted with myself, and with relationships. I needed some alone time to get my act together. I was scatterbrained, confused, angry, and frustrated. I was lost and had precious few people I could talk to. I didn't want to share my feelings with my family, and there was only so much Dr. Salamon could say. My decisions were ultimately up to me, and I wasn't very happy with myself. I needed a friend, and I found one in our new principal at school, Amelia.

Amelia and I developed a close working relationship as well as a profound friendship. We spent hours deep in conversation ranging from educational philosophy and practice to psychology and religion. Our talks were intense and meaningful. I shared my feelings of loneliness and my estrangement from God. As a gift, she bought me the ***The Purpose Driven Life*** written by Rick Warren. I didn't immediately read the book but kept it for when I was ready to renew my relationship with God. I started the book about a month later and brought it with me to Florida on a visit to see my parents. I finished it during my visit with them. When I finished the book, I was ready to re-establish my relationship with God, if He would have me.

I asked my mother to take me to church with her. She is a Methodist and started going to church regularly once she and my father moved to Florida. She always told us that she was forced by the Catholic Church to agree to raise us in that faith, or they would not marry her and my father. Thus, we were raised Catholic while she retained her Methodist faith.

I found the people at her church welcoming and warm. The Pastor's sermon was not doom and gloom, but joyous and comforting. This was not the type of sermon I remembered from the church experiences I had, but the service format had a lot of similarities that were also familiar. Immediately upon returning home to New York, I called the Methodist Church in my neighborhood. It was late on Saturday night, the night before Easter. I expected a recording of the times for Easter services the next day. I wasn't prepared to get a person, and to my surprise, the Pastor answered the phone. I asked my questions, and he asked my name. I gave him my name and told him that I was a Catholic who was looking for a new relationship with God.

He said, "You'll be in good company. I look forward to meeting you."

I went to church and met the Pastor and fellow parishioners. I loved the upbeat, encouraging words of the sermons, and continued going every Sunday. I found a faith and church community that changed my entire perspective on my relationship with God. I continue living a life of faith and cherish my relationship with God to this day.

I was free once more to concentrate on my new mission, obtaining my certification in School Administration and Supervision. I desperately needed to get out of the classroom for the sake of my students and my own mental stability. Although I was then stable on the new medications, I needed the ability to leave the environment if I was triggered. I also wanted a new challenge, but needed to remain in the field of education.

I chose an urban setting, Queens, New York, to study, as I truly believed that my peers would challenge me to be the best I could be. All my previous post-graduate work had been completed in suburban colleges and universities. Queens College offered me a wider demographic of students, and had a reputation for challenging, rigorous requirements. I needed that type of environment to keep my mind off my personal life and focus all my attention on my career plans. I worked hard and learned a great deal. I obtained my certification and pursued my next goal with a vengeance.

I remained in the classroom, but interviewed for assistant principal positions when they became available. When the Assistant Principal of my school returned from maternity leave, she and Amelia were struggling to work well together. By the end of the year, her relationship with Amelia collapsed, and she transferred to another school in the district. This was my chance, and I did all I could to secure the AP position on a tenure track. I interviewed for the position and was hired as the Assistant Principal in the fall of 2005.

My first year as Assistant Principal went very well. It was a tremendous relief not to have the responsibility for a class of students, meeting their needs, creating individualized curriculum, creating lesson plans and units, parent conferences, and the endless paperwork that accompanies a teaching position. I was able to leave my desk when necessary to go to the bathroom or take a brief break outside to smoke a cigarette or two.

The flip side of that coin was that now my responsibilities extended to the entire building of over five hundred students and ninety faculty and staff. The stress was different, but constant. I walked in each morning wondering what kind of day it was going to be. My 7:30 a.m. phone call to the substitute hotline gave me my first clue. There were days when substitutes were not provided, and I needed to get creative fast in order to have the building up and running by 8:30 a.m. when the students arrived. Coordinating busing for these students required scheduling over twenty buses to come to and go from school four times each day. There were always mini-crises that needed to be managed. Endless scheduling details needed to be created and managed. Evaluating teachers challenged my skills cognitively and creatively, and working with parents and students offered me the opportunity to put into practice my psychotherapy skills on a daily basis.

My office was also used as a therapy room for teachers who needed to vent or who came to me with problems they trusted me enough to talk to about. I worked ten- to twelve- hour days without a lunch break. It was exhausting work, and challenging, and I must say I didn't always manage the level of stress as well as I should, but Dr. Salamon was there to help me sort through my feelings and helped me temper my reactions when triggered into a rage episode. I also had my renewed faith and dependence on God for help, and with His help, I experienced success.

CHAPTER **23**

FALL FROM GRACE

Liz's fall from grace was quick
She couldn't see it at all
She lost control of her mind and heart
Causing her to take the fall

She quit her job on impulse
She had no plan in place
She hooked up with a crack head
She shot a clerk in the face

She and Tony were desperate
They had no money for drugs
They stole and hurt the innocent
And were labeled dangerous thugs

Her crimes were cruel and heartless
The punishment severe
Twenty years in prison she received
Leaving me to shake with fear

I once again sought treatment
For this cruel twist of fate
I fell into the grips of hell
A place I know, but hate

Lori-ellen Pisani

SEPTEMBER 2006, STARTED off as a good school year for me. I was in my second year as a tenure track assistant principal, and I decided in December 2005, that it was time to purchase my retirement home in North Carolina. Liz and I went on an adventure during Christmas break of 2005. We traveled all over North Carolina to find the setting that most reminded me of the small-town village I read about in the ***Mitford*** series of books by Jan Karon. I fell in love with the idea of living in a town like that and wanted to find it. However, in the books, Mitford was on the West Coast near the mountains, where it snowed every year. I wanted to get away from the snowy, harsh winters of New York, so we kept our search confined closer to the middle of the state. I also wanted to be close to Duke University for continued study as well as their excellent hospital, just in case I needed it.

We came upon a small town about thirty minutes outside the Triangle area of Raleigh, Durham, and Chapel Hill. It was close to the highway for easy travel and had all the stores I was familiar with in New York. It also had a townhome community development that was in the construction process. We toured the models, and I fell in love with the largest one they offered. The prices were incredibly reasonable. I developed a relationship with the sales representative that I have maintained to this day. She walked me through the process and introduced me to the mortgage broker affiliated with the development.

"I found it," I said to Liz, as we returned to New York.

It took a lot of preparation to get the down payment together and complete the mortgage process, but it was worth it. The home I chose has three bedrooms and two and half baths, a master bedroom suite on the first floor, and a loft for an office/library on the second floor overlooking the open floor plan below. It was large enough to have guests, and cozy enough for me. The development had yet to build the swimming pool and clubhouse. I was purchasing the home during phase one of the planning process. I was pleased and proud to finally have a home I could look forward to living in when I retired. I wanted to buy at that time, so that my mortgage would be half paid off, at least, by the time I planned to retire in 2020. I was putting my life in order. I was, for the first time in a long time, content. But my contentment wouldn't last for long.

Things were not going well for Liz. I asked her to go along with me because I knew she liked adventure, and I needed her outgoing personality and legal background knowledge if I was to find a home I wanted to buy. I was not at all confident doing this on my own. Her confidence made up for my lack of it. She was excited to go, and it gave her a break from the tumult of her own life.

Liz's psychological state had continued to decline since 2001. She raged out of control one minute, then cried hysterically the next. The fact that she smoked pot every single day since she was thirteen years old didn't help with her mood swings.

She was still working for Bob in 2006, but their relationship was not at all professional or healthy. They behaved more like a battling husband and wife rather than business associates. It was a bizarre relationship to anyone looking in from the outside.

He paid her partly off the books to save on his expenses. She didn't mind, since it put more money in her pocket and helped with her tax liability. She had health insurance but no retirement investment plan.

I was disappointed in the decisions she was making. I was convinced that she was bipolar, just like me, but she was not taking her illness seriously. I tried my best to speak with her about this and let her know that it was not her fault. I learned after further study that we inherited it, and we have to live with it, but we can't do it alone. We needed professional help. In 2004, she finally agreed to see a psychiatrist and try medication. She complained often and bitterly about her medication regime and insisted that she was not bipolar. Her psychiatrist was forced to close his practice due to his own health crisis. She was disappointed by this and did not seek help again for a long time.

She continued to spend money she didn't have on fancy clothes and a sports car, and bought a house she couldn't afford in an exclusive community in Connecticut. It was during the housing boom, when sub-prime mortgages reigned supreme. She was able to buy this house with no money down. If she had applied for a conventional mortgage, she never would have qualified.

In the spring of 2006, Liz started calling Debby and me to ask for money. She was having trouble making payments for her car, insurance, mortgage, food, and utilities. This was in part due to the fact that the house she bought was a money pit. It needed huge amounts of repairs to the septic system and roof, for starters. We tried to point some of these issues out to her before she purchased the house, but she was having none of it. It was her dream home and her income for her retirement.

Her plan was to get a reverse mortgage when she was eligible, and to live off that income. She was convinced the house was a million-dollar home when actually, it was a shack that any other buyer would have torn down. The other residents in this community tore down the shacks on their properties and built actual million-dollar homes. Liz was convinced the property value on her home was close to theirs. Another selling point for her was that it was in a community that had access to a private beach. Liz was a beach lover, and this home was her oasis. It was also a drug haven. Liz was smoking pot at an alarming rate and started drinking as well. It affected her work and her relationship with her boss. Tension in the office was high, and she fought bitterly and frequently with Bob.

I had had enough. I spoke to my family and Bob and told them I was going to call an interventionist. For some stupid reason, her boss told her of my plans and she called me to say that there was no way she would agree to go into rehab. I canceled the intervention. I wasn't going to spend three thousand dollars just to have her walk out in a rage.

Her relationship with her boss continued to decline. She raged at him to the point where she threw a computer at him and tried to run him over in the parking lot. Bob called me to tell me she was out of control.

I told him, "No shit. Why the hell did you blow my plan out of the water?"

"I couldn't cover the rehab costs. My practice isn't doing as well as it was, and I'm in the middle of a very expensive and contentious divorce. It's costing me a fortune."

"To be honest, I don't give a damn about your divorce. My sister is spiraling out of control. That's my concern. Something bad is going to happen. I hope you're ready for it. You blew the last chance I had at getting her help."

"I'm sorry about that, but there's nothing I can do," he concluded.

"There's nothing I can do now, either," I said. "Goodbye."

Within three weeks of my conversation with Bob, she went into a rage and quit her job. She had no savings and no means to pay expenses. Now, the shit was really going to hit the fan, and Liz's choices would lead to her destruction and my next breakdown. Liz was desperate for money. She called us frequently, but we were in no position to help her. Her desperation led her to do something illegal and immoral.

Liz had been secretly gathering evidence of Bob's infidelities and illegal practices over the years. This evidence would help his estranged wife immensely in her divorce action. In exchange for money, Liz fed this information to his wife. The money wouldn't last forever, but it would give Liz time to find another job. Instead of looking for another job, she wasted her time on the beach every day smoking pot and drinking with her neighbors. The money she was receiving as part of her "deal" was running out. Time was running out, and Liz was spiraling rapidly out of control.

In August 2006, I was in North Carolina with my brother and his new wife, closing the sale on my new home. I received a phone call from my mother in Florida who informed me that Liz had checked herself into a psychiatric facility in New York. I told my mother that I'd be home just as soon as the closing was completed. Upon my return, I went straight to the hospital to see Liz.

Our meeting was tearful and frightening. She wasn't making much sense, but I knew she was in deep trouble. She was angry, tearful, and an all-around mess. She babbled on about how Bob's behavior drove her to quit. He was crazy, and she needed to get away from him. There was no point in my explaining that her behavior was responsible for the state she was in. I was at a loss for words.

Liz had no insurance to cover the cost of the hospital stay. While I was visiting her, she tried calling Bob to ask about COBRA insurance, but he wasn't answering the phone. I explained that she quit her job and wasn't entitled to COBRA. She went into a rage and screamed at me, "I had to quit! He was driving me insane! The job was killing me! I'm entitled to COBRA, and you have to tell him!"

"What? Me? I don't know if I can do this, Liz," I said tearfully.

"You're my only hope. You've got to help me, please, please, please," she blurted out through her tears.

"I'll do my best," I promised.

"I love you, Baby Sis," she said as she hugged me goodbye.

"I love you too, Big Sis," I replied through my own tears.

I don't know why Bob agreed to see me, but he did. I went to his office with my head down and my heart pounding. It took every ounce of control I had not to scream at him for blowing my last chance to help Liz. When I stepped through the door, his new legal assistant showed me into his office. Bob and I shook hands, and I sat down across the desk from him.

"Thank you for agreeing to speak with me," I began.

"I've known Liz and your family for almost sixteen years. I couldn't say no."

"This is a very sad occasion," I replied.

"What's happening?" he asked.

"I'm not sure if you are aware that Liz has checked herself into a psychiatric facility and has no means or insurance to pay for the help she needs. I am asking you if you would be so kind as to extend to her the ability to participate in COBRA to help with the expenses. I fully understand that she quit of her own accord. I also think you might agree that her mental stability was in serious question before she quit. My understanding is that the stress of work and trying to keep the practice going was getting the best of both of you, and that might have contributed to her decline. She no longer has a job and will most likely lose her home. She needs this opportunity to regain stability and start over.

As you will remember, I tried to intervene before, but it didn't work out. I need your help, she needs your help, and given the fact that she has been by your side for sixteen years, I believe she deserves your help."

"You make a good argument. However, I'm struggling to keep the practice alive, and I've since found out that Liz has been giving my wife information to use against me in the divorce proceedings."

"I wasn't aware of that," I lied. "If that is indeed true, then it is testament to her psychological downfall. I can certainly understand your anger. It is a betrayal and unforgivable. I don't know what else to say except that I'm in danger of losing my sister forever. She has attempted suicide once before, and I am not at all certain, given her circumstances, that she would not attempt it again and this time, succeed. I am not above begging, sir. I am begging you now. Please, I beg you, please help her."

"I know you've done all you can to help her in the past. I am angry at what she's done, but I will try to help her. I can't make the full payments to COBRA--are you in a position to make payments for her?"

"I will make it work. You have my word," I replied with a sigh of relief. He filled out some paperwork, gave me some papers for Liz, and asked for a check for four hundred dollars. With his contribution, that would give Liz one month's coverage. I wrote out the check and gave it to him on the spot.

"I'm grateful to you for your help. Thank you. I don't think we'll be seeing each other again, so let me wish you well, Bob," I said as I stood up and extended my hand.

"I wish your family well. It's a terrible shame the way things went down, but it is what it is," he said as he shook my hand and walked me to the door. I got into the car, said a prayer of confession for my lie, and lit up two cigarettes in a row. It took fifteen minutes before my hands stopped shaking enough to start the car and drive home.

I went to see Liz again the following day. When I explained that she now had COBRA for one month, a big smile crossed her face. She hugged me, looked me in the eye and said, "I knew you could do it." Her eyes left mine for a moment and locked onto someone else's eyes. I looked in that direction to see a tall, lanky young man walking in our direction. "I want to introduce you to my friend, Tony," Liz said. Tony and I shook hands, and we all sat on the couch together, Liz unnaturally close to Tony. I thought, *Oh shit. This is all I need: a crazy sister who has fallen for a crazy guy. This isn't going to be good.*

We exchanged pleasantries for a while, and I got up to leave. I shook Tony's hand, and hugged Liz goodbye. I whispered in her ear, "Be careful, Liz; you are not stable enough yet to make any decisions regarding a relationship."

She whispered back, "Don't worry; we're just good friends."

Shortly after Liz's release, Tony was released and went to live with her in her soon to be foreclosed upon house. From September to December, Liz was calling constantly for money, and I gave her what little I could. I had no idea that Liz not only had started smoking pot again, but also started smoking crack with Tony.

It was December 18, 2006, just before we were to break for Christmas. I was at work, on the phone in the main office, coordinating my substitutes' assignments. I was on one phone when the other line started to ring. Amelia answered the phone, and with a serious look on her face said, "Lori-ellen, it's for you; it's your sister."

I thought it might be Liz, since she was the only one who called me at work. I put my caller on hold for Amelia to take and pushed the button for the other line.

"Liz?" I asked.

Over the phone, I heard crying for a moment, and then my sister Debby's voice. In a loud, almost shrieking voice Debby yelled, "Lori-ellen, it's Debby. Liz has been arrested and she's in jail!"

"What happened?" I almost yelled back in alarm.

"I don't know. I got to work, and someone approached me and said, 'Is Elizabeth Pisani your sister?' I said yes, and she showed me the local newspaper with her name in the headlines. Apparently she and that shithead boyfriend of hers robbed some stores over the weekend and were caught. They're locked up."

"What's the bail?"

"Half a million dollars."

"WHAT! Did she shoot someone for God's sake?" I screamed.

"She had a pellet gun, and yes, she shot someone. We've got to get to the arraignment. I don't know what time it will be, so meet me at the courthouse as soon as you can."

"Jesus, Mary, and Joseph--Lord have mercy; I'm on my way." I grabbed my things and headed out the door to Superior Court in Connecticut. I ran into the courthouse and approached the desk. "Excuse me, Officer, I am here for the arraignment of Elizabeth Pisani--can you direct me?" I asked.

"It's upstairs. Put your things on the belt and walk through the metal detector. Leave your cell phone at the desk. They're not allowed in the courtrooms. The room is upstairs, #104," he explained.

"Thank you, sir. Can you tell me what she is being charged with?"

"Let me look on my sheet," he said, as he started to look through his papers. "Elizabeth Pisani is her name?"

"Yes, sir."

"Well, it says here that she is charged with five Class A felonies, including three armed robberies, possession of a firearm, and assault with a deadly weapon. Added up, she could get sixty-five years if convicted."

"Lord have mercy," I said, as I tried to steady my weakening knees. I gathered my things, dropped off my cell phone, and took the stairs to the second floor. I opened the door to courtroom #104, and saw the back of my sister Debby's head as she sat in the front row. I slid in beside her and gave her a kiss on the cheek. "I just spoke to the guard downstairs. He told me what she's charged with, and if convicted, she can get sixty-five years," I whispered.

"Take a look at this," Debby said, as she handed me the newspaper with all the details printed out on the front page. The article, which took up half the page, described how Liz and Tony had been caught at her house after they robbed a convenience store at gunpoint. Liz shot the eighteen-year-old clerk in the face with a pellet gun. She wanted more money, and the clerk wasn't moving fast enough. She got away with only twenty bucks and jumped into her Saab with Tony as the getaway driver.

The clerk, who, thank God, was not seriously injured, was able to give a description of Liz. There were also security cameras recording the whole crime. Another witness, who was getting gas at the time, was able to get the license plate. Once that was traced, the police surrounded her house, phoned Liz inside the house leaving messages ordering them to surrender or they would storm the place. The article also stated that they were linked to two more armed robberies that same weekend.

It's all Tony's fault! I hated the bastard from the moment I laid eyes on him! He got her hooked on crack," Debby seethed.

"How long was she on crack?" I asked.

"A couple of months. He's a crack head, and her great idea to help him get off it was to do it with him!"

"What are we going to do? There's no way in hell we can make this kind of bail."

"We can't do a damn thing. Once we're outta here, we have to get over to her house. Her cats are still in there."

"How are we going to tell Mommy? And what about Daddy? He's not going to be able to manage this at all. Wait, look, the door is opening," I said and pointed to the door.

A line of people dressed in paper-thin white jump suits and chained together started walking through the door. Liz spotted us, and her mouth fell open. She mouthed "How did you know?" at us. I held up the newspaper. She was unrecognizable. She looked exactly like the *Scream* painting. Her hood was up, and under it, all I saw were bloodshot eyes as big as saucers, sunken cheeks, and pursed lips. She was scary-looking.

When Tony walked in several people behind Liz, Debby jumped up from her seat and started screaming, "You bastard! You should rot in hell for what you did! You are a no-good, crack head, and I hate you for what you did to my sister! I tried my best to get you away from my sister, and look what you did!"

For a few moments, there was complete silence in the courtroom. The bailiff started coming our way, and I pleaded with him not to throw us out due to the extreme stress my sister was experiencing. "She's got to calm down and be silent, or I will have no choice but to escort you both out." "Yes sir I understand," I replied still in a pleading voice. I grabbed Debby by the waist, as she was now leaning over the railing with her arms outstretched as if she were trying to grab him. Debby sat back down and put her head in her hands. Liz kept her head down and started to cry. I think I was still in shock. All I could hear was Liz's court appointed attorney saying, "Not guilty, your honor," and with that, they were led out of the courtroom. Liz looked back at us for moment. This time I yelled, "I love you!" before she disappeared.

Debby and I sat for a moment to collect ourselves. We were both shaking, Debby with rage and me with fear. We didn't speak. We were lost in our own thoughts. I looked up to see the bailiff approach. I was scared for a moment that he was going to give Debby a summons or something for her outburst, but he didn't. He handed me a small piece of paper and said, "This is from your sister." I opened it up to find the name "Mike" written on it with a phone number.

"Who's this guy?" I asked Debby as I showed her the paper. "I don't know, but we've got to get outta here and get to her house," she answered. And with that, we were off.

I followed Debby in my car to Liz's house. We were both still in shock over what we had witnessed a half hour earlier in the courtroom, but we were on a mission. Liz had two elderly cats that had not been fed in two days. As pet lovers, our whole family always treated our animals as family members, and making sure these cats were alright was our first priority. We were determined to see that her cats did not suffer as well. There was nothing more we could do for Liz except make phone calls.

We reached the door only to find a padlock from the police department on it. We went around to the back, and sure enough, it was locked as well. Debby and I looked at each other.

"What are we going to do?" I asked.

"We're going to have to break in," Debby responded.

"This is friggin unreal; now all we need is to get busted ourselves for breaking and entering," I said with a measure of disgust. "What if the cops are casing the place, looking for more suspects?" I asked with no small measure of fear. We peeked through the kitchen window, which was in front of the house, and saw the cats wandering around.

"We can't leave the cats. We've got to get in there. We'll leave something unlocked in the back of the house so we can get in again when we need to. Let's stop wasting time, and get in there," Debby stated with authority in her voice.

"Okay, this is going to be interesting. Let's get this kitchen window open, and I'll climb through it. Keep a lookout, and give me a boost," I said with even more fear creeping through my body. We jimmied the window open. I climbed on a plastic chair left on the porch, and Debby pushed me through. I landed in the sink. The skirt and blouse I was wearing now had water and food remnants on them, but it didn't matter. I climbed out of the sink to get to the back door. Luckily, we were able to open the door from the inside despite the padlock on the outside. I quickly let Debby in, as I didn't want her standing out there any longer than absolutely necessary. I was afraid the police were coming back, and I didn't want the both of us locked up as well.

Immediately upon entering the house, we fed and cuddled the cats for few minutes. We wanted to make sure they were not dehydrated. They ate heartily and went on their way as if nothing unusual was happening. Debby and I sat at Liz's dining table to make some kind of plan.

I remembered I had the slip of paper in my pocket that the bailiff gave me. "We should call this Mike guy and see what he has to say. He must be someone who can help, or she wouldn't have given us his number."

I picked up the phone and dialed the number Liz wrote under his name. The person on the other end picked up after four rings.

"Mike here," he greeted me.

"Umm, hello, my name is Lori-ellen Pisani. I am the sister of Liz Pisani. Do you know her?"

"What is this about?" he asked rather gruffly.

"Umm, well, Liz handed me this slip of paper, and I'm not sure why. It only has your name and number on it. I'm not sure how she knows you, and why she wanted me to call you at this time. May I ask how you know Liz?"

"I'm a bail bondsman. I've worked with Liz before. What does she need?"

"Well, Liz was arrested Saturday night. Her arraignment was today, and the bail is set for five hundred thousand dollars."

"Jesus Christ! What the hell did she do?"

"Umm, well, she got mixed up with a guy who was a crack addict. They must have run out of money, so they started robbing convenience stores with a weapon. The last robbery they attempted, Liz shot the clerk in the face with a pellet gun."

"What are the charges?"

"There's a list of them, all felonies, adding up to about sixty-five years in prison if convicted. They've got her on video tape."

"She's in deep trouble. Where is she being held?"

I told him. "Look, I don't know a thing about bail and how it works. We don't have that kind of money," I said.

"You would need at least ten percent of it, depending on the terms of bail. Do you have that, or collateral you can put up?"

"No, and I seriously doubt if any family member is going to get a second mortgage to get her out of jail."

"I guess you're outta luck, then. Good luck to her," Mike said.

"Thanks for your time, and the information--goodbye." I said and hung up the phone. I looked at Debby with astonishment.

"What the hell was she thinking, giving us this number?" I yelled. "Did she really think that we'd sell our souls to get her out with a half million dollars in bail money needed? Why the hell didn't she give us a lawyer's number or something that we could actually use!"

"She's probably in withdrawal and doesn't know what she's doing," Debby countered. "Let's try Uncle Joe; maybe he knows someone."

I dialed Uncle Joe's number and prayed he was home to answer my call.

"Hello," he answered.

"Uncle Joe, it's Lori-ellen, your niece," I stumbled out.

"I know who you are. What's happening?"

"I have some bad news, and we need your help."

"Christ! What happened?"

"Liz has been arrested for three counts of armed robbery, assault with a deadly weapon, and possession of a firearm, but I'm not sure anymore of the actual charges. There are five Class A felonies against her. She was seen on video surveillance. She's in jail, and we don't know what to do. Her bail is set at a half a million dollars."

"Jesus Christ!" he shouted. "What the hell is wrong with her?"

"She hooked up with a crack addict, and when the money ran out they robbed three convenience stores, and Liz shot a clerk in the face with a pellet gun."

"This is going to kill your mother and father," he said.

"We haven't called Mommy yet. Debby is with me, and we thought we should call you first to see if there's anything you can do. If there is, then at least we can tell Mommy there's a plan. None of us can afford to bail her out."

"There is no plan! I'm not licensed to practice in Connecticut and don't know of anyone who is, but I can make some calls. That's all I can do."

"I'll give you my cell number. If you get anyone, please call me as soon as possible."

"Alright. Let me work on it. Jesus, she really did it this time. She may be looking at the rest of her life in prison, for Christ's sake! I can't believe this! Okay, let me go. I'll see what I can do and get back to you. You call your mother. God, I hope she can handle this, on top of your father," he concluded.

"I hope so, too. Thanks, Uncle Joe. We'll be in touch." I hung up the phone.

Next, we had to decide who was going to call our mother. "I'll do it," I said. "I seem to be on a roll. I'll put her on speaker so you can jump in if you want to." With trembling fingers, I dialed my mother in Florida.

"Hello," she greeted me.

"Hi Mommy, it's Lori-ellen," I said in a trembling voice.

"What's the matter?" she asked with concern in her voice.

"Mommy, you need to sit down. No one has died or has been in an accident, but I have some terrible news." There was silence on the other end. "Mommy," I continued, "Liz has made a terrible mistake. I'm here at her house with Debby."

"What happened?" my mother's voice trembled through the line.

"Liz was arrested for armed robbery and assault with a deadly weapon. She and her boyfriend were high on crack and robbed three stores at gunpoint. Liz shot a clerk in the face with a pellet gun during the last robbery. She was arraigned today, and bail is set at half a million dollars. We already spoke to a bail bondsman, and none of us has the kind of money needed to get her out. We also spoke to Uncle Joe, who is looking for a Connecticut lawyer to help us," I spat out as fast as I could.

Again, silence on the other end, but I could hear my mother sobbing. Never in my life had I ever seen or heard my mother cry, and here she was eighteen hundred miles away, sobbing into the telephone. "Thank you for telling me. Keep me posted," was all she could manage to say before she hung up the phone.

"Lord help me, I'm going to lose my mind," I said as I hung up the phone.

As it was now after five o'clock and we could make no more phone calls, Debby and I fed the cats again, made sure we left a window in the back of the house open a little so we could get in again, turned off the lights, and headed to her house. We called our bosses, who already knew the situation. Liz's name was plastered all over the front pages, giving Debby's boss the heads up, and I was standing in front of Amelia when the phone call came in from Debby. Both our bosses were sympathetic and empathic. We updated them on what was happening and told them we wouldn't be in the next day. There was too much to do. They wished us well and left us to figure out our next steps. We called a few family members to fill them in, and after we hung up with them, we sat at Debby's kitchen table drinking coffee and smoking cigarettes. Neither one of us could imagine eating. The thought made us nauseous.

"We need a plan," I began.

"We've got to take care of the cats first," Debby replied.

"Okay, but we've got a problem. I can't take them. I've got Baby Girl, my cat, who would eat them alive. It would be war in my house," I said.

"I can't take them either. I've got Cody, her dog, who would do the same. We're going to have to take them to a no-kill shelter. We don't have time to ask around. We also have to get her things outta there before they secure the house for good."

"The only thing I can think of is getting started tomorrow, and I'll come up on the weekends to help clear out the house. What are we going to do with Tony's stuff?"

"It can rot for all I care," Debby said seething.

"Okay, we're gonna need boxes and garbage bags," I said quickly, to get her mind off my comment about Tony's things and back on track about the plan.

"I can pick some up at work," Debby said more calmly. "I've got some here to get started."

"Where are we going to put her stuff?"

"I can store most of it in my garage. We're not keeping clothes, only those things she may need for court. She won't be getting outta there for a long time, and I don't have the space. Everything goes except her papers and personal things. I'm not touching his crap. I'm not touching it, and neither are you," she said, her anger flaring again.

"Alright. It's a plan. We'll deal with whatever comes our way as it comes. I can't think anymore. My head is killing me," I said, exhausted.

We could do no more by the time we finished making a plan. It was late, and since I wasn't going to work the next day, I slept at Debby's. We got up early the next day and went over to Liz's. I borrowed a pair of sweats and a sweater from Debby, as my work clothes were not suitable for what we needed to do.

For the next four weekends, and with Debby going to the house during the week, we cleared out all of Liz's personal belongings. Debby took the cats to a shelter, and they were adopted together almost immediately. This was a huge relief to us. We kept an eye on the newspaper coverage. Liz and Tony were front-page news for almost a week. They were dubbed the "Bonny and Clyde" of Connecticut. The public was angry, especially with Liz for shooting the young lady in the face. "Let them hang," was one comment posted on the internet.

We spoke to the lawyers my uncle found, only to realize we couldn't pay their large retainer fees and subsequent fees for court. Liz would have to use a public defender. We met with real estate agents in an attempt to "short sell" Liz's house. It wasn't worth what she paid for it. The house would end up in foreclosure. We kept our mother informed of what we were doing. She decided not to tell Daddy, since his medical condition was deteriorating, and she wasn't sure how he would take the news. It was to be kept a secret from him for the rest of his life.

In one conversation with my mother, she railed, "I hope she never gets out. I will appear at every parole hearing and tell the panel that she should stay in jail for the next sixty-five years. She's always had this streak in her, and now it cost her her freedom. That's it. I'm done."

Oh my God, I thought. *How the hell am I going to tell Liz not to contact Mommy?* I decided to write Liz and let her know to give Mommy some time—that she was in shock, hurt and disappointed. I would let Liz know when she could contact her. As time went on, my mother's heart softened. It took almost two months for my mother to speak to Liz.

I cannot say the same for Louis. He had, in the past, broken off his relationship with Liz for other reasons. They didn't speak for years after an argument they had over Louis's girlfriend at the time. He blamed Liz for interfering in his life. When the apartment building Louis and my father owned needed to be sold, Liz interfered again and Louis lost $100,000 in the process. This incident sent him over the edge. He let me know that she was dead to him, and that it wasn't necessary for me to keep him apprised of her case. He meant it. To this day, he has not spoken with her. She tried writing him letters. He didn't respond. She asked me to plead her case to him. He wasn't interested. Her actions were and remain unforgivable in his eyes.

Liz's case occupied all of Debby's and my spare time for the next several months. Paperwork had to be filed to secure a public defender, as well as clear us for visitation. It was a living nightmare. Liz did not want us to come to all her court appearances. I spoke to her attorney, who told me this was a very high-profile case in Connecticut. He was looking at any plea deal he could make. They had her on video. Eyewitness accounts were reliable, and Tony was singing like a canary to anyone who would listen in his own attempt to get a plea bargain. Going to trial was too much of a risk. He told me that she might be looking at serving time for at least ten to twenty years with a plea bargain. It was my breaking point.

I was in full-blown mania throughout the entire time Debby and I were taking care of Liz's things, speaking with attorneys, and real estate agents. It was February 2007. I was on overload, and knew I needed help. I worked with Dr. Salamon to adjust the medications, but I needed more. I thought seriously about calling Dr. Mintz. I started with him, and he knew me best, but I reconsidered this option as I wanted to talk about what was happening with me now. I had changed over the years. So much had changed since I'd last seen him, and I didn't want to spend a great deal of time catching him up to where I was now. I wanted to start immediately with the crisis I was in at the moment.

I researched therapists online and found one who studied psychoanalysis. She was also on my insurance plan, which helped. Her name is Renee Pepper. She is a clinical social worker. I called to make an appointment. When I arrived at her office, I was as nervous as when I first went into therapy with Dr. Mintz. Once again, I asked myself, *Where do I start? I'm all over the place. She'll think I'm nuts if I walk in and start rambling on about Liz. I need to give her my history first, and then I can dive in.*

Renee opened the door and greeted me warmly. I handed her the forms I was given to complete and stepped inside and sat down.

"What brings you here today, Lori-ellen?" she began.

"What brings me here is that I'm in crisis, and in trouble. You need to know, and you will read in my history, that I'm bipolar type II. I'm in frequent contact with my treating psychiatrist, Dr. Salamon. His information is on the forms," I answered.

"That's good to know. Thank you for telling me. Now, what is the crisis about?"

"Well, you'll come to know about my dysfunctional family as we go along, but right now, I'm dealing with my sister Liz's huge fuck-up that has taken me on a roller- coaster ride. Please excuse my language," I said with embarrassment. I didn't know her at all and the "F" bomb was just dropped. I wasn't sure how she dealt with cursing.

"I don't mind the 'F' word; go on."

"Thank you for understanding. The short of it is this. In the course of three days, my sister Liz, whom I believe is also bipolar but doesn't accept it, committed three armed robberies and shot an eighteen-year-old young lady in the face because she didn't move fast enough to hand over the money. She's facing what amounts to possibly sixty-five years in prison. If that is her sentence, she will die in prison. She's already forty-six years old. At this point, I'm done. I'm so exhausted in every possible way. I have no strength to carry on, and I'm crashing from mania into a deep depression. I don't care if a bus runs me over. It would end the misery I'm in."

"Are you actively suicidal at this time?"

"No, more depressed, probably from exhaustion, but I have had suicidal thoughts in the past. I don't want to get to that point again, so I came to you."

"And I'm glad you did," she replied.

"I'm desperately afraid that through Liz and my father, I am looking at my future."

"Is your father in prison too?"

"He was, when I was about sixteen, but that's not what I fear. I'm so afraid that I'll either do something horrific in a rage that will send me to prison, or become a vegetable like my father."

"What do you mean by vegetable?"

"He's not paralyzed, but he is what I would describe as catatonic. He is an undiagnosed bipolar who was once the man of the hour until his world fell apart. He lives in Florida with my mother, who is not mentally ill and has taken on the responsibility for his care. He is non-functioning."

"We'll get to that, I'm sure. We need to talk more about your immediate situation," Renee explained.

I spent the rest of the session in tears as I explained my history with Liz and how I didn't think I could deal with her possibly spending the rest of her life in prison. Before I left, Renee explained that given the circumstances, my feelings were within the normal range, but if I were to have any suicidal thoughts, I was to call both her and Dr. Salamon immediately. She would call him before our next appointment to introduce herself and get more information about my history. This comforted me, and I was able to go home and sleep through the night for the first time in over a month.

I met with Renee once a week for months. During that time, I brought her up to date on the family history, and my journey thus far. Liz's case dragged through the court for what seemed like an eternity. Cases like these always do. In November 2007, Liz's attorney was able to reach a plea deal with the District Attorney. Liz's sentence was handed down. She would spend the next eleven years in prison, and nine years on probation. Liz agreed to the plea bargain, and I tried to figure out how to deal with my sister in a maximum-security prison two hours away for the next eleven years. If she had to serve the eleven years, she would be released in 2018. She would be approaching fifty-eight years old.

Liz's case was not the only thing preoccupying my mind during this time. My father's health was deteriorating rapidly, and soon after Liz's sentence was handed down, I had another crisis to get through. My father was dying.

CHAPTER **24**

MY HEART JUST TOOK A PICTURE

My heart just took a picture
A snapshot in my mind
A smile, a kiss, a moment in time
When you showed me you were kind

My heart just took a picture
Of us in frames of gold
Memories that are forever etched
In my heart as I grow old

My heart just took a picture
Of you as my angel nearby
To you I can call on when in need
To console me when I cry

Lori-ellen Pisani

WHEN MY PARENTS moved to Florida in 1997, my father was not in good physical or psychological condition. The mini-strokes, loss of his businesses, homes, and job took their toll on him. He no longer drove. My mother, who, up to that point, never liked driving on highways let alone finding her way around unfamiliar places, put the pedal to the metal so to speak and took over every aspect of their lives. She had to. My father rarely spoke. He spent over twelve hours sleeping each day and got up only to eat. At night, he watched TV aimlessly. He changed channels constantly. The only shows he watched consistently were *M*A*S*H* and war movies.

My mother found doctors who managed his diabetes. They all remarked how depressed my father was, but there was nothing they could do about it. He refused all treatment, and as the years passed, he sank deeper and deeper into his own world. His memory deteriorated to the point to where I wasn't sure he knew who I was anymore.

I made it my business to get down there at least twice a year, usually in the summers and during Easter break. It was torturous for me to see my father sitting on the couch smoking cigarettes and changing TV channels. I couldn't believe I was witnessing the slow death of my father. I imagined that this was similar to what the children of Alzheimer's victims experienced. I lost the father whom I both feared and loved. In front of me was a man I no longer recognized. I didn't know what to say. Although he'd call my name if he wanted something, I wasn't sure he remembered who I was. I asked him once if he remembered the nickname he gave me as a child. He didn't. He never asked any questions. He wasn't interested in having a conversation. I sat silently with him on the couch, just to keep him company.

My visits always ended the same way. I'd go over to the couch, kiss him on his cheek, and say, "I love you, and I'll see you again." I wanted to say those words to him. I wanted him to know that I forgave the past and held dear the good times. Invariably I left in tears, although I never let him see me cry.

Since my father never exercised, and ate sparingly, the diabetes was out of control. My mother and his doctors did all they could do to manage it, but the disease was winning. His eyesight deteriorated beyond the point of laser surgery correction. He refused all efforts my mother and his doctors made to get him to agree to surgery. My mother had timers going off at different hours to remind her to put drops in his eyes to preserve the little sight he had left.

Circulation was impeded to his feet, and as a result, my father had stents inserted into the arteries in his legs and heart, and lost his big toe due to an infection that wouldn't heal and the onset of gangrene. I flew down for this surgery. Although he made it through the procedure, the doctors were very concerned about his depression. They thought that the intensity of his depression might prevent his healing and he might not survive. He was transferred to a nursing home for a while to heal. My mother could not manage on her own with him, given his size, and his weakened state. He needed to learn to walk without a big toe, and if he fell, my mother could not catch him.

I walked into his room to find him curled up in the fetal position in bed. No one really knew if he was awake or sleeping, since he kept his eyes closed most of the time and refused to speak. I sat in the chair at the side of the bed, staring at him, not saying anything out of fear. On my last day, I asked my mother to leave the room so that I could speak to him. I was convinced it was the last time I would see him, and I wanted to tell him something. She agreed and left the room.

"Daddy, it's Lori-ellen," I whispered in his ear. "I'm here. I've been sitting by your bed every day for a week, but now it's time for me to leave, and I want to tell you something. You don't have to speak, but if you can hear me, just listen."

He didn't move, but his breathing was regular, not the breathing pattern and snoring he usually had when he slept, so I guessed he was awake. "Daddy, I wanted to say thank you. You might think that's a strange thing to say, but it's not. You see, all the bad times I had as a kid, all the yelling, screaming, hitting, and fighting taught me something. Those bad times made me fight to succeed and prove to everyone in the family that I was worth something. I waited until I went to college to ring the opening bell for round one. It was my chance to free myself from the pain and start over. You gave me that chance by sending me to school. I kept ringing that bell with each award, scholarship, and degree I received. And now, I'm able to fight my own battles and win. I have a successful career and can stand on my own two feet.

"I made it, Daddy. I survived. I have won the fight, and now it's up to me to keep moving forward. I have said goodbye to the past. All is forgiven. You are my father, and I love you. I will keep you in my heart forever, and when I remember you, I will smile. Daddy, I pray you make it through this surgery, but that is up to you. It is your choice, and I respect that. Daddy, I have one request. If you decide that it's your time to go, would you be my guardian angel? I want to be able to speak to you from my heart, call upon you for help, and feel your spirit in my soul. I want to make you proud."

At that moment, my mother popped her head inside the room and told me that we had to leave to get to the airport. "One more minute," I said. She could tell I was crying but didn't come in. She closed the door again. She knew what I was doing.

"Daddy, you don't have to answer or say anything. It's time for me to go. I need you to know that I love you with all my heart, and I pray that you will be my angel in heaven."

As I leaned over to kiss his forehead, I saw tears streaming down his face. I had my answer.

As it turned out, my father survived the surgery and was able to return home in about four weeks. I didn't quite know what to do. I had already said my goodbyes and now he was back home. *What was there left to say? How would he respond to seeing me again? Part of me thought, he probably won't remember what I said, so stop worrying about it. The point is that I said what I needed to, and that's all that matters*. The other part of me felt like a damn fool. I took off the angel pinky ring I bought immediately upon returning home. I put it in my jewelry box. It wasn't time yet, but it would be soon enough.

I went down again in August 2007. I did the usual thing by sitting on the couch silently while my father changed channels with his remote. He had a few major health scares between his surgery and my next visit. He lost half his blood volume due to a botched colonoscopy. The doctors said that his size saved his life. Even though he didn't eat much, he was still a good-sized man. He required several platelet and iron infusions since his kidneys were only functioning at ten percent, and his red blood cell count was very low. He was growing weaker, and time was running out.

I went with my mother and him to the doctor to hear the latest test results. The nurse who started working with him upon their arrival ten years prior came into the room with tears in her eyes. She didn't speak to my father, who was sitting there with his head down and silent. She asked my mother if she wanted her to say what she needed to say in front of him, or should we go in another room.

My mother got up, and said, "Dan, wait here. I'm going to speak to Jan for a minute." I followed her into the next room.

"His organs are shutting down," she said. "He doesn't have much time left. It's hard to tell how much time, since he's been through so much and survived even when we all thought he wouldn't. I can tell you that the process is now in full swing. He won't bounce back as he had in the past. I'm sorry," she said, and hugged my mother.

My mother hugged her back. "Thank you for all you've done for him for the past ten years. It's because you and Dr. Lin cared so much that he made it this long. You are good people, and I will never forget what you've done for him," she said with tears in her eyes.

"He was one of my favorite patients. He's my big teddy bear. He always said, 'Yes ma'am' to whatever I asked him to do. He's so sweet and gentle," she said, dabbing her eyes. She regained her composure enough to say, "The doctor, who wasn't in the office at the time, will give you a call."

I stood up and said, "On behalf of his children, we'd like to thank you as well. My mother has always had wonderful things to say about the care my father received here, and we are grateful." Jan hugged me as well. We returned to where my father was waiting. I didn't know what my mother was going to do. I was going to follow her lead.

"Dan," she said, "you're done for today. Let's go home." She never told him what the results of the tests revealed.

While my father slept, she called Uncle Joe, who made plans to fly down immediately. I called Debby and Louis to let them know what the results were. Both wanted to know if they should come immediately or wait. I didn't have an answer but told them that we believed death wasn't imminent. He had between a few weeks to a few months. They decided to wait.

He didn't get out of bed much anymore. He slept for seventeen to eighteen hours. My mother tried the best she could to get him up to eat. She was successful most of the time. He would get up, eat dinner, and go back to bed. If he did get up, it was in the middle of the night when she and 1 were sleeping. I couldn't hear a thing with my door closed, but my mother awoke with each of his stirrings, and watched to make sure he made it to the couch. He stayed for a few hours, flipping channels aimlessly, then put himself back to bed.

For days after we returned from the doctor, I lay in bed at night praying for the words I would say to my father as I left him for the last time. I fully expected him to be asleep when I left. Since I had already said my goodbye, I certainly didn't want to repeat it again. But I knew I didn't want to say the word "goodbye." *What would I say?*

The morning I was leaving, I walked into the living room to see my father sitting on the couch. I was in shock. I didn't expect to see him awake during the day. I gasped, and said, "Hi there. Good morning." He looked at me, nodded, and returned his gaze to the TV. "Do you want anything?" I asked.

"No, thank you," he replied, to my amazement.

I quickly dressed and packed the last of my things. I had ten minutes before it was time to leave. *Dear God, give me the right words to say, I prayed.*

I walked back into the living room and sat down beside him. I stared at the bulldog tattoo he got in the Marine Corps. I remember asking him as a kid what the bulldog was for but couldn't remember the story he told me about it. I wanted to hear the story one more time.

"Daddy, what does the bulldog mean?" I asked.

"Huh? I don't know," he replied. I missed my chance. I would never have it again.

My mother walked into the room to tell me it was time to go. She deliberately walked immediately to the car, knowing that I had to say something to my father. She wanted me to have a minute alone with him once more. I looked to the ceiling and said a silent prayer. *Please help me, God. I don't want to upset him, and I don't want to say goodbye. Please give me the words*. I turned to my father and said, "Daddy, I have to leave now, but I'm not saying goodbye. I will say I love you, and we will see each other again."

I leaned over to give him a kiss. He puffed out his cheek, just as he did when I was little. He looked at me with knowing eyes, closed them, and nodded his head in agreement.

I got up, my legs like jelly under me, and headed for the door. I took one last look back and said in a loud voice, "Thank you, Daddy. I will always love you, my angel," and headed for the car. I sobbed all the way to the airport. My heart ached like it had never ached before. I cried through the airport, on the plane, and on the train home. No one knew what to do with me. People let me pass them in line, the stewardess offered me a drink, and seas of people parted to let me through the airport. I was oblivious. The pain was crushing me. I was in trouble again. Once home, I called both Dr. Salamon and Renee. I made appointments with each of them and worked with them to get me through. Despite all their efforts, however, I sank deeper.

In October 2007, I hit bottom. I couldn't handle the opening of school with all its stresses and demands. I couldn't get a grip on my emotions regarding the imminent loss of my father and my sister's imprisonment. She wouldn't be able to go to his funeral, and I was going to have to go to the prison at some point to tell her that our father died. I didn't know how she would react, and if it was anything like what I was feeling, there would be more trouble than I could handle. I cried at the drop of a hat and raged when colleagues complained about anything. I was all over the place and couldn't manage my emotions.

For the first time since I had been working with Dr. Salamon, he asked me if I thought hospitalization was in order. I had already considered it and rejected it on the basis of how it would be received by the school district. I spent so much time fighting to keep my illness a secret and was successful. Yes, there were colleagues who were also close friends and knew that I was bipolar, but no one on the district level knew it, and I was desperate to keep it that way.

We talked about a leave of absence, but I couldn't take that chance either. I decided to take a day off here and there, when needed, to help me cope. My medications were adjusted again, and I met with Renee every week. It was one of the slowest walks through hell, which I never want to take again but know that I will. I was in a battle for my life, and I wasn't at all sure I was going to win this one. I worked hard with Dr. Salamon and Renee to keep up the fight. Slowly, very slowly, I regained my balance enough to function properly, but knew that I was one step away from losing it. I could fake it through the work day and fall apart at home. It worked for the time being.

By December 2007, it became apparent that my father had only a week or days to live. It was also the first-year anniversary of Liz's incarceration. Debby, his first born and favorite, flew down to be with him. I had already said my goodbyes. I asked Louis if he wanted to go, but he declined for his own reasons. It wasn't my place to judge anyone's decisions, so I didn't press him on the issue.

Louis was in the process of closing down the union he had started with my father. He had managed for ten years to keep it going. The insurance it provided helped immensely with the costs associated with my father's care. When we found out in August that my father didn't have much time left, Louis decided it was time to shut it down.

We had been trying for weeks to make arrangements to pick up the office furniture, but we couldn't get it together. Amelia graciously agreed to store it at school. We could use most of it anyway. I asked District personnel if they would send trucks to help me. I had a good relationship with those in the Buildings and Grounds Department. One of the guys, Domenick, had dated Liz several years earlier, and they remained friends. He was devastated to hear what had happened, and when I asked him to help out with the furniture, he spoke to the Department Director, who agreed.

Daddy was in the hospital. His red blood cell count was so low they couldn't pump enough platelets into him. He was dehydrated, and his kidneys were barely functioning. He was slipping in and out of consciousness. Debby called me every day at work to give me an update. He was sinking fast and was moved to the hospice unit in the hospital. He was not in pain, for which I was immensely grateful. Time was running out.

December 21, 2007, 12:30 p.m. My cell phone rang. I was standing in the main office by the teachers' mailboxes when I heard the ring and looked to see that it was Debby. I had just spoken to her about an hour before. She told me then that Daddy's breathing was labored. It was going to be today. They were deciding whether or not to give him a shot of morphine to help ease any discomfort. I guess they did.

"Hello," I answered.

"Daddy's gone," Debby replied with a low, deep sigh.

"Are you alright?" I asked.

"Yeah. It was hard, but I'm glad I came."

"I'm glad you were there too. You were his number one and always will be."

"I can't believe it."

"Neither can I. Is Mommy there?"

"Yeah."

"Let me speak with her for only a minute. I won't keep her."

"Hello?" my mother said, sounding exhausted.

"Hi, Mommy. I just wanted to say thank you for all you did for Daddy. You were an amazing nurse--kind, loving, and caring towards him, and I am and always will be deeply grateful. I thank you from my the bottom of my heart for what you did," I managed to get out before my throat closed.

"Thank you. I've got to go now. There's a lot to do."

"I know. I just wanted you to know how I felt."

"Okay. Talk to you soon. I love you," she said.

"I'll call the family on this end," I said. "Take care." And I hung up the phone. I didn't get the fact that she said, "I love you," for the first time in my life, for a very long time.

I looked up from where I was standing to see everyone who was in the main office staring at me. "My father's dead," I said.

"Oh my God!" was the general response as they crowded around me to give me hugs and condolences.

"What can I do?" asked Amelia.

"You can help me finish the job at the union office. We can't seem to get the trucks over there to clear out the office furniture," I replied. I needed closure.

I don't know what Amelia said or did, but I came out of the ladies' room to see three trucks in the circle outside school. "The trucks are here," Amelia said.

I gave her a hug and jumped in one of the trucks. I had yet to call Louis. He didn't know I was coming, and he didn't know Daddy had died. I dialed his number on my cell. When Louis answered, I said, "Louis, I'm on my way with trucks to pick up the furniture."

"I'm ready," he replied. *You're not ready for the second half of what I have to say,* I thought.

On the way over, I called my cousin Tracey, Uncle Joe's daughter. I knew he was flying down to see my father. My mother called him when my father was moved to the hospice unit. "Tracey? It's Loriellen," I said when she answered the phone. "I'm calling to let you know that my father has just passed." The truck driver and guy sitting next to me were dumfounded. They shot a look at me like, *What in the hell are you doing sitting here in a truck with us when your father has just died?*

Tracey screamed into the phone, "NO! My father is on the plane now! He didn't make it in time! Oh my God!"

"This isn't going to be good, Tracey. What should we do?"

"I need to call Steven, her son. I'll have him meet my father at the airport and drive him to your mother's house. I can't trust that my father won't call from the plane once he lands, and I don't want him driving under these conditions."

"Sounds like a good plan. Thanks," I responded.

"Uncle Connie was a very special person. My sister and brothers are going to be devastated."

"Do you want me to call them?" I asked.

"No, you have enough to do. I'll make the calls to the family on this side."

"I appreciate that. I'm on my way to close down his office right now."

"Honey, I'm so sorry. Please give our love to Debby, Louis, and your mother. Oh my God! What about Liz?" she asked, suddenly remembering that Liz was in prison.

"I'm going up there. I'll call them to let them know why I'm coming, and hopefully they can give us some privacy. I have no idea how she will take it, so I'll also let them know to keep an eye on her. She might get suicidal."

"Let me know if you want me to go with you. I'd be happy to go," Tracey responded.

"Many thanks on that, but it would take too long to get you cleared. I need to do this and get it over with. There's a lot to do on this end. I've got to plan the funeral."

"I'm available to help with that too, if you need it."

"You're a godsend. I will let you know. Now, we've both got things to do, so we'll hang up now, and be in touch real soon, okay?" I said as we approached the office.

"Love you, cousin. Take care, and call me if you need me. I'm calling Steven now, so he can meet my father's plane."

"Love you too," I said as I hung up the phone. I looked over at the stunned driver and guy next to me and said, "I know this looks weird, but if you think about it, it's closure. My father is gone, and now his office will be closed. It's a difficult situation, and I certainly didn't plan it this way, but God has a funny way of working sometimes. We just need to go with it. When we get there, give me a few minutes. I need to tell my brother. He doesn't know yet. I'll let you know when to come in."

"Anything you need, lady. We're here for you."

"I appreciate that, and I also appreciate how awkward this must be for you. I am grateful."

"No problem," the driver said. And with that, the trucks arrived at the union office, and I jumped out to see Louis.

On impulse, I kissed him on the cheek when I saw him. "What was that for?" he asked. "I have something else to tell you," I said.

"He's dead, isn't he," he said flatly.

"Yes," I replied.

"What time?"

"Around 12:30." Louis looked at his watch, turned away from me, and walked away. I left him alone for a few minutes and went outside to have a cigarette. I told the guys to wait a few minutes. They stood silently, almost at attention.

I walked back inside to find Louis walking around the office. I said, "We don't have to do this today. It was freaky the way the trucks showed up after we've been trying to get them here for weeks."

"No, let's do it. Get the guys," he said. I went back outside and waved my hands for them to come in. They made short work of clearing the office furniture, and within a half hour we were on our way back to school. Before we left, I gave Louis a hug, and told him I'd see him later.

It was over. My father had died, and his last business venture was closed down. There was nothing left to do but tell Liz and pray she wouldn't attempt suicide. I called the prison to inform them of the purpose of my visit. They agreed to give us a private room, with a guard, so I could tell her the news. I also informed them of her propensity for suicidal thoughts and actions and asked if she could be taken directly from our visit to the infirmary so she could be watched. They agreed to that as well.

Liz had no idea I was coming. Usually, our visits were arranged in advance by letter, but there was no time for that. I went to church early and made the two-hour drive to the prison in time for early visiting hours. I passed through security, stored my belongings, and was escorted into a room adjacent to the main visiting area. A guard stayed with me while they brought Liz from her cell into the room. I was afraid that she would know immediately that something bad happened when she was told I was there unannounced, but I was wrong.

Liz came bouncing into the room with a big smile on her face. She looked at the guard to see if it was alright to hug me. Normally, we get one hug across a table and are not allowed to touch during visits. I looked at the guard, too, fearful that this smiling sister of mine was going to freak out big time once I told her.

"Hey there, Baby Sis, this is a nice surprise! How are you?" she asked.

"I'm okay, how are you?" I said, knowing that she was either oblivious to the situation or in serious denial. I braced for the worst.

"Well, I've been busy with my painting and writing, and there's this new girl on my tier who…" she rambled on. I let her go on for a few minutes, while I tried to figure out what to say. The guard looked at her watch. I didn't have much time.

When Liz stopped rambling for a minute, I jumped in. "Liz, there's another reason for my visit," I said in a low, slow tone. "I have some news that will make you very sad," I started and grabbed her hand. I looked at the guard who nodded that it was okay for me to touch her.

"Daddy?" she asked, shocked back into reality.

"Yes. He passed away on the twenty-first. He went peacefully and without pain. Debby and Mommy were with him the whole time."

Liz immediately broke down into sobs. I rubbed her back and remained silent for a few minutes. "I'll never see him again," she sobbed. "And there's no way I can go to his funeral. I'm so mad at myself. I screwed everything up, and now my father is dead," she continued as she sobbed.

"Liz, what's done is done. Try to think of it this way. You couldn't speak to him before, but now you can. His spirit is alive, and you can call upon him at any time. You can say all you need to say, and ask him to be your guardian angel, like I did. Just close your eyes and think of him. He will come to you. He will listen. You need to forgive yourself and forgive him. Only then will you find peace of mind and heart." I looked over at the guard for any kind of help, but she was busy dabbing her eyes with a tissue.

"I just can't believe it."

"We all knew this was coming. What's most important is that he passed without pain. He is whole and at peace with Nanny, Poppy, Chrissy [his beloved cat], and all his friends and relatives that have gone before. Just think – can you imagine the conversations he's having now? What I wouldn't give to be a fly on a cloud to hear that!"

Liz chuckled at that remark and picked her head up. She stopped sobbing and looked at me. "I'm so selfish," she said. "I didn't ask how you were doing."

"I'm alright. I'm working with my doctors to help me through this, and I strongly suggest that you take advantage of any counseling that they offer you here. You can't do this alone, Liz. Promise me you will speak to a counselor immediately after I leave. Promise me," I said in an authoritative tone.

"I promise," she said as she began to weep again. The guard stood up indicating that our private time was over. She allowed us to go into the visiting area to continue our visit. I made sure I talked about anything but my father's death for the next half hour. When I got up to leave, I hugged Liz across the table and told her that I loved her. She said the same, and we walked toward the metal sliding doors. The doors opened, and I walked through. As the door slid closed behind me, I looked back to see a guard putting her arm around Liz while she escorted her from the room.

I prayed all the way home that she wouldn't attempt suicide. I played music as loud as I could bear it, to take my mind off what I had just done. When I got home, I flopped on my bed and cried myself to sleep. I soon learned that Liz did see a counselor and was deemed fit to return to her tier. She was not suicidal, but severely depressed. They would manage that through counseling. I was relieved, as I did not think I could survive one more heartache.

I continued to work with Renee on a regular basis for the next two years. Although there were times of intense pain, I was able to pull through it and regain my footing. I focused intensely on my work at school and took time to enjoy my home in North Carolina.

The worst, I thought, was over. The man I feared and loved most in this world was gone. I had survived an abusive, horrific childhood, a divorce, cancer, and countless other health scares. I was still standing. I was winning the war.

It was time to move on toward retirement and a life of peace. I had my retirement date etched in my brain--June 30, 2020--and with each passing June, I grew more and more convinced that I was going to make it, come hell or high water. I was going to fight through whatever battles came my way. My colleagues respected my work and valued the help I was able to provide them both professionally and personally. I couldn't honestly say that my life was joyous. It wasn't. It was okay. I hadn't been on a date in more than six years. I lost my precious Baby Girl to cancer, and I could still be triggered into rage easily, but I could manage it. My plan was set. It was as good as it was going to get.

I was in a place of manageable chaos, and with the help of Renee and Dr. Salamon, I didn't need a medication change for nearly three years. I was able to decrease my sessions with Renee to once every eight weeks. My appointments with Dr. Salamon, however, remained the same. This schedule I would never change. My story would end here, but life as a bipolar is ever-changing.

EPILOGUE

May you run and not be weary
May your heart be filled with song
And may the love of God continue
To give you hope and keep you strong.

May you run and not be weary
May your life be filled with joy
May the road you travel always
Lead you home... lead you home...

-verses from Methodist Hymnal

IN THE BEGINNING of 2010, I thought that my life was finally in order. I had ten more years until I could retire from my position as an elementary school assistant principal, with full pension benefits, to my home in North Carolina. I had two additional sources of income with my Roth IRA and my 403(b) plan. In retirement, I could work if I wanted to, but wouldn't have to. I could travel and do all the things on my "bucket list." My new life could begin at fifty-seven rather than working until sixty-five or older. I was content. I wasn't prepared, however, for the email that greeted me upon my return from mid-winter break.

On the morning of February 22, 2010, I opened my school email to find one that had been sent by my administrative union's lawyer. He explained that the District might possibly eliminate positions or lay off administrators, including me, due to major budgetary shortfalls. The email stated that the lawyers were holding a meeting in late March to explain our rights. I printed the email, and went straight to my principal, Amelia.

"Did you see the email from the union lawyer?" I asked.

"I haven't had a chance to get to it. I came back from break to over 100 emails."

I explained what the email stated, and asked, "What's happening? I remember in October, the Superintendent explained that the District was facing a major budget deficit due to a decrease in State funding. Is it worse than I thought?"

"We've had a lot of budget meetings, and we [the school principals] have been asked to submit three budgets from the least amount of cuts to the worst-case scenario."

"Am I in danger of losing my job?"

"I don't think so. Your position is safe for the 2011-2012 school year, but I cannot guarantee what's going to happen for the following year. The District is facing an eleven- million-dollar budget gap, which is unprecedented, and we just don't know what's going to happen. If there are cuts in administration on the high-school level, those who lose their positions may bump those on the bottom of the seniority list."

At that point, I sat down and put my head in my hands. *Good God. I must have had my head in the sand. I knew that New York was facing a huge deficit, and that the Superintendent warned of cutting the budget, but I never even thought about losing my position.*

"I wouldn't worry about it too much."

I have to worry about it. I didn't plan for this. In one fell swoop, I may lose my job and medical insurance, house in North Carolina, have to move to a smaller apartment in New York, and lose everything I've worked for, for the past twenty-three years in this district. I don't have a fallback plan, and I have no one in my life who can pick up the pieces but me. I needed to make some phone calls.

I walked back to my office in a daze. My legs felt like jelly, my head was spinning, and I was feeling like I was about to lose my mind. *Oh my God; what in the world was I supposed to do?* I called my financial planner, Bill, and asked for a meeting as soon as possible. I called the district personnel office and spoke with the Assistant

Superintendent for Human Resources. She informed me, "At this time, we are not thinking of eliminating your position, but I understand your need to know where you are on the seniority list. You are third from the bottom."

With that information, I put my coat on, grabbed my pack of cigarettes, and went outside for a smoke. *Oh my God,* I thought. *I am ruined. All is lost. I cannot believe this. I may lose everything, and I have no plan.* I began to pray, *Dear Lord, I am confused, frightened, and at a loss for words. Please help me. I cannot handle losing everything I've worked so hard for. I don't know what to do first. I need your help. In Jesus' name I pray, Amen.*

Tears sprang from my eyes as I finished my second cigarette. I tried as best I could to compose myself and get back into the building without being seen. If anyone asked what was wrong, I'd say "allergies" and keep moving. Once inside my office, I closed my door, went to my desk, put my head in my hands again, and sobbed. I made it through the day and went straight home.

In the silence of my apartment, I looked around and contemplated my life. Once again, the tears came. *You stupid fool,* I told myself. *This is a punishment for pride.* I thought I had everything in place. I thought I was on solid ground. I had a good paying job with benefits, two residences, and investments that would enable me to retire early with full benefits. I was set, and I was proud of my achievements. That was the sin I was being punished for. For two years, I watched the news and couldn't relate to the unemployment figures and the heartbreaking stories of families who lost everything in the market crash. I felt sorry for them, but I was too far removed to feel their pain. I was feeling pain now.

I mentally calculated my monthly expenses. There was no way unemployment would give me what I needed to keep up. Then I took out my pension benefits book. *What if I retire now, with twenty-three years of service?* I thought. I quickly calculated that I would earn about forty thousand a year. Then I could go down to North Carolina and get a job to make up the monthly shortfall. I wouldn't have New

York expenses anymore, so that should help. I had to make at least seventy grand a year a year in total, so I would need a job that paid about thirty thousand, and that would see me through. With my credentials, I should be able to find a job for that amount of money.

I opened the book and read through it more thoroughly a second time. To my horror, I discovered that if I retired at the end of the present school year or the next, I wouldn't be eligible to receive my pension payments until I turned fifty-five, and that my yearly income would be much lower since I retired before age fifty-five with less than thirty years in the District. I stared at the page. *Jesus help me. I can't even retire! Mother of God, can this get any worse?*

For the next two weeks, I plotted and planned. I was desperate not to have to sell my home. With the economy in shambles, who's to say that I'd get what I paid for it anyway? I never thought of selling it before, so I didn't care what the market was doing. It was my sanctuary, and now I was forced to put it on the rental market. Having strangers live in my home sent my emotions reeling once again. I didn't want anyone in that home but me. That's why I spent twenty thousand dollars to furnish it the way I wanted it to be. Quite frankly, it looked like I robbed someone's castle. My taste is very old-world European. All the furniture was over-sized, upholstered in rich fabrics. My bed was a huge canopy bed that took up half the master bedroom. I didn't care what anyone else thought of my designs, I loved it, and that's all that mattered to me. I had clothes and linens, kitchen utensils, pots and pans all set up, so that I could jump in the car and go whenever the mood struck me.

Now that I had to put the house on the rental market, I was going to have to move out of the house completely to make room for strangers. *Would they wreck the house? Would I have to repaint and replace the furniture and appliances? How bad was this experience going to be?* I didn't want to be a landlord. I had that experience once, and it was a disaster. I didn't want to deal with strangers, their demands, and collecting rent. I considered this situation to be a huge loss emotionally, and part of my punishment. I cried for days over the loss of my home, for that's exactly how it felt. I was losing my home. I would regain it after ten years of penance.

I emailed the realtor who sold me the house, Terry. We kept in contact over the years, and I trusted her. I wrote to her and explained my situation and asked for help. She immediately replied that she was "on the case" and would help in any way she could. I was immensely relieved. She put me in touch with a property manager, Sally. Sally and I spoke, and I was reassured by her professionalism, experience, and expertise in the field. She was also a full-service property manager who would take care of the rent, have repairs made when necessary, inspect the house regularly, and help with the moving of my things. She took me step by step through the process. It was tough, but she made it easier.

In a span of two weeks, Sally inspected the house, took pictures for the listing, and had a mover come in to estimate the cost of moving and storage. I set up an account with a bank that is also popular in the south so that she could directly deposit the rent minus her monthly fee and storage fee. Now, all I had to do was get down there and pack my clothes and personal effects. I made the plan for the week we were off from school for spring break.

I also made another plan. Since I needed money, I decided to begin looking at the career choice I had made for my retirement years. Years ago, I was the reader for a book on tape. It was Robert's textbook I used while in graduate school studying for my master's degree. I read it for blind students who were in the program with me and had no other means to study. The "studio" was an empty apartment, and my equipment consisted of a microphone connected to a boom box. If I made a mistake, I had to rewind to the previous section and start over. The finished product was crude and unprofessional, but it served its purpose. Nonetheless, I enjoyed the voice over work, and always had it in the back of my mind that I would return to it someday.

In addition to the plans I had put in place in case of a layoff, I also took the time to use my medical insurance to investigate why, at age forty-seven, my body seemed to be failing me. I'd had two bouts of very painful pleurisy (inflammation in the lungs), and I was constantly exhausted. I sweated in bed so profusely each night that I ruined sheets and mattress covers. My joints ached, and I generally felt like crap. I had gained nearly sixty pounds since 2004, mostly in my stomach area. I looked nine months pregnant and those who saw my stomach, but didn't know me well, were constantly congratulating me on the pending birth of my baby. It was hugely embarrassing and my condition took its toll on my confidence level and self-esteem. I tried every diet I could find and exercised like a maniac, but I couldn't lose the weight. I was frustrated and angry. I thought, *something has got to be wrong. Why can't I lose the weight? Why am I growing instead of shrinking? Oh my God, I thought. This is it. I've got cancer again, on top of everything else!*

I made the rounds of my doctors: internist, gastroenterologist, infectious disease specialist, gynecologist, endocrinologist, all with the hope of finding out why I couldn't lose the weight no matter what I did. Half of me was convinced I had a tumor the size of a watermelon in my stomach, and once they found it, all would be well. My gynecologist ran tests to see if I was in peri-menopause – nope, that wasn't it. The endocrinologist ran tests for my thyroid – still functioning. The infectious disease specialist I was referred to couldn't figure out why I was even there, but did run a test for inflammatory disease – again normal.

I went to see a gastroenterologist and furnished him with a litany of my family's history of gastrointestinal issues and my own background relating to my digestive system issues. The first question he asked me was, "Do you eat dessert?"

Immediately I was triggered. I looked at him as if he was in danger of physical bodily harm. He actually said to me, "You have a funny, kind of scary, look on your face. Are you alright? I see you are on mood-stabilizing drugs."

I replied, "After all I've said to you, that is your first question? I think you need to keep talking, because so far, I'm not at all impressed."

I truly believe I scared him. What he knew, and what I found out later, was that he lived directly across the street from my school. He started to ramble about tests he could order and things we could do. I said, "Now you've got the right idea; keep talking." I left his office with a script for a medication to help my digestive system start working properly, and an order for an abdominal CAT scan. I was so pissed off, that after leaving his office, I went straight to the grocery store and bought a box of chocolate donuts. I ate them all within an hour of returning home.

When all the tests came back normal, I was forced to take stock of myself. *Boy, Lori-ellen, when you screw up, you really go big,* I said to myself. As much as I wanted to believe these doctors were complete imbeciles, tests don't lie. I should have been thankful I didn't have cancer, but I was miserable. I couldn't stand looking at the diet commercials where I'd see celebrities in their before and after pictures once they'd lost thirty or more pounds. The infomercials for diet products and exercise gadgets sent me into spasms of rage. I started binging at night. I ate entire boxes of cupcakes, apple puffs, ice cream bars, cookies, just about anything I could get my hands on. The weight poured on until I reached almost two hundred pounds. I had done some serious damage. When my eating got to the point of ridiculousness, I took one weekend to sit quietly and reflect on the damage.

I realized that although I thought I had grieved the loss of my father and precious kitty cat, Baby Girl, three years prior, I had not. I felt tremendous guilt for having made the decision to euthanize my cat when she became desperately ill. I knew in my head that it was the right thing to do, but my heart ached for her. She was the love of my life, and I missed her beyond all measure. She gave me unconditional love; a love I craved all my life but never received.

In fact, I missed love and companionship beyond all measure. For years, I made excuses that I didn't have time for a relationship. My work was my relationship, and it took all I had just to keep up. By this time, I had lived alone for sixteen years, and hadn't been on a date since 2006. I couldn't imagine having another person in my life.

I needed my alone time. I didn't have the energy to give to another person. These excuses, however, didn't fill the giant hole in my heart, so I filled it with food.

Food also helped me to stuff my rage back down my throat so that I didn't explode with anger against anyone. I knew I had the capacity for violence once triggered, and it scared me. To cope, I used words to figuratively cut people's throats when they triggered my rage. So, I suppressed my rage with food. It had to be junk food. Nothing short of a sugar fix could squelch the burning fire inside.

Food had been my comforter, my friend, my life force, and my mechanism for coping with rage and depression, and now it had become my enemy. I wanted my life back in balance. I wanted to feel better about myself. I wanted to look people in the eye again. I wanted the pregnancy comments to stop. I wanted to have a fighting chance at finding peace of mind and heart. I wanted to be able to handle whatever the District had to throw at me.

My internist recommended a medically supervised diet program through the medical group where all these doctors were. I resisted it as I kept searching for any other medical reason for the weight gain. After my weekend of self-reflection, I knew it was my last hope. I made the appointment. The doctor I saw was both an internist and specialist in obesity. She ordered another battery of tests before my visit, and I was sent a packet of papers to complete along with a food diary. I looked at the food diary and sighed, *Well, if I'm going to do this, I'm going to do it right. If it goes in my mouth, it must be written down in the diary.* As much as it pained me, I wrote it all down. I had the tests done and waited for my appointment.

With my food diary in hand, I went with head down into her office. I weighed in at 196 pounds, and my waist circumference was 41 inches--my all-time record. I was disgusted. While I waited for the doctor, I practiced what I would say. The computer had the results of all the tests done in the past two years, as well as the results for the tests she ordered. A few minutes after I was seated in the exam room, a beautiful woman with a picture-perfect figure walked in and introduced herself. I was immediately embarrassed. She looked straight at me, and said, "Talk to me."

I reviewed all I learned about myself the past weekend, and my triggers for eating, and my experiences with the doctors I sought help from in the past. She listened carefully, taking notes, and reviewed the results from the tests she ordered.

"In addition to everything you told me," she began, "you also meet the criteria for metabolic syndrome and insulin resistance."

"Excuse me?" I responded in shock.

"Your blood work shows that your body is not using insulin properly. You are pre-diabetic and have a fatty liver, which isn't good."

How did you find it?"

"It all depends on the types of tests ordered. In this program we look for specific things in your blood to tell us how your body metabolizes food and processes insulin. If you're not looking for it, you won't find it."

"I can't believe it. Diabetes runs rampant in my family. My father died from complications of the disease. I just thought I had the bipolar gene passed from him, and now I find I might be headed down this path too. It's a lot to take in."

"Well, luckily, you are here in time, and we can work with this. I'm going to start you on a diabetic medication to help with the insulin resistance, and I'll put you in the induction phase of the diet program. You will see me again in two weeks, but you will weigh in once a week."

Still in a bit of shock, I followed the doctor to another office, where a nurse walked me through the program in detail. She gave me the supplements I needed to take and tallied up the bill--$320. Yup, this was going to be real expensive. She made my appointment for ten days later, as my school schedule didn't permit a one-week appointment. I took my packages home and read over the material. A trip to the grocery store for fresh fruits, vegetables, and lean proteins cost me another hundred bucks. *Damn, I hope this works,* I thought.

I was faithful to the diet, keeping my food diary, and praying that this would be the answer. I refused to get on the scale at home, fearing the worst. I didn't feel that in ten days I had lost that much weight, despite the major change in diet. When I saw that I'd lost only two pounds in ten days, I was immediately in despair. The doctor explained that she had one patient who lost thirty-five pounds in a year and half and was thrilled. She had underlying health issues like I did. That information didn't help me. I knew something else was the reason for not losing more weight. Then the doctor hit me with what she really thought about the lack of weight loss.

"I'm having a real problem with your psychotropic drugs," she said.

Oh no, I thought to myself. All the other doctors mentioned that my meds might be the reason for not losing weight, but I dismissed it because I had been on this combination for several years and my weight remained relatively stable.

"But I've been on this combination for several years, the weight gain associated with them should have stabilized," I countered.

"It's not only the weight gain, but the weight retention. These drugs are weight- loss resistant. You may want to think about changing your medications."

My heart immediately sank, and tears formed in the back of my eyes. I had vowed never to switch meds again after the hell I went through to find this combination. And now, I found out that it is precisely this combination that was preventing me from losing the weight.

I didn't see a choice here. Either I could continue to gain weight and become a full-blown diabetic with all its complications, or be a guinea pig once again and try other bipolar meds, risk their side effects, and possibly lose mental control. I was distraught. I couldn't believe that I might have to choose between two evils: diabetes, or out-of-control bipolar disorder. I felt the sudden urge to eat everything in aisle four of my grocery store.

I was in trouble and in danger. With a low voice I said, "You have Dr. Salamon's contact information. Please call him to discuss this, and I will follow up with him."

With that, I left the office and drove towards home. As I reached the turn that would take me to the grocery store, I told myself, *This is a battle, and you're going to do all you can to win it. Don't you dare make that turn. Go home, cry, scream, throw something, do whatever you have to, but don't give up.*

I did just that. I went home, cried, screamed into my pillow, and threw it around the room. I made my high-protein dinner and went to bed at eight o'clock. I was exhausted in every possible way.

The weight management doctor called Dr. Salamon to discuss the change in medication. I emailed him to let him know my feelings about changing medications. I told him that of the two evils I faced, I needed to lose the weight or risk serious complications from diabetes. I didn't connect the insulin resistance with my eyesight that was getting worse rapidly. I was no longer a candidate for laser surgery to correct my vision. It deteriorated too rapidly, and I had borderline glaucoma. I was already putting drops in my eyes twice a day. My fear was that I was going down the same path as my father, and I needed to fight back. It was worth the risk of experiencing side effects of new bipolar medications.

I called Dr. Salamon the next day to discuss the change. He agreed that my health was more important, and started me on a new anti-depressant very slowly to minimize side effects. I lost three pounds the following week. At the time of this writing, I am continuing this process and pray to God daily for help. I cannot, with any confidence, tell you that I have won the war, but I am still fighting the battles with everything I've got.

Eight years have passed. It is now 2018. I have so many more stories to share about the events that took place during the eight years since I finished this book, and perhaps, one day, I will.

My prayer is that my story, as it was until 2010, helps you and your loved ones keep fighting with me, and that you find peace of mind and heart.

May God bless you, and keep you safe in His loving embrace,
Lori-ellen Pisani

CPSIA information can be obtained
at www.ICGtesting.com
Printed in the USA
LVHW020304280120
645026LV00004B/719

9 781478 795773